AF478266

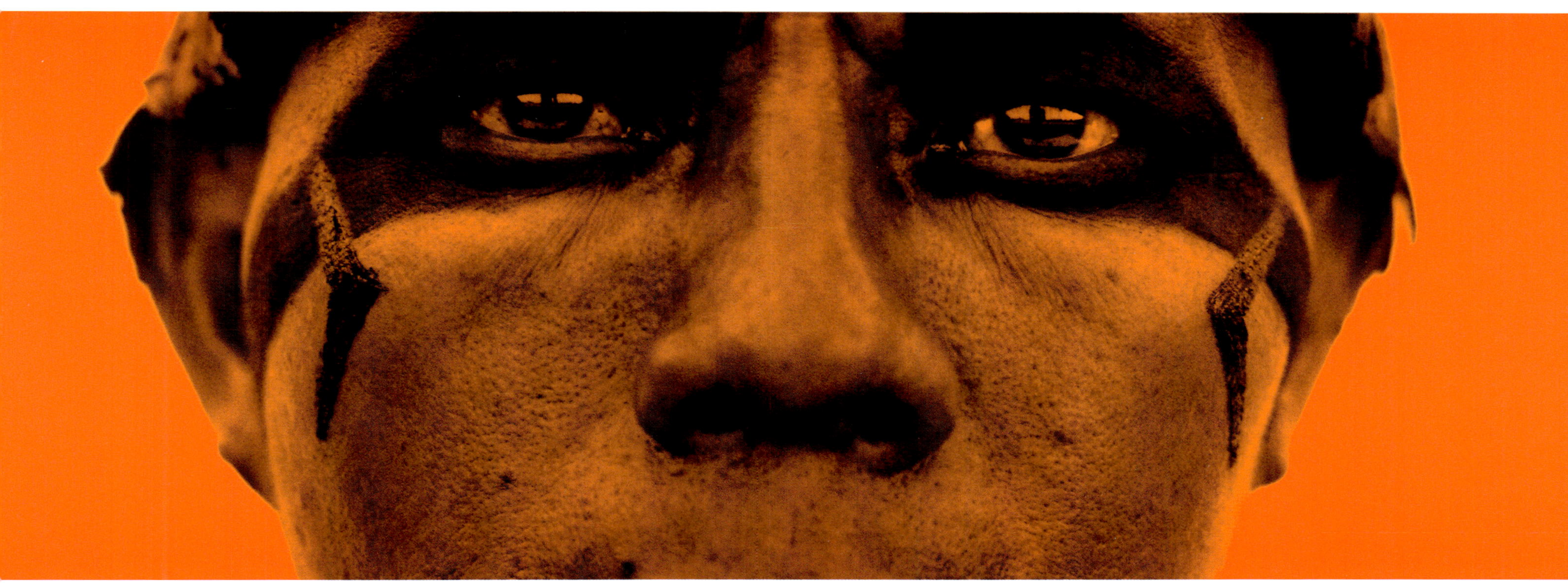

powerHouse Books, New York, NY

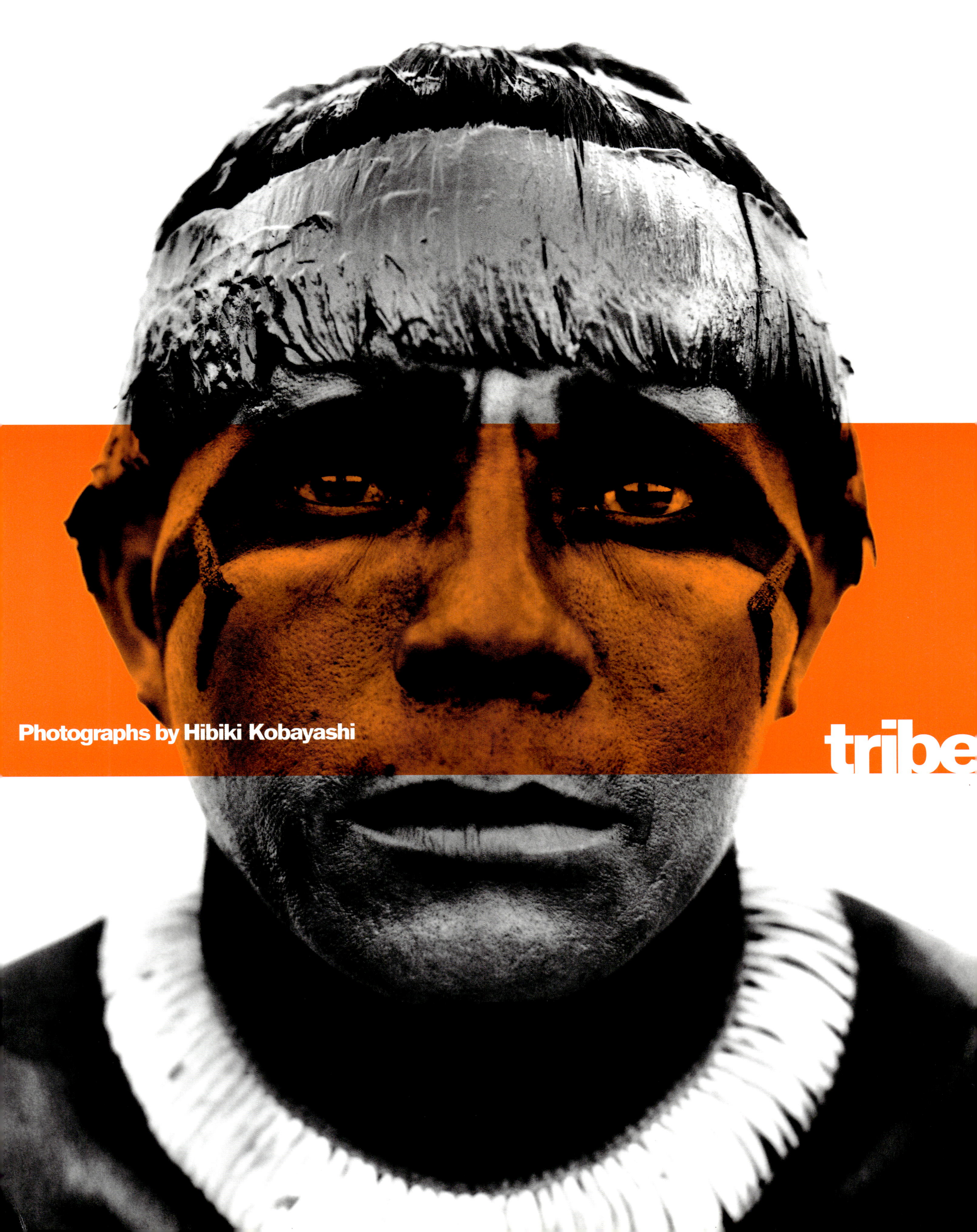
Photographs by Hibiki Kobayashi
tribe

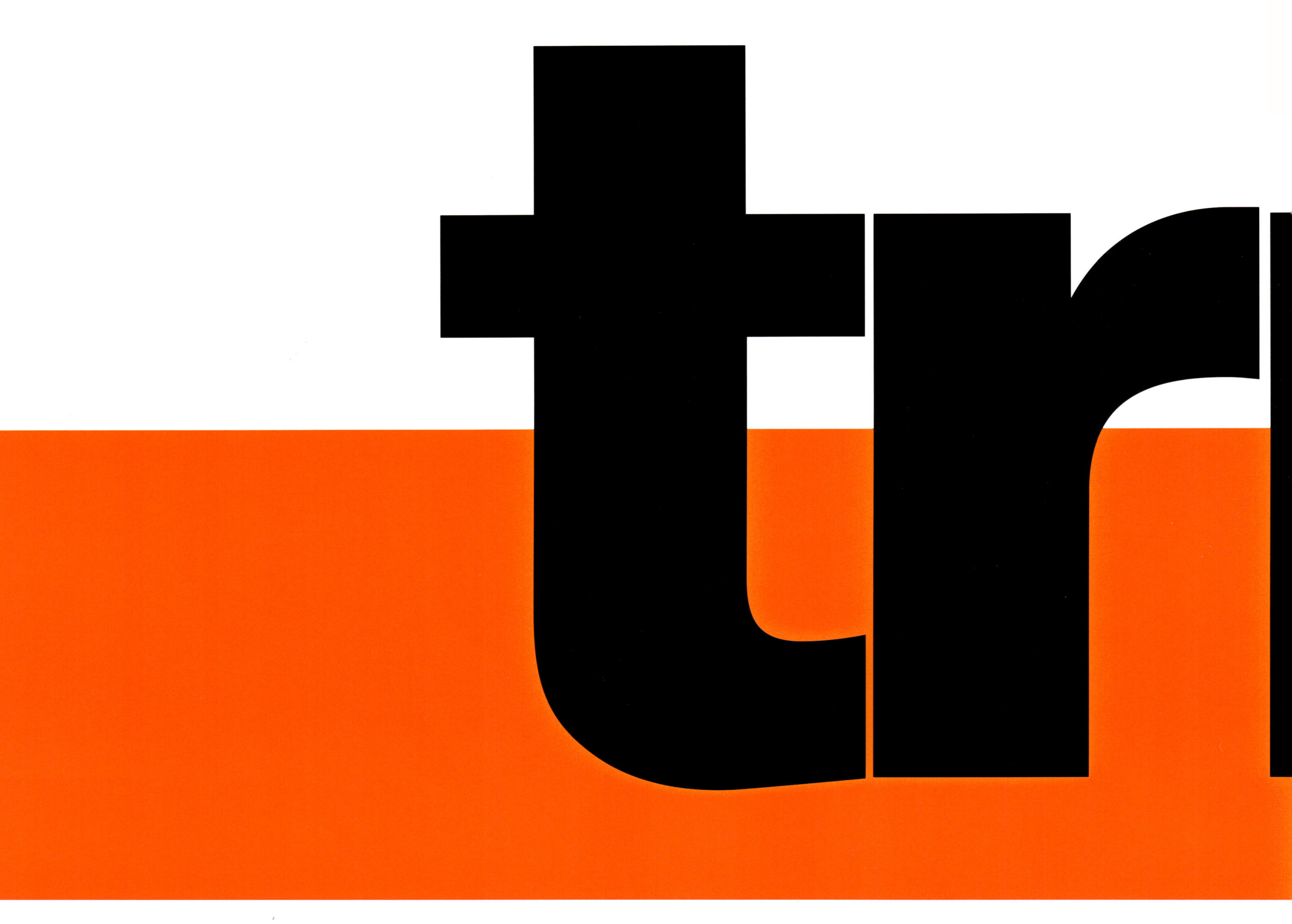

Tribe: Photographs by Hibiki Kobayashi

First published in the United States of America in 1998 by powerHouse Books,
a division of powerHouse Cultural Entertainment, Inc.
180 Varick Street, Suite 1302, New York, NY 10014-4606, telephone 212 604 9074, fax 212 366 5247
e-mail: info@powerHouseBooks.com web site: http://www.powerHouseBooks.com
Original edition published in Japan in 1998 by Korinsha Press & Co., Ltd.

Library of Congress Cataloging-in-Publication Data:
Kobayashi, Hibiki, 1955—
Tribe / photographs by Hibiki Kobayashi ; art directed by Fabien Baron.
p. cm.
ISBN 1-57687-032-4
1. Portrait photography. 2. Indigenous peoples--Portraits.
3. Tribes--Pictorial works. I. Baron, Fabien. II. Title.
TR681.I58K63 1998
779'.93058--DC21 98-9179
CIP

ISBN 1-57687-032-4
Special thanks to JAICA (J.O.C.V.), AMAZON, F.M.V., VALIS, DK, AYUMI K. INC.
Photograph printing by Monique Thompson, Sixty-Eight Degrees, New York
Tritone separations by: Toppan Printing Co., Ltd.
Printed and bound by: Toppan Printing Co., Ltd.
A complete catalog of powerHouse Books and Limited Editions is available upon request; please call, write, or hit our web site.
10 9 8 7 6 5 4 3 2 1
Printed and bound in Japan

Art direction by Fabien Baron, design by Patrick Li and Koji Katsuta / Baron & Baron

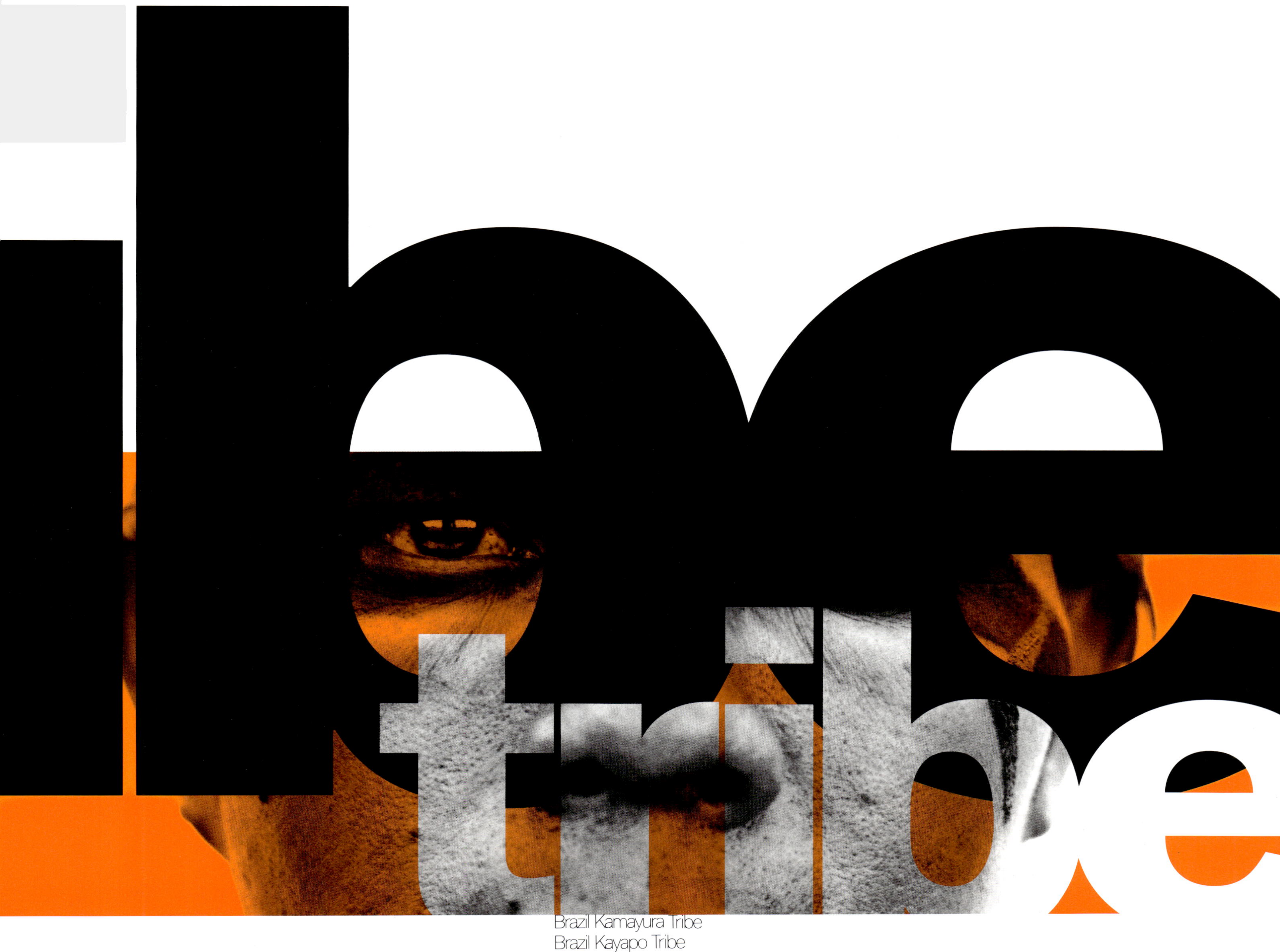

Brazil Kamayura Tribe
Brazil Kayapo Tribe
Kenya Samburu Tribe
Kenya Turkana Tribe
Irian Jaya Dani Tribe
Ethiopia Amhara Tribe
Yemen Beni Husheich Tribe
Yemen Shafa Tribe
Yemen Beni Suraym Tribe
Jordan Beduin Tribe
Mustang Tibet Tribe
Nepal Newar Tribe
Nepal Parbate Tribe
Nepal Tamang Tribe
Nepal Tharu Tribe
Thailand Lahu Tribe
Thailand Lisu Tribe
Thailand Meo Tribe
Thailand Padaung Tribe
Irian Jaya Chié Tribe
Borneo Iban Tribe

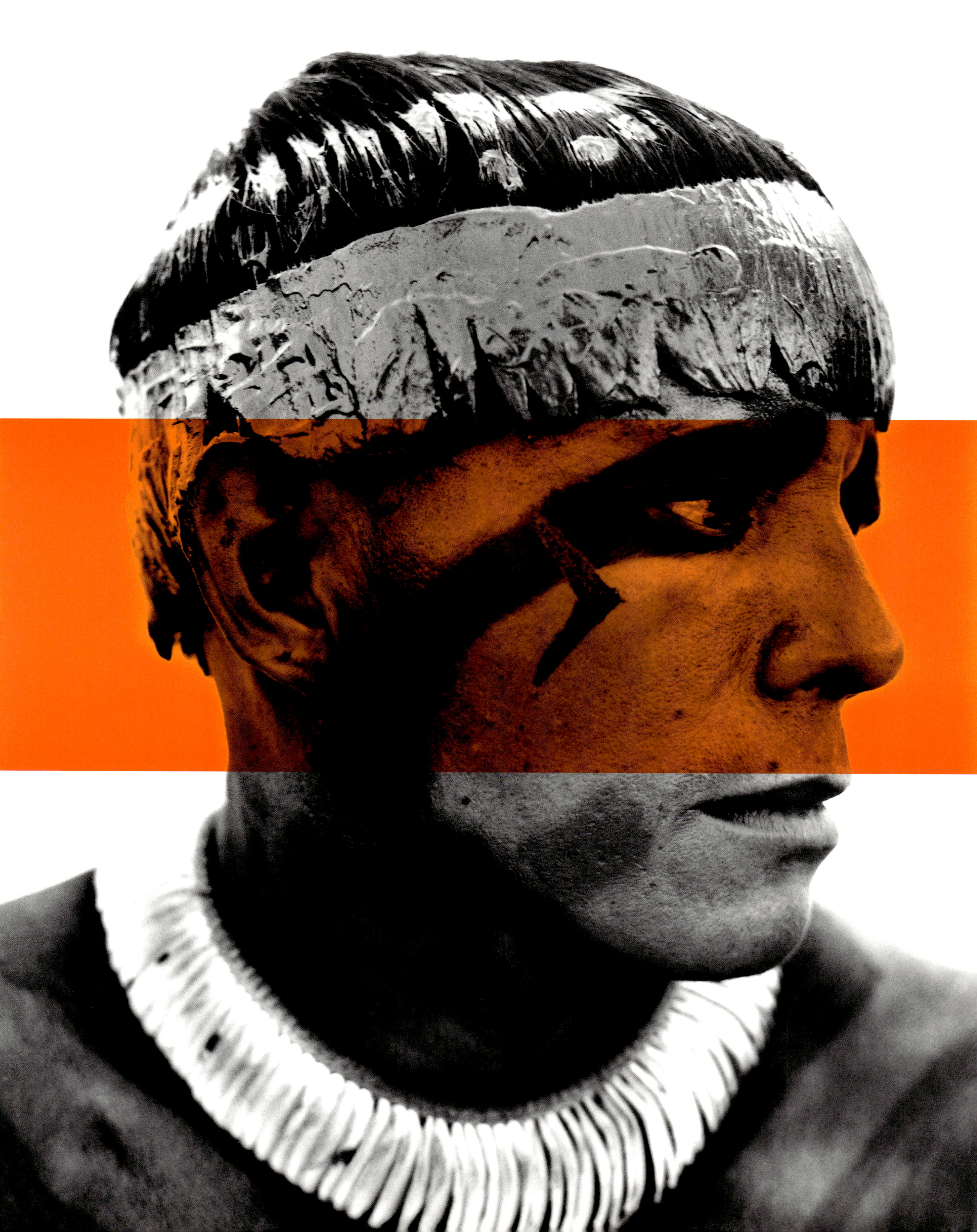

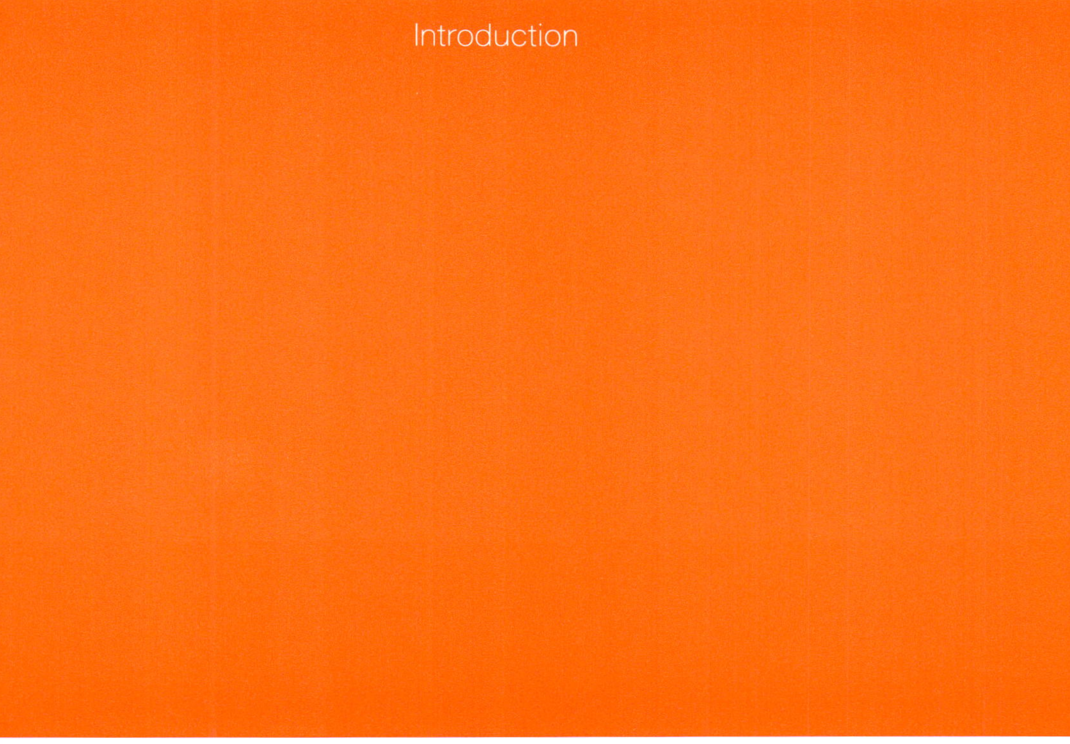

Introduction

"Global population grows by a remarkable 1 million more births than deaths every four days. If a bomb as destructive as the one that destroyed Hiroshima had been dropped every day since August 25, 1945, it would not have stabilized human numbers." (*The Lancet*, England, September 15, 1990).

One of the key elements in Hibiki Kobayashi's photography is the way it makes you stop and think about the fairness with which it was undertaken: the openness, the innocence, the calm and the patience, the understanding of others . . . the whole business of welcoming diversity as opposed to what's really happening down here on earth. Territorialism, tribalism, xenophobia, selfish greed, pecking-order pride in the rat race, franchise-mania, artificiality—distance from nature—eliminating diversity wherever we trample. Bhopal, Love Canal, Chernobyl and beyond . . . Hey, wait a minute—if we're so great (we know our numbers are great), why are we enemies of nature, enemies of every continental land mass and even of ourselves? And slowly, slowly as we grow, adding a million souls to the earth every few days, we expertly adapt to the damage we cause. In the confusion of stressful changes, behavior declines. Political leaders lie, traditions are abandoned, authenticity fades away. Innocent people are caught in a world at war, over-populated, over-stressed refugees. Time out. Full stop. Hibiki Kobayashi is up-to-date with these looming dilemmas. He quietly presents a great variety of innocent looking, very different peoples, indigenous, authentic in nature, down to earth, part of natural history and our one and only, fast evolving, exploding, shrinking globe. They represent a quiet and humble reality. We are probably too late to realize the importance of it. There is little time and less and less space to readjust our sights. We are destroying things faster than we can understand how big a mistake we've made, naively suffocating our once huge and diverse world. Like a cancer we have spread over and deeply into the body of the host. With monotonous predictability, rapacious cunning, exponential explosions of people and pollution, we squeeze in more and more, constantly adjusting to the destruction we inflict.

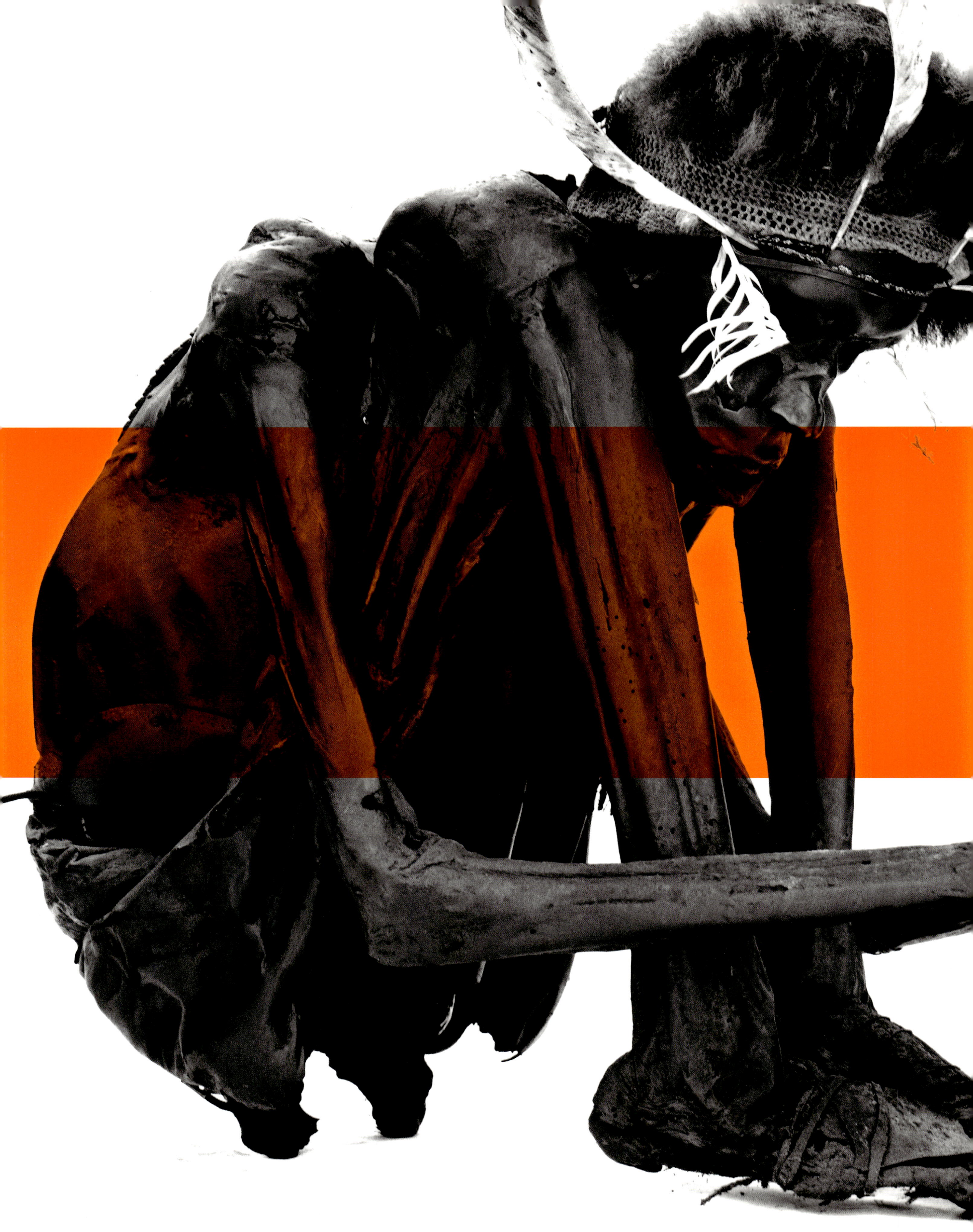

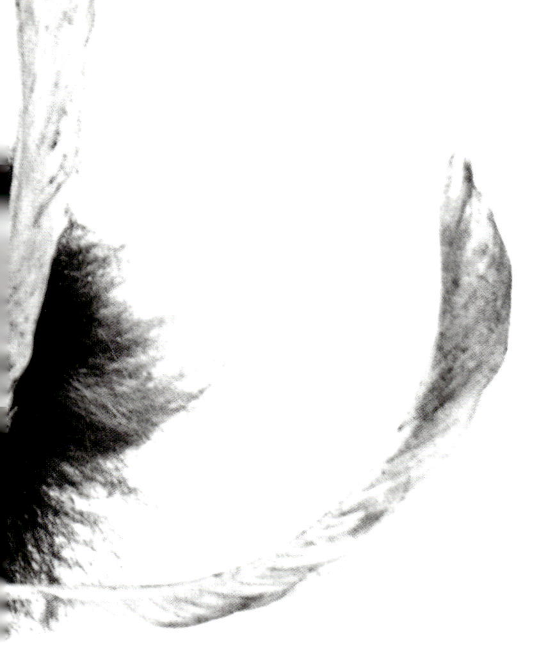

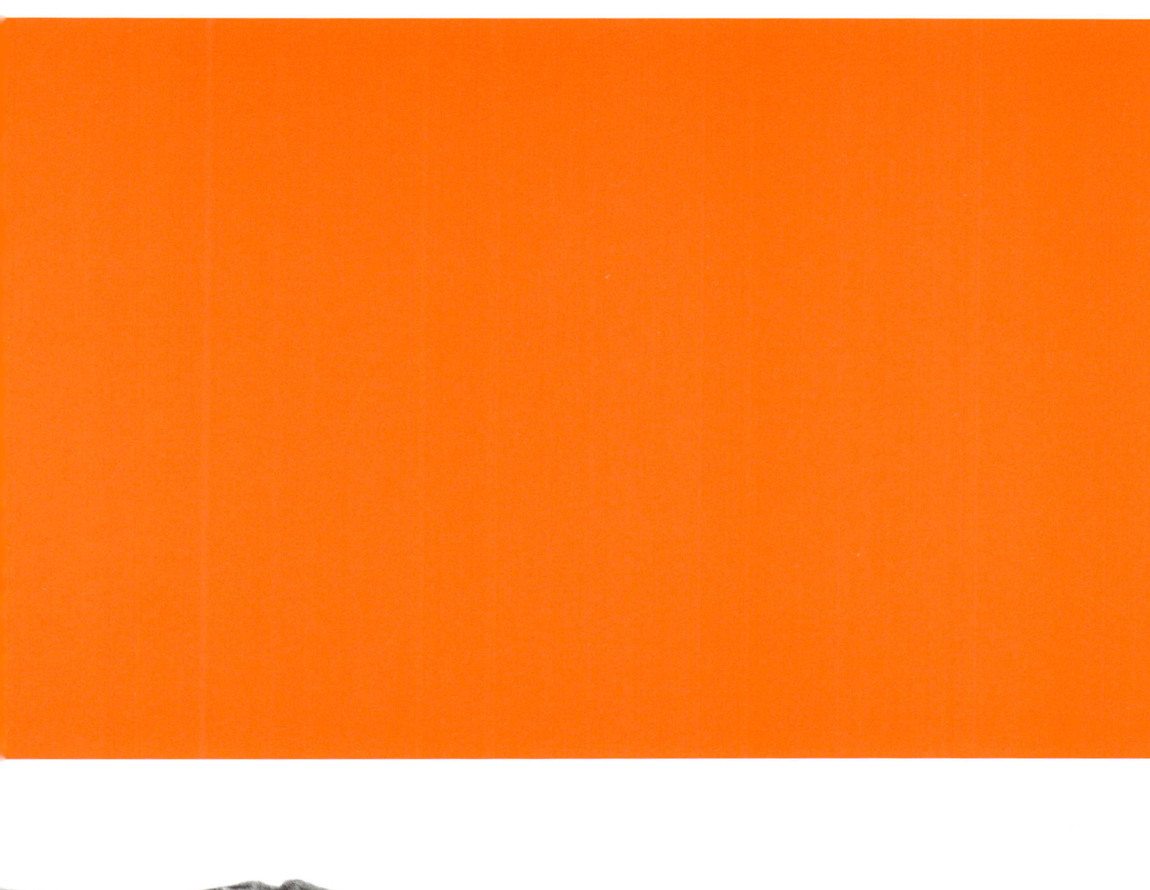

The people in Kobayashi's images are presented quietly, self-contained in their outside body shells. You see in their eyes a far-off connection, a consciousness of something very important and elusive. It is a very educational experience just slowly going through these pictures. They show us a whole range of different ages, sexes, and tribes, those completely authentic and those compromised, pure and intermixed, decorative and plain; they show us everything, straight into the eye of the camera. There's nothing self-conscious, arty, uptight, or limited in this presentation. No gimmicks. I am personally interested in this kind of presentation because I live in Kenya, a country with over seventy significantly different tribes, and I want to say "Vive la différence!" We have to try to outgrow our perpetual inborn rivalry: tribe against tribe, hill top to hill top—raiding, looting, and cattle rustling as national sport—the same unevolved, bloody, dangerous, primitive behavior in Bosnia, the Middle East, Rwanda, Liberia, and the Sudan as in Los Angeles, Detroit, and Washington, D.C. ...almost everywhere. *We must become* more compassionate and understanding, before it is too late. *We must start* to think about these things—yesterday. If there is to be a livable, recognizable, enter-without-fear Kenya of tomorrow, let's say, it won't be because of the Kalenjin wars against the Kikuyu, or Luos overtaking the Turkana, or the "haves" squashing the innumerable "have nots." It will be because of some miracle, some radical turn in our consciousness late in the game—the Dalai Lama comes to mind ...Carl Jung, Elisabeth Kübler-Ross, Stanislav Grof. Do we need an invasion from outer space to finally bring us together? Certainly more humble and open-minded works like this book of Hibiki Kobayashi's can help us to start to rethink our global game plan, our purpose on earth.

Peter Beard

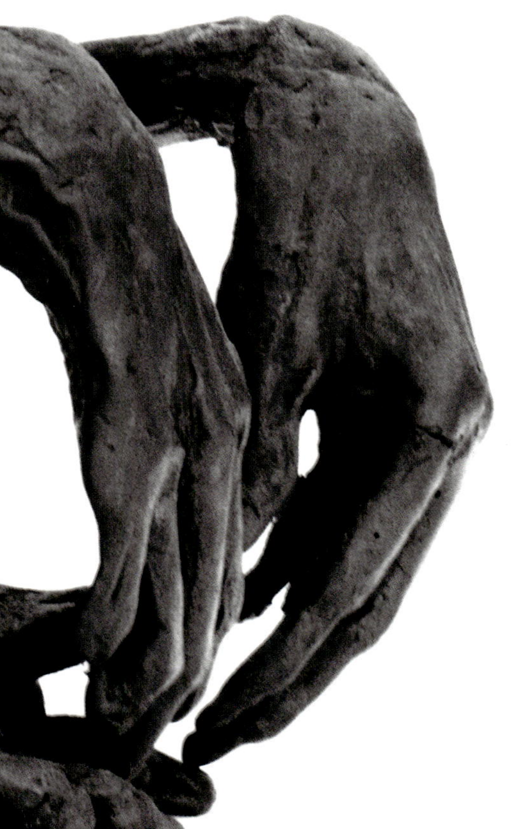

Foreword

I remember an episode from my first trip to Africa. I was traveling from Nairobi to Lake Rudolf near the border of Kenya and Ethiopia. It was a four-day journey of many bus rides. Along the way I saw two men, herding several dozen cows, disappear into the savannah. Naked from the waist up, they wore tribal garb and carried spears. This was my first encounter with African tribal people. They were people of the Turkana tribe. Dwelling in homes made of earth, wood, and cow dung, they lived the same nomadic life that their ancestors had for centuries. When I met these people in their village, I encountered something unique. I did not understand a word they spoke, but I sensed something from their eyes, their voices, and their faces. Their presence was worlds apart from that of people who believe only in material things. I was overwhelmed by the power of their existence. I was moved by a profound impulse to photograph them. I have never felt more compelled to capture an image on film. In the ensuing five years, I traveled to Asia, the Middle East, Africa, New Guinea, and the Amazon, photographing portraits of more than three thousand people. This encounter in Africa took place in November of 1990, but the passionate excitement of that meeting remains with me to this day.

Hibiki Kobayashi

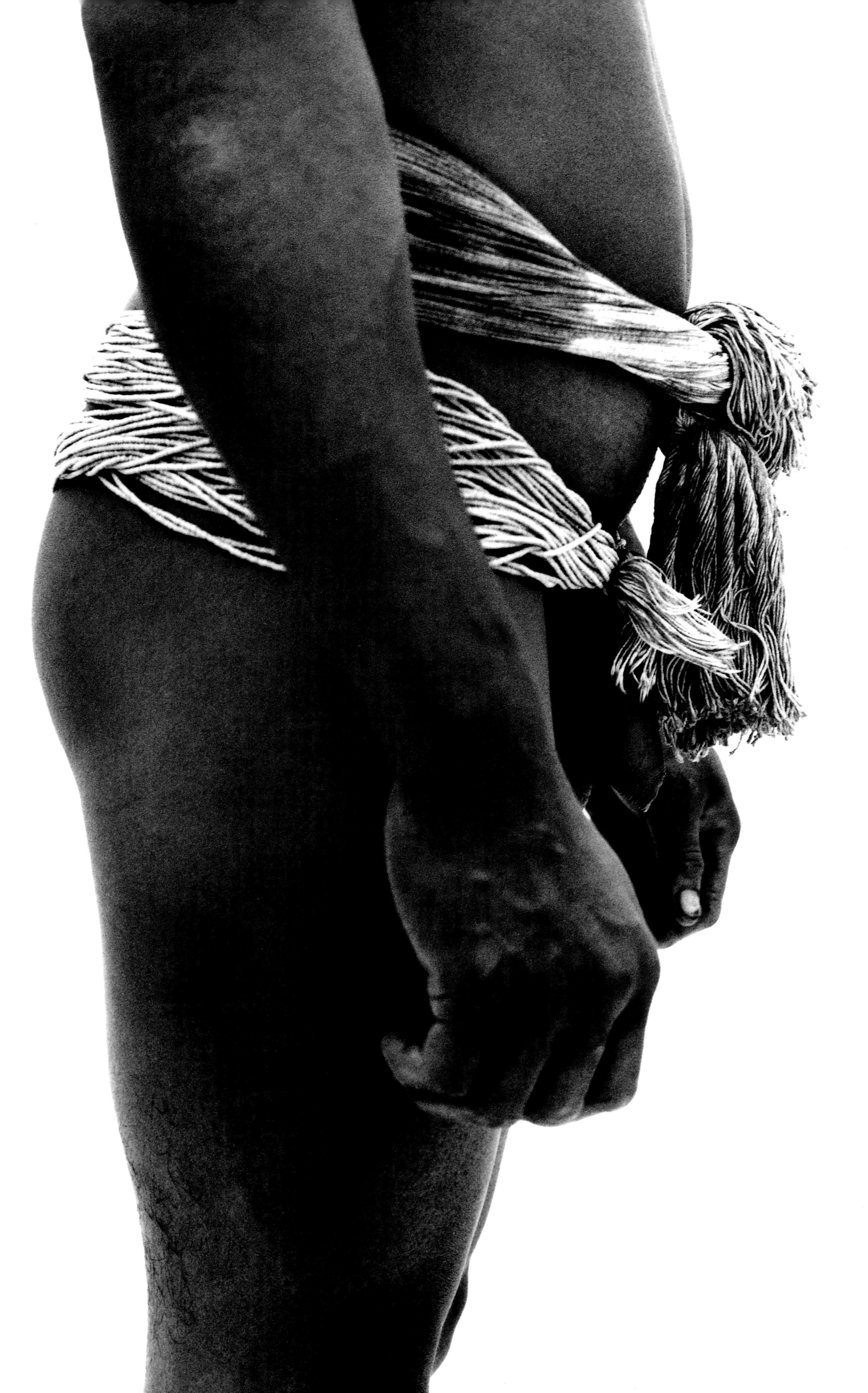

Brazil Kamayura Tribe

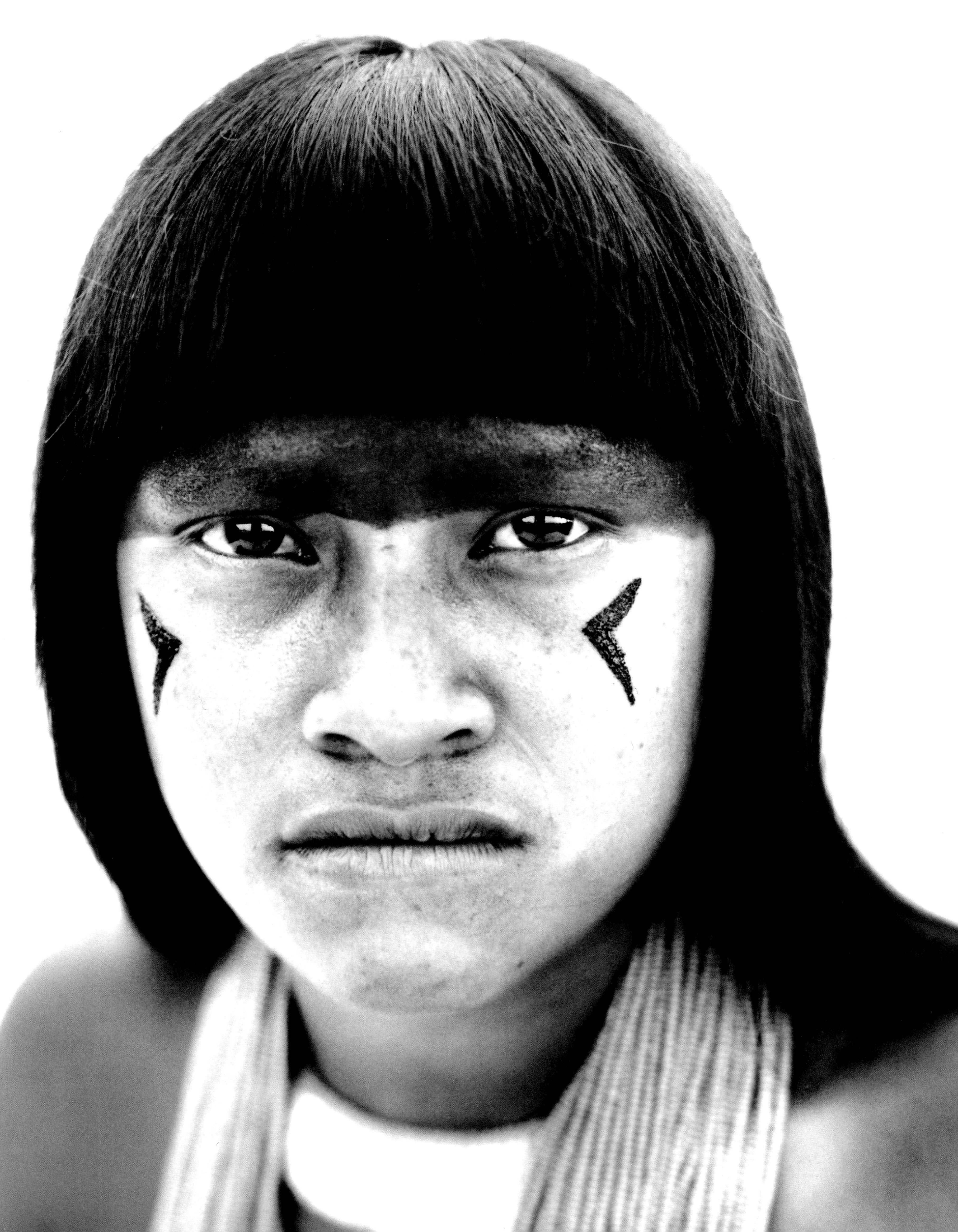

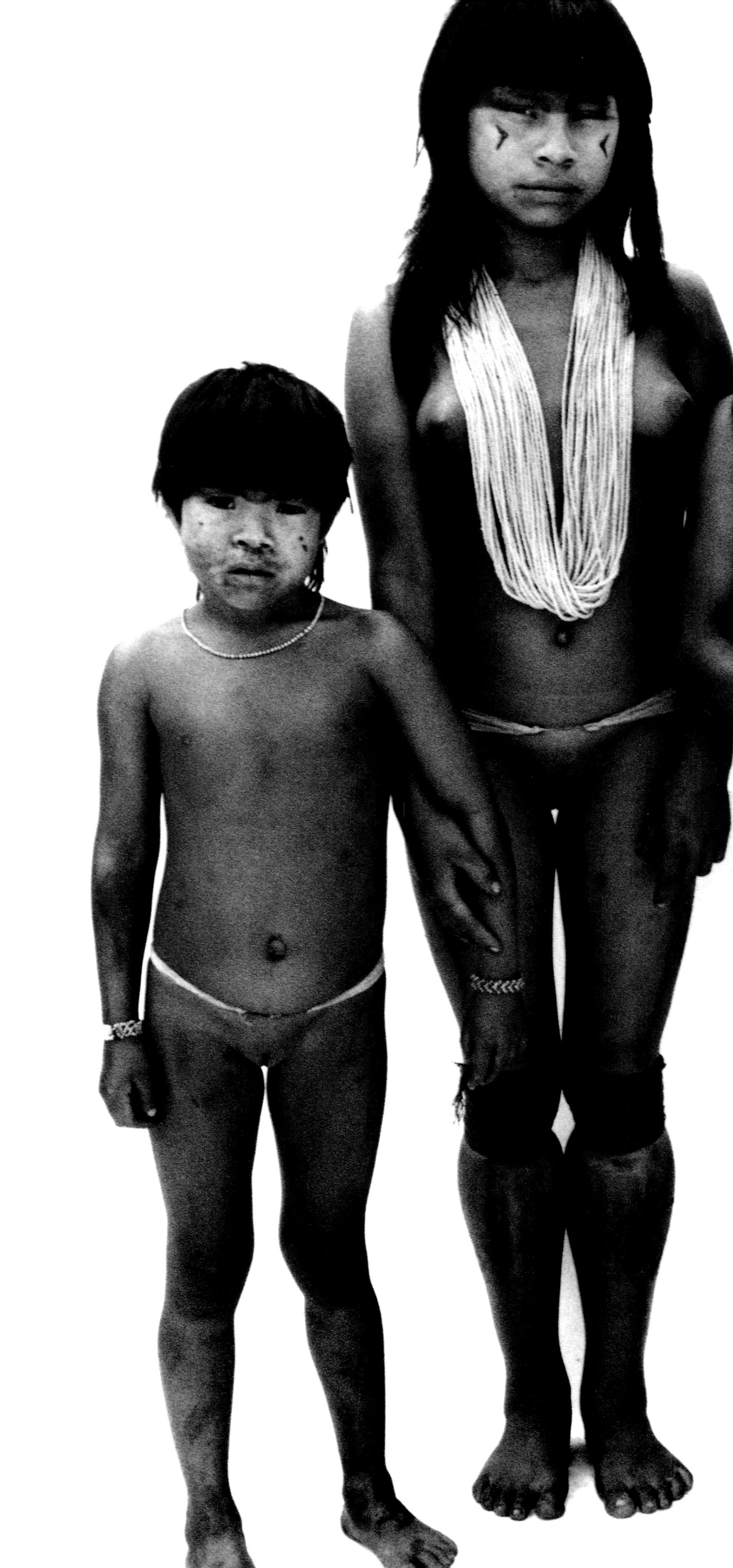

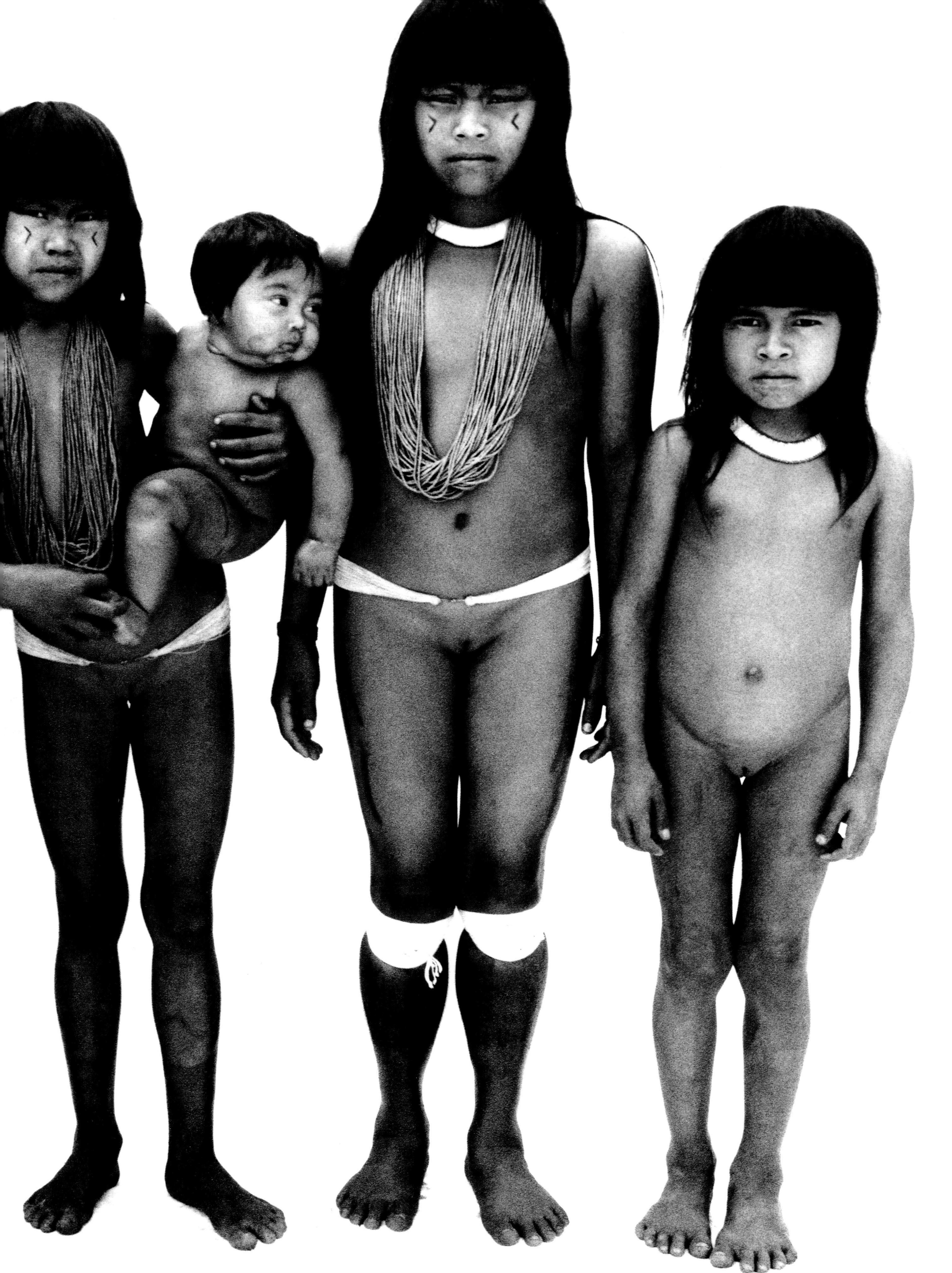

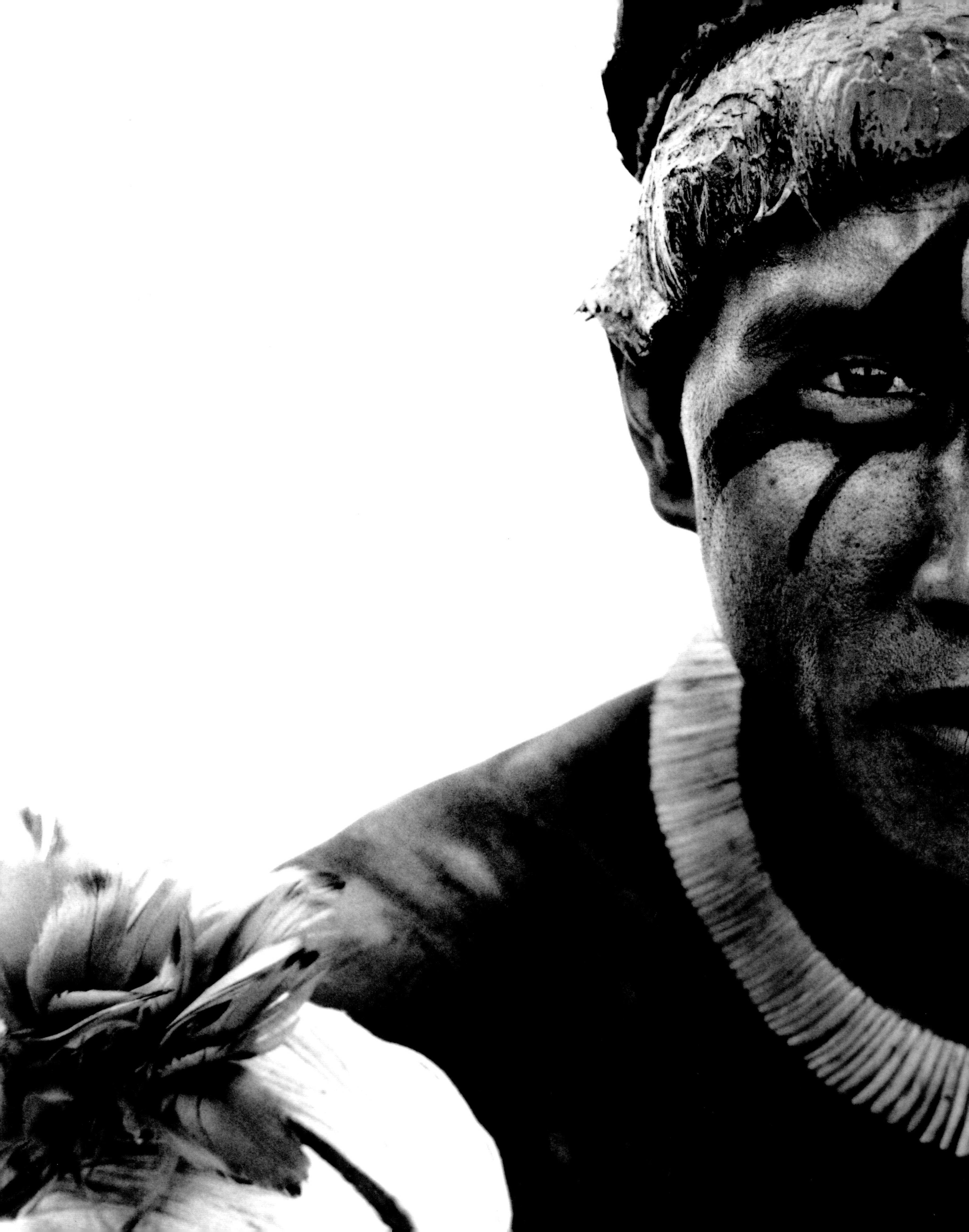

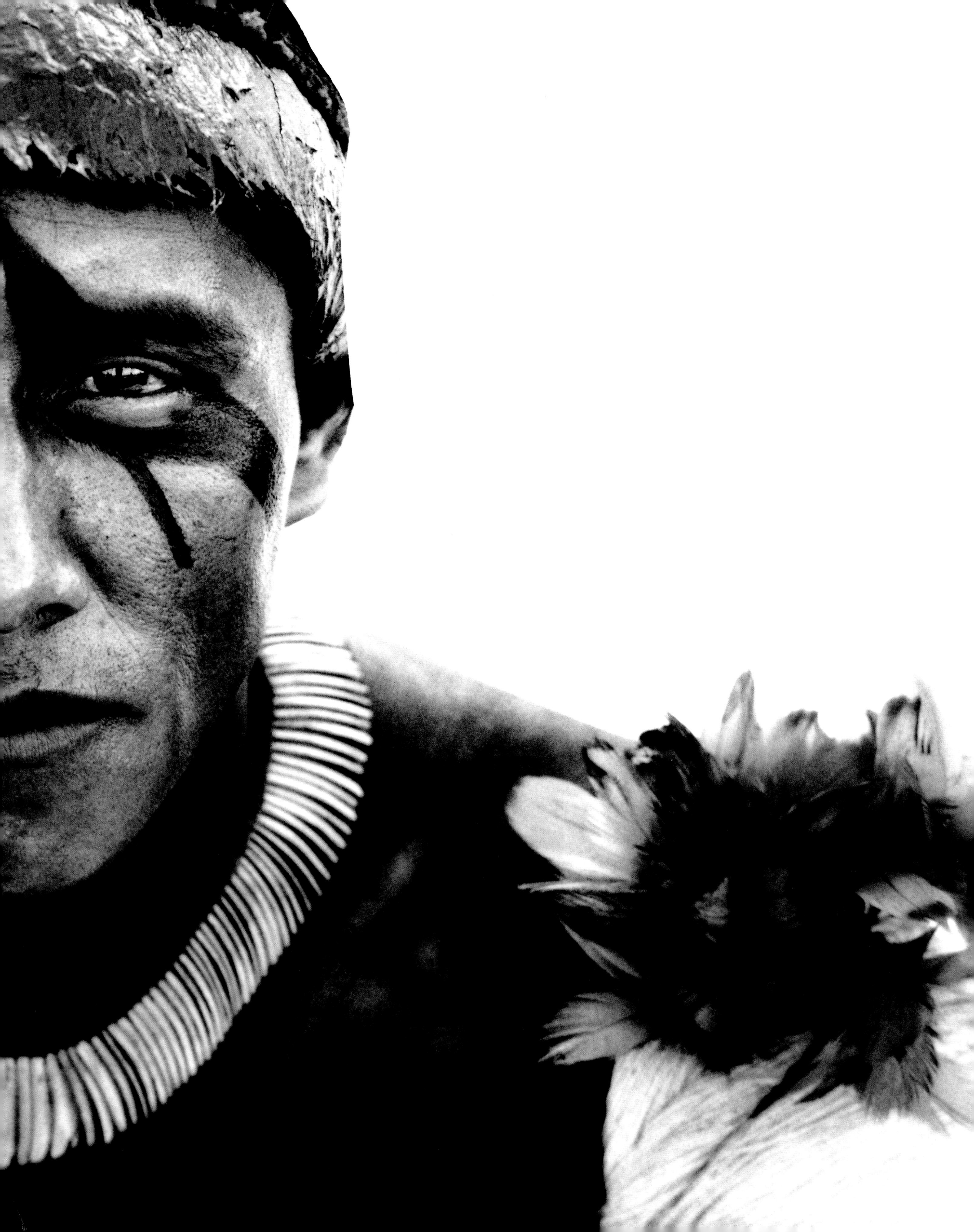

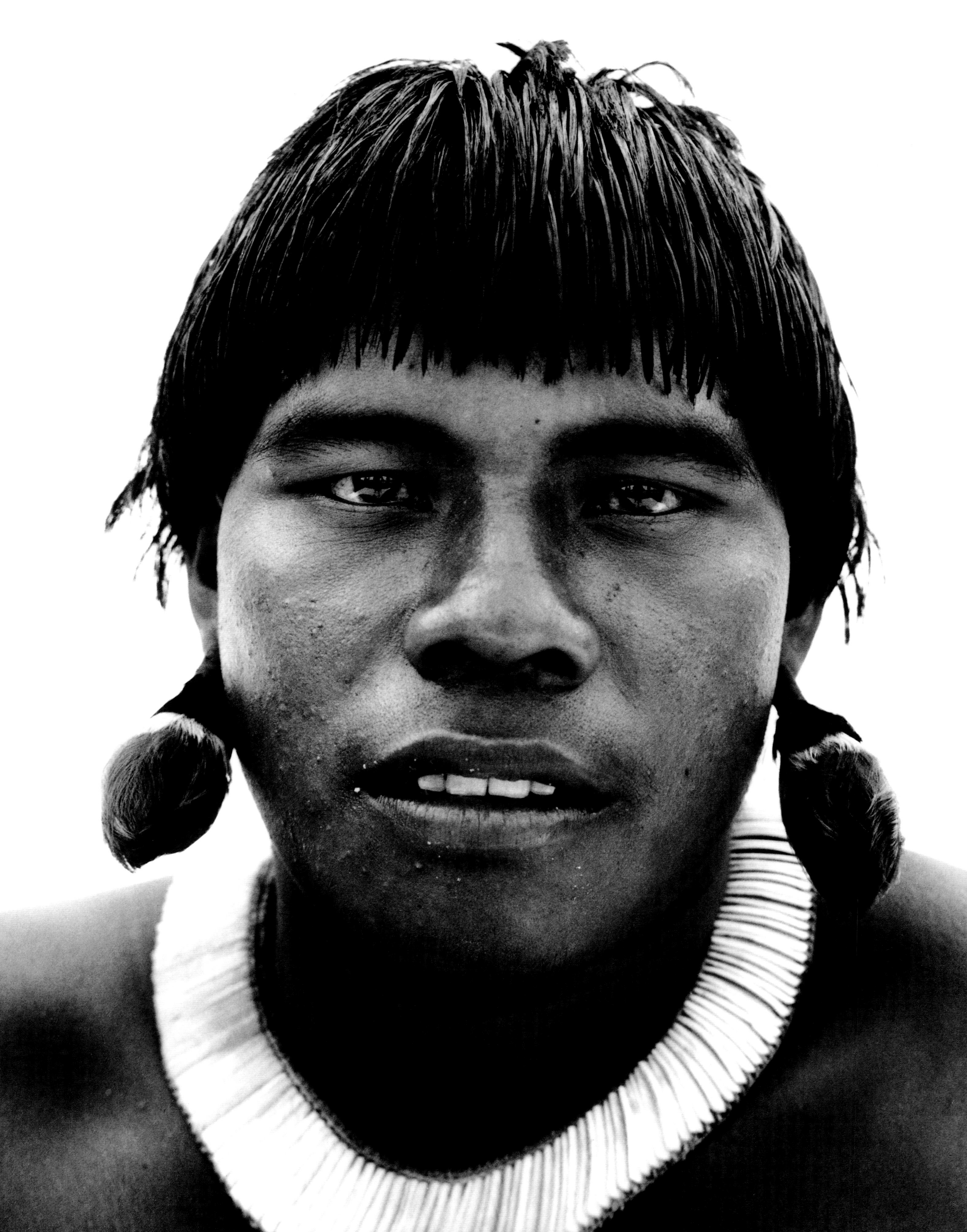

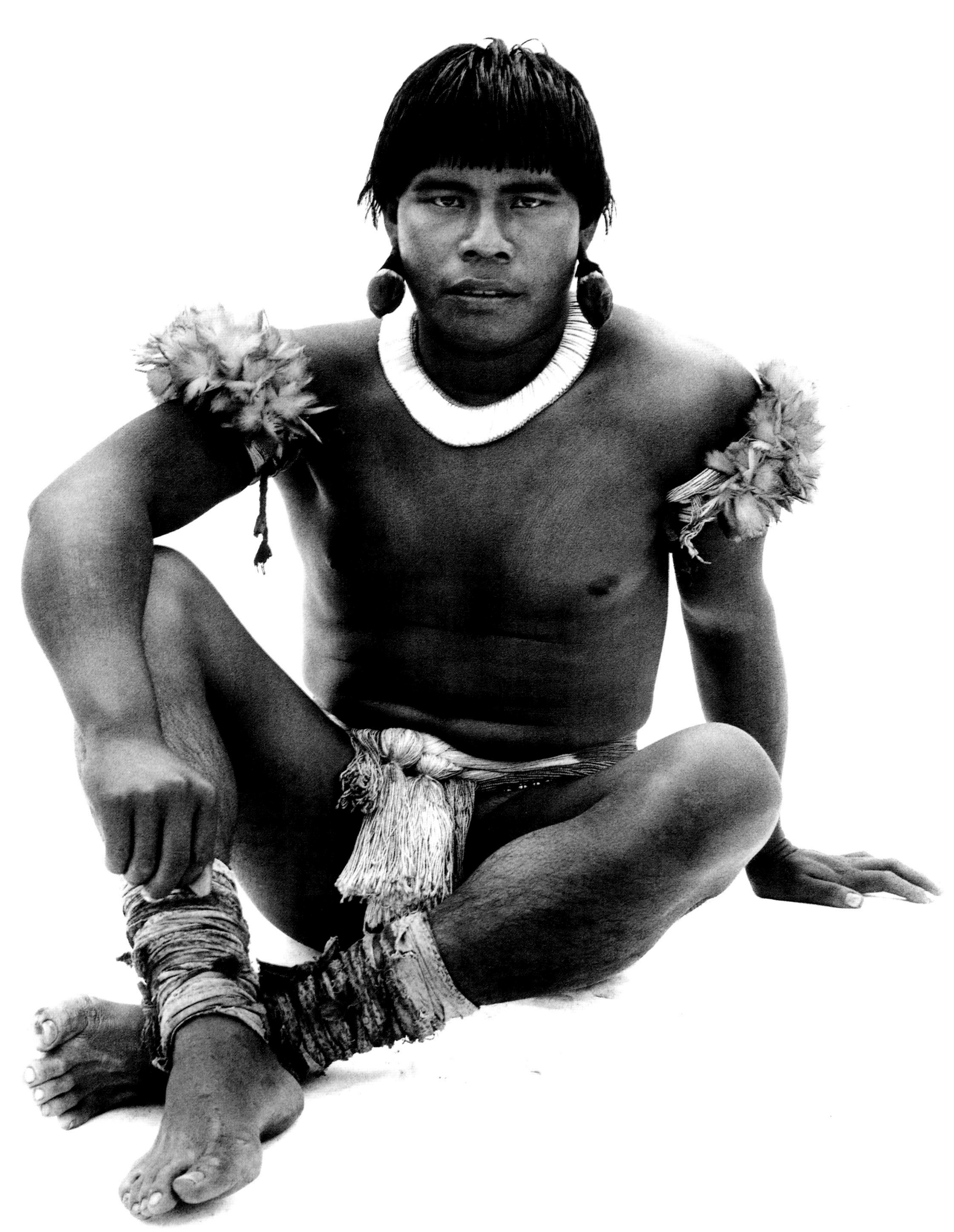

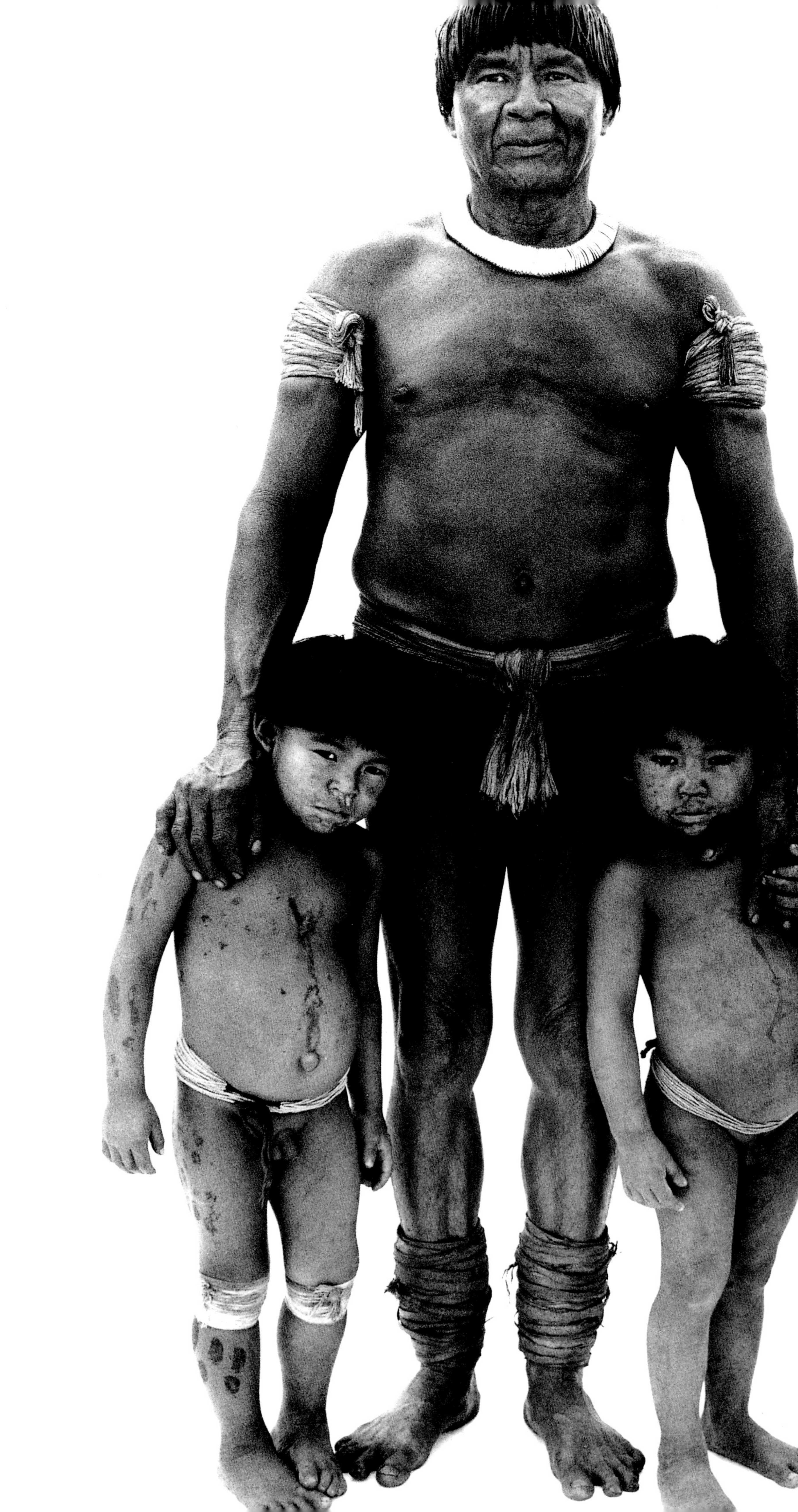

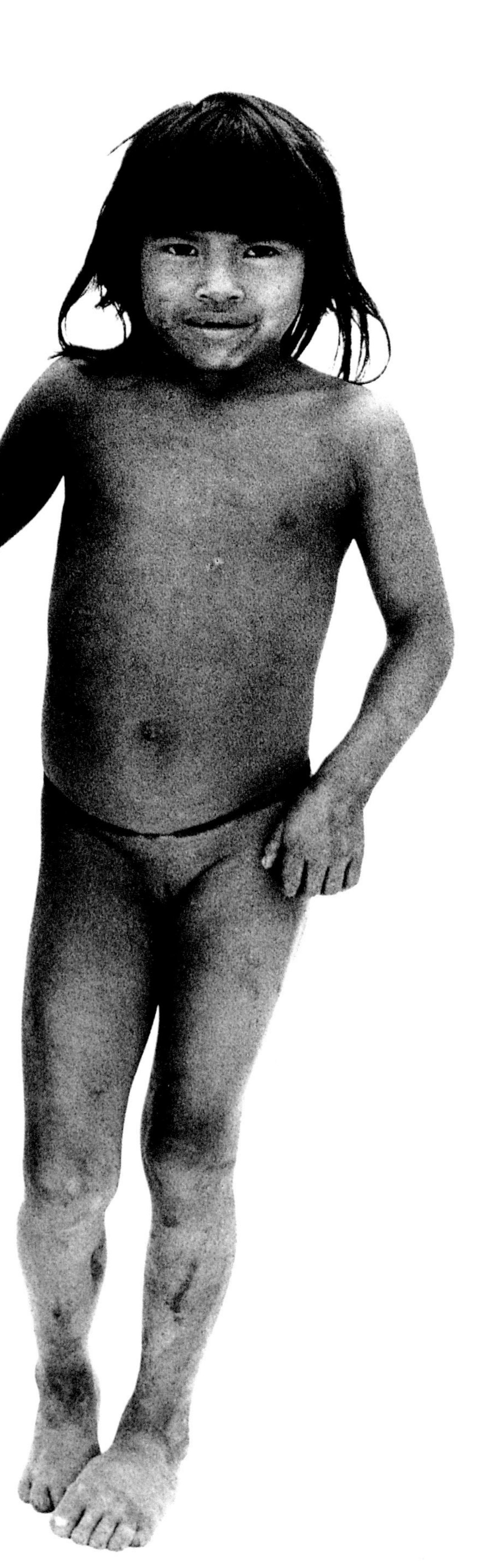

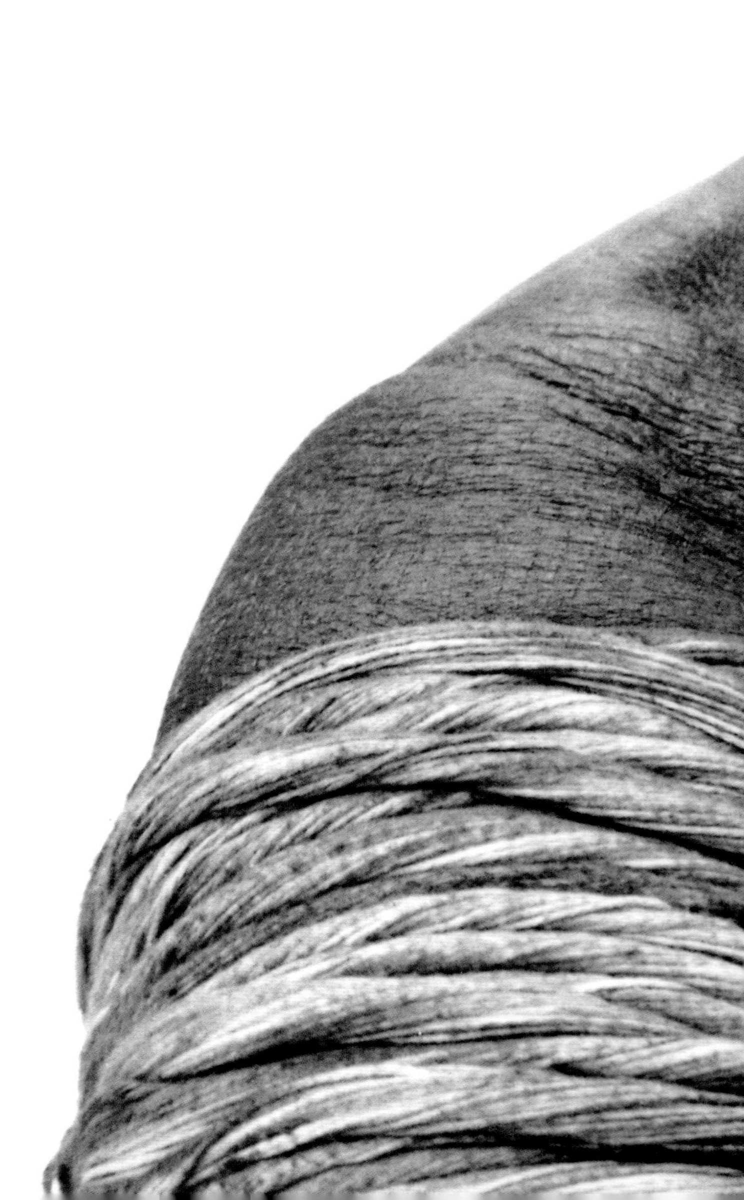

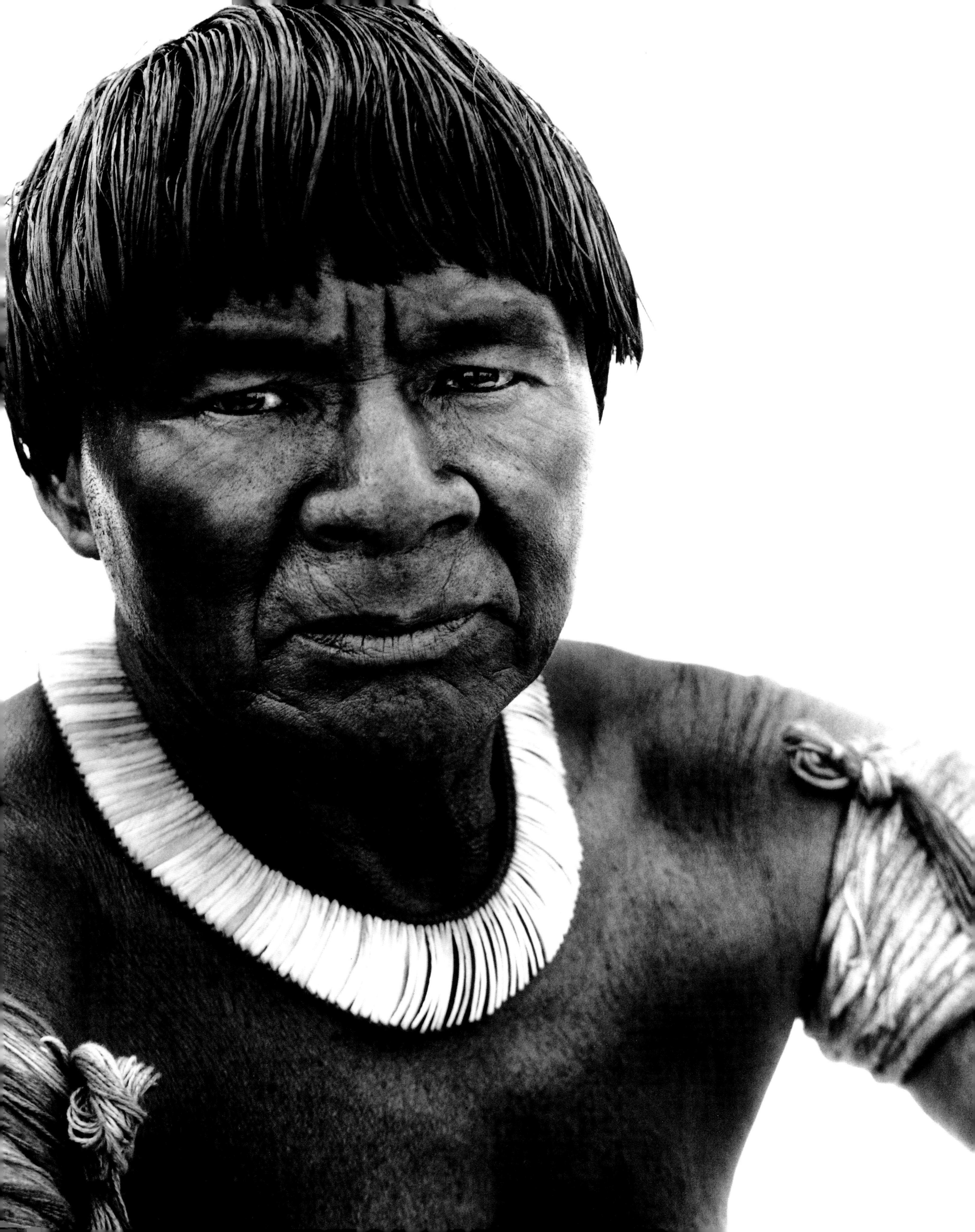

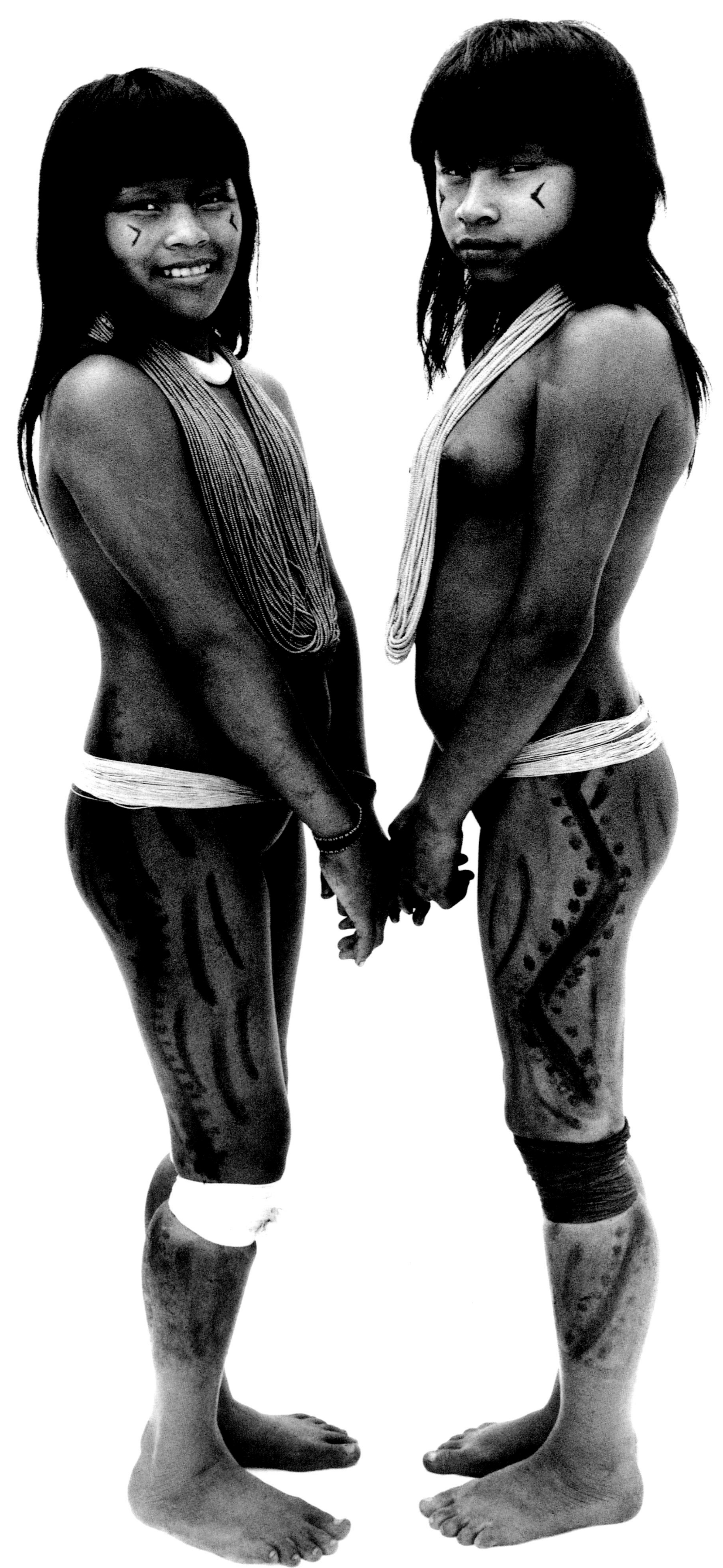

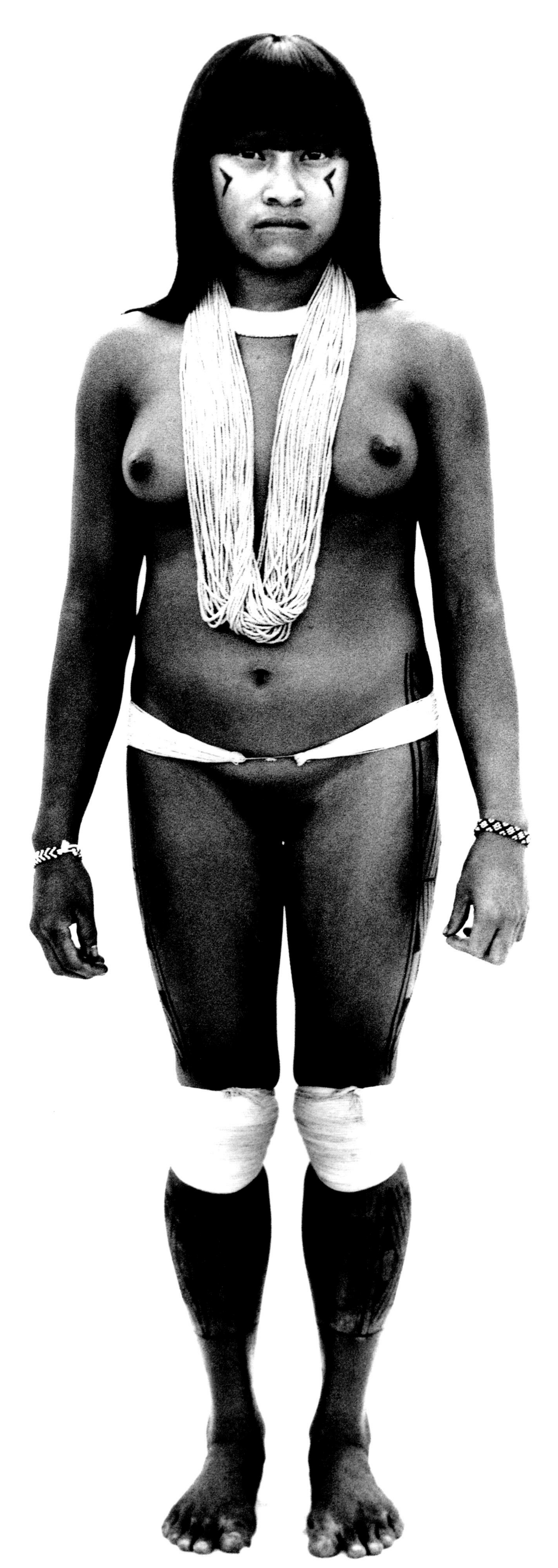

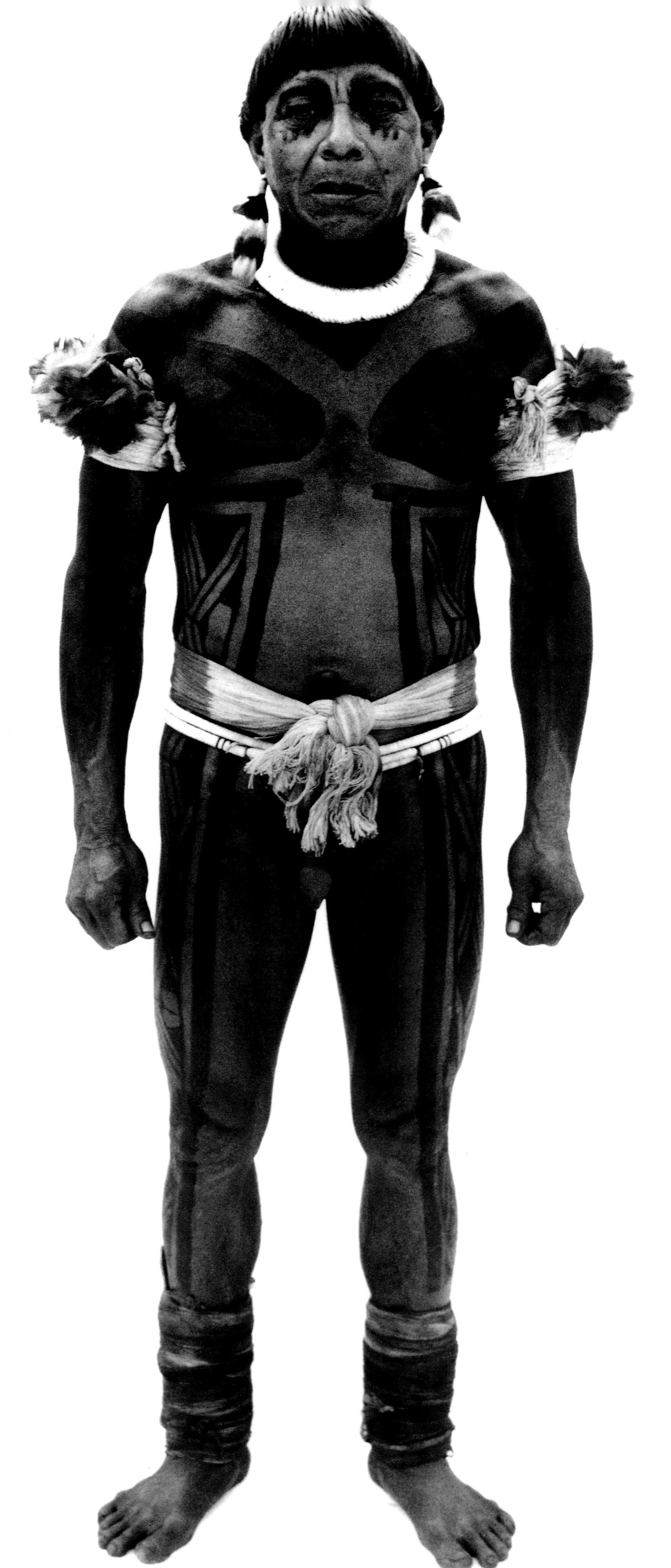

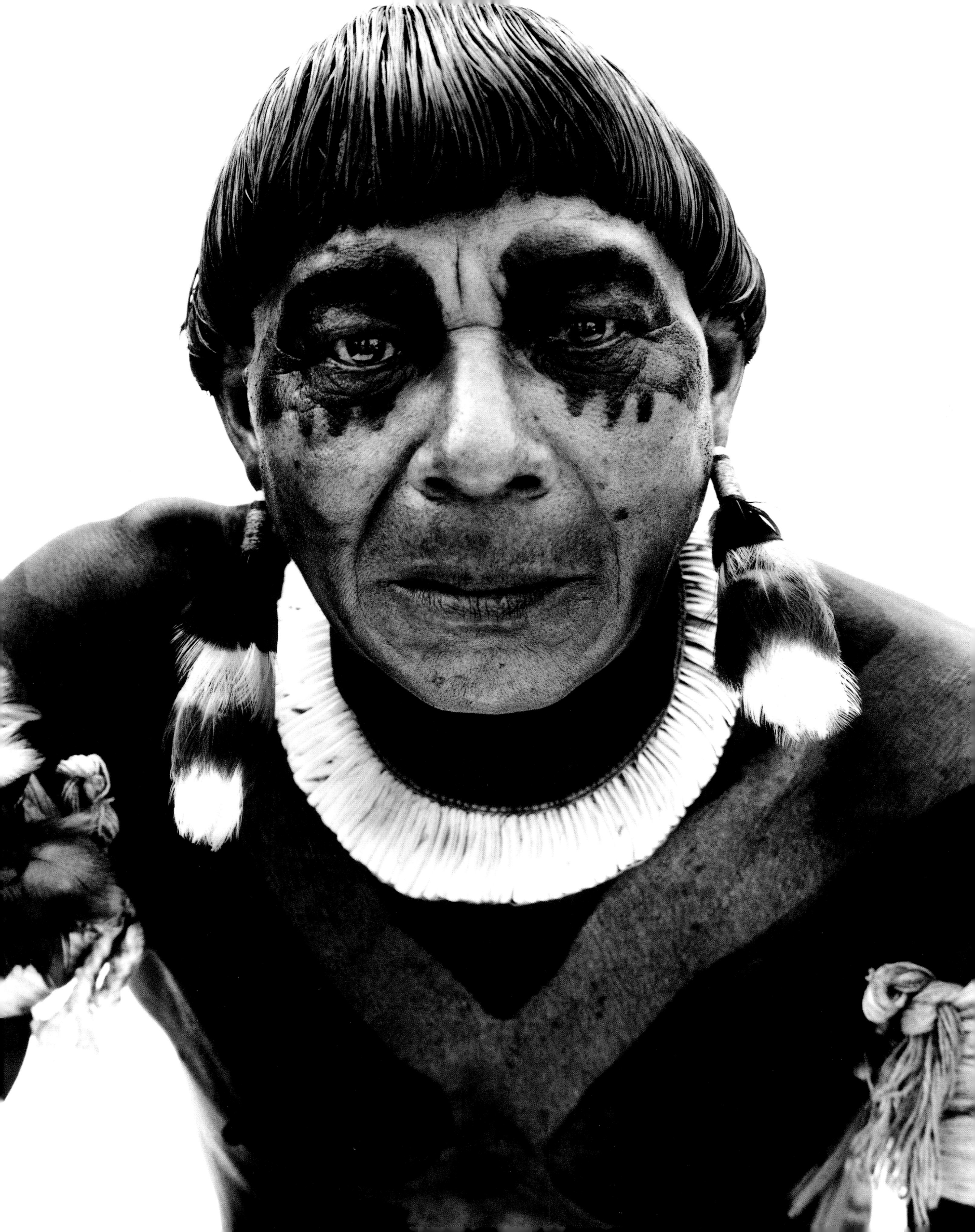

Brazil Kayapo Tribe

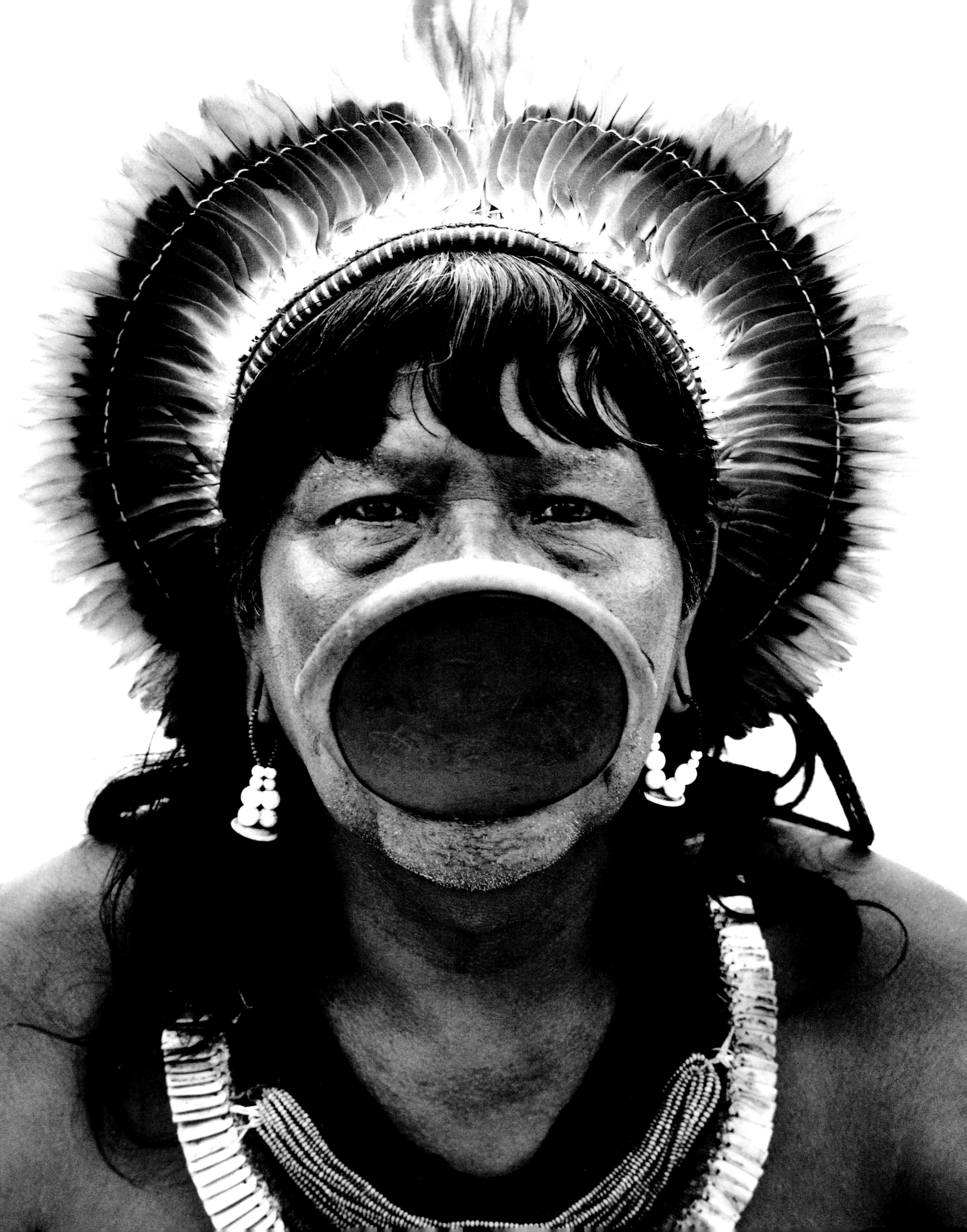

Kenya Samburu Tribe

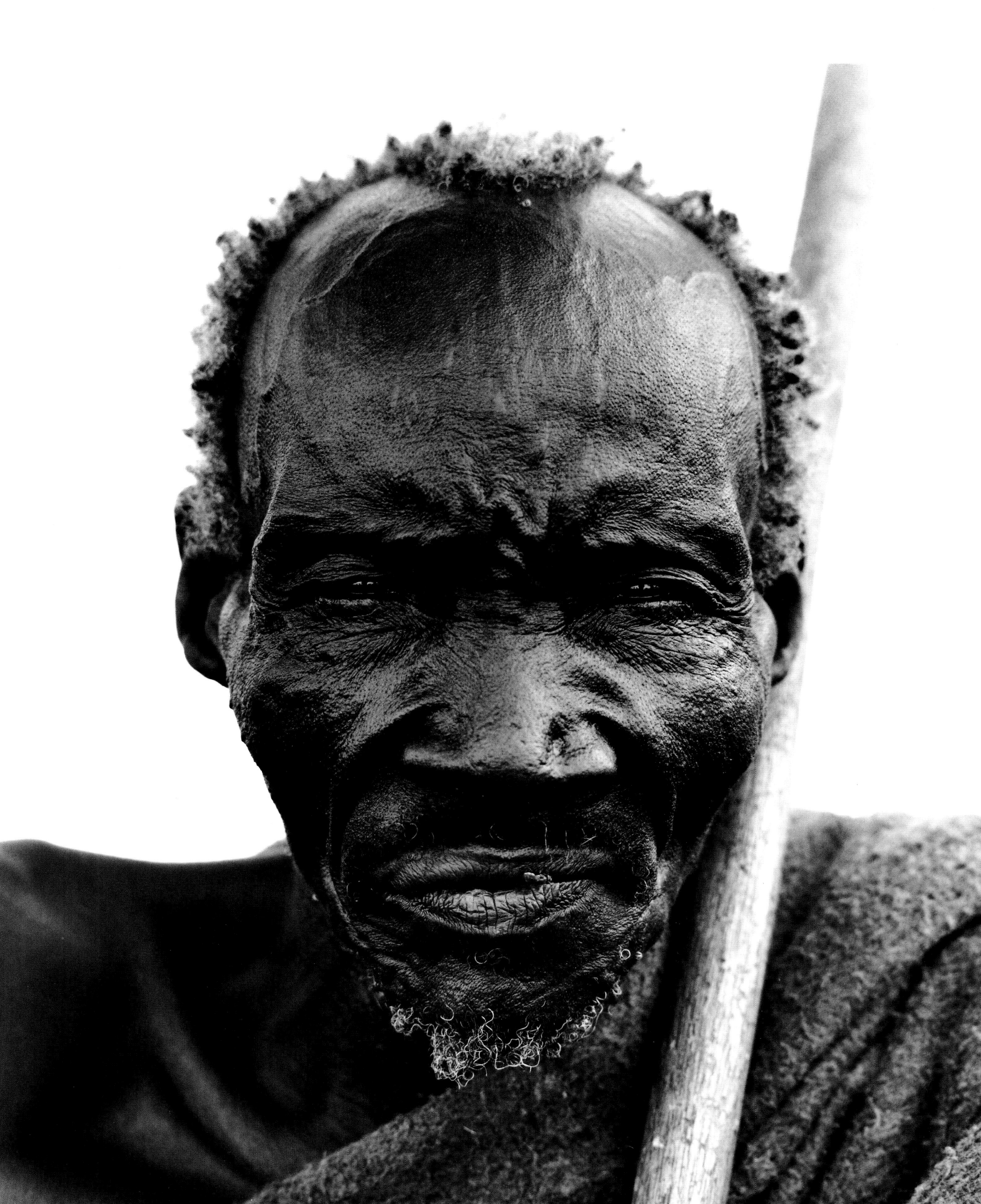

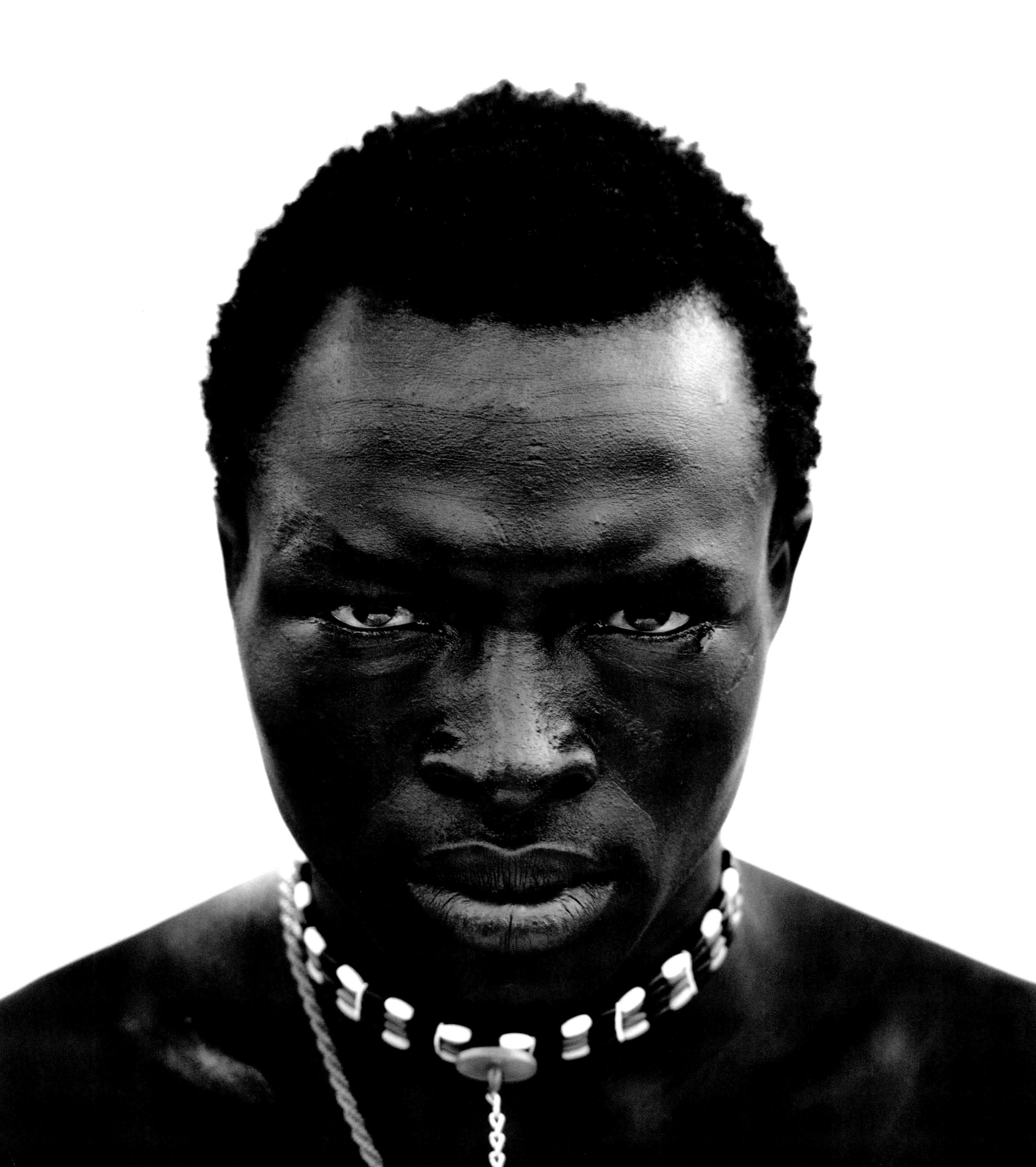

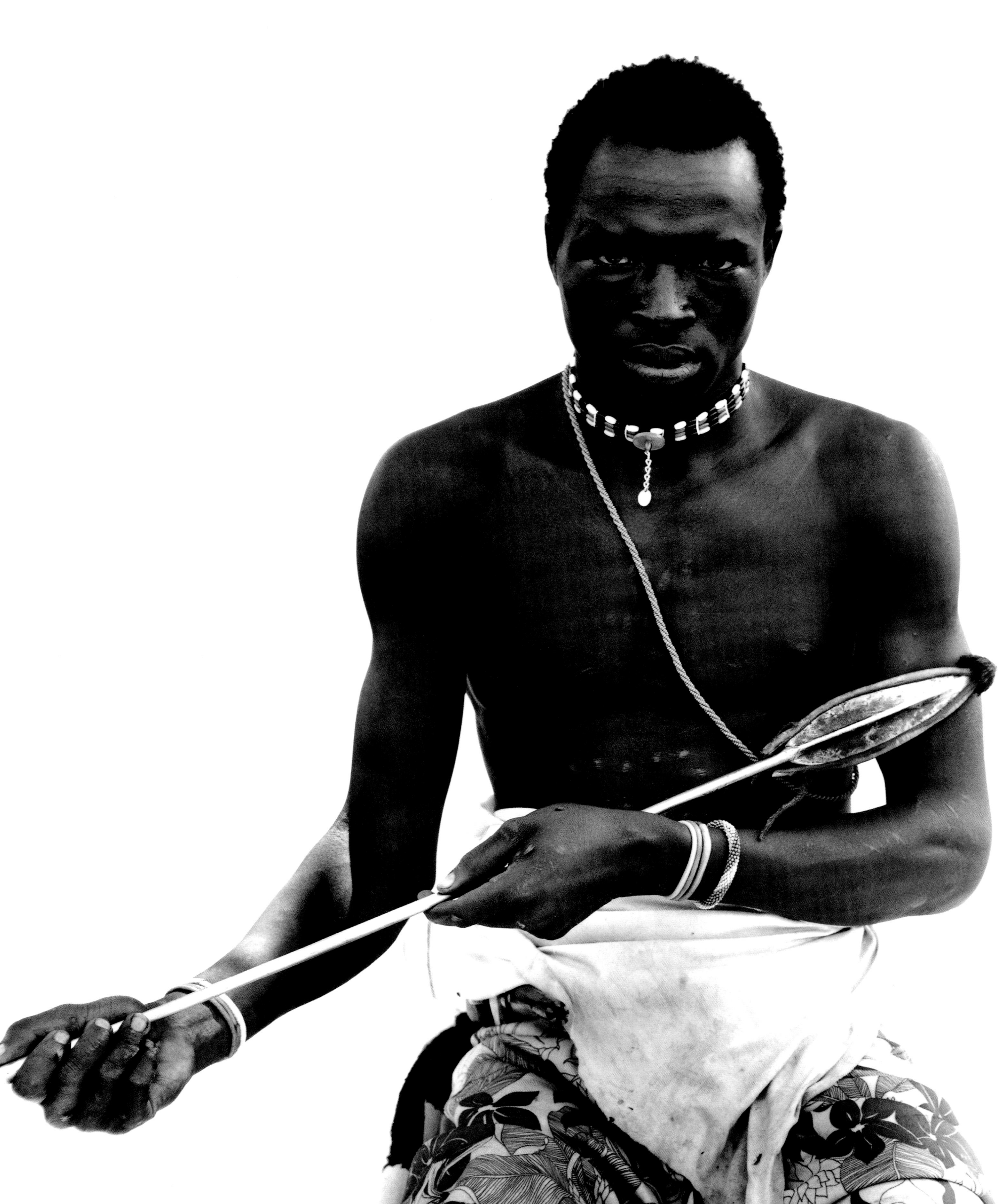

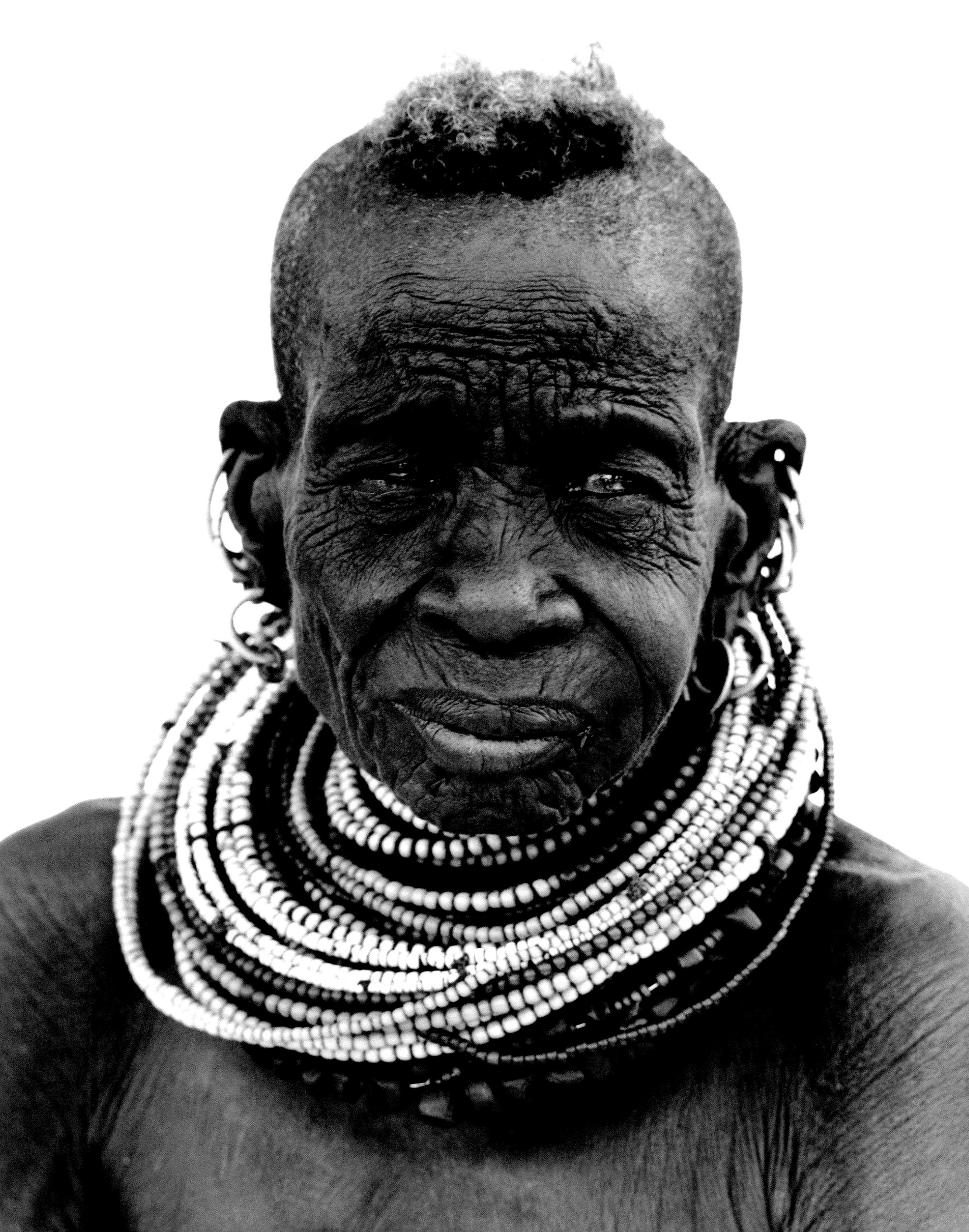

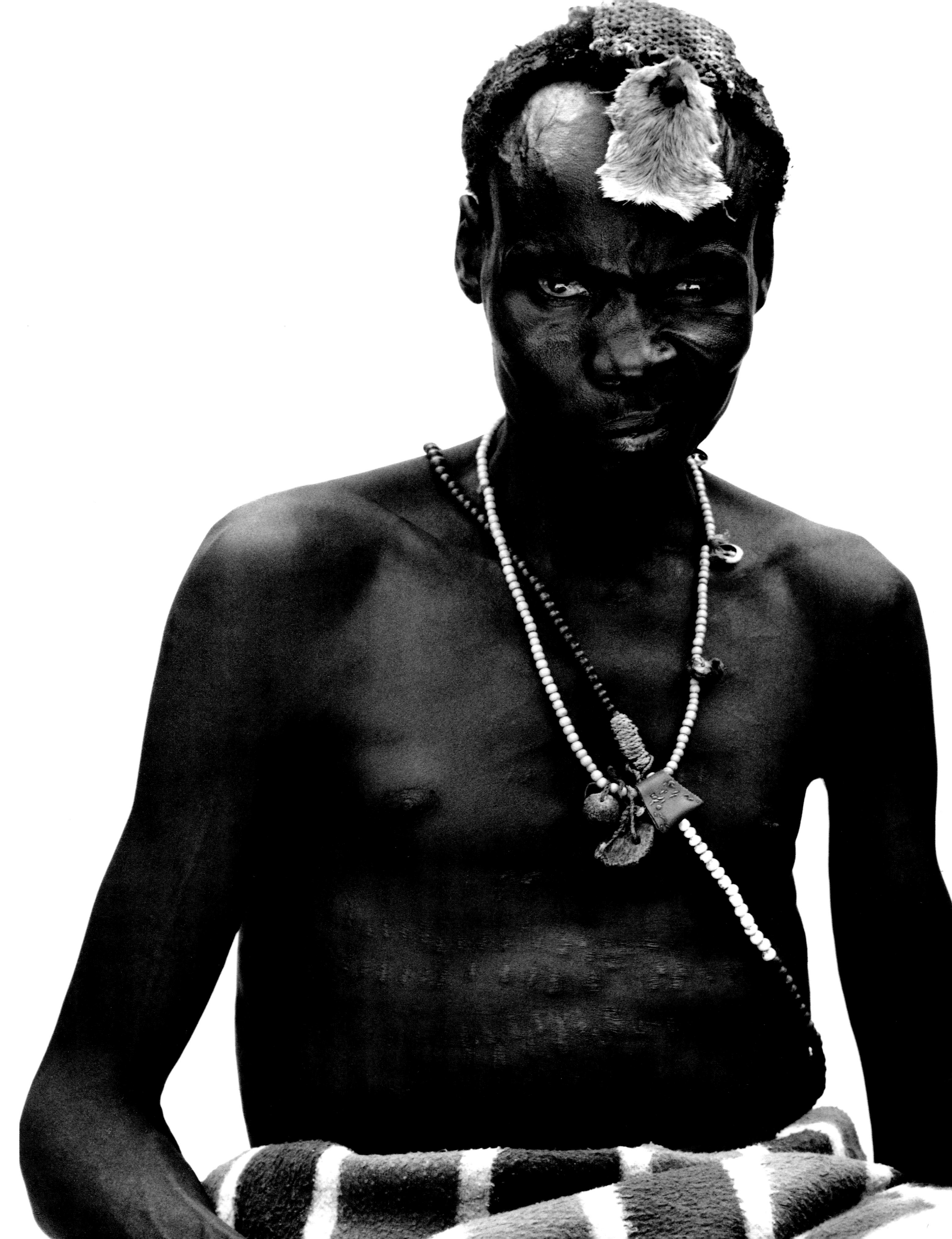

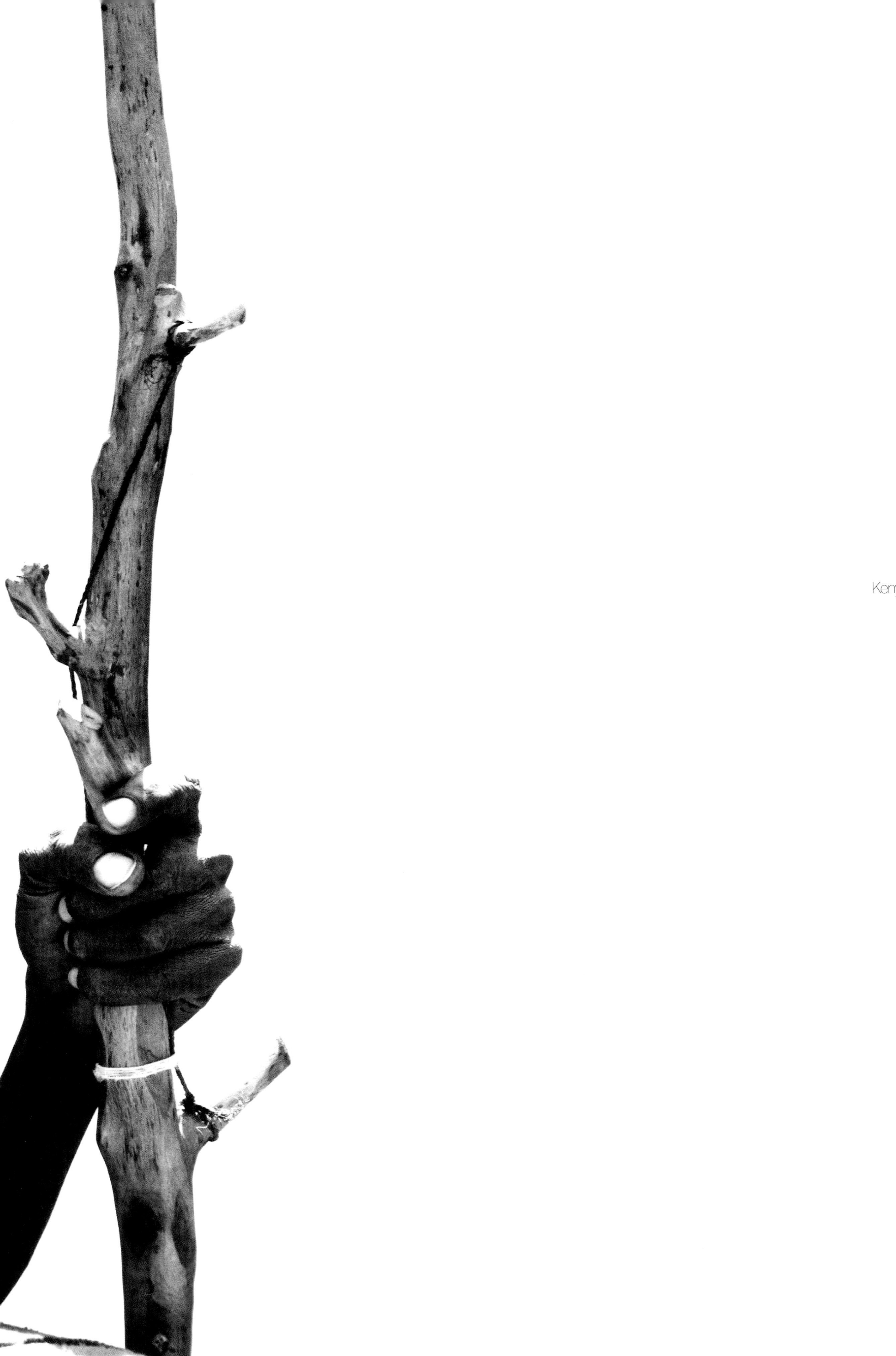

Kenya Turkana Tribe

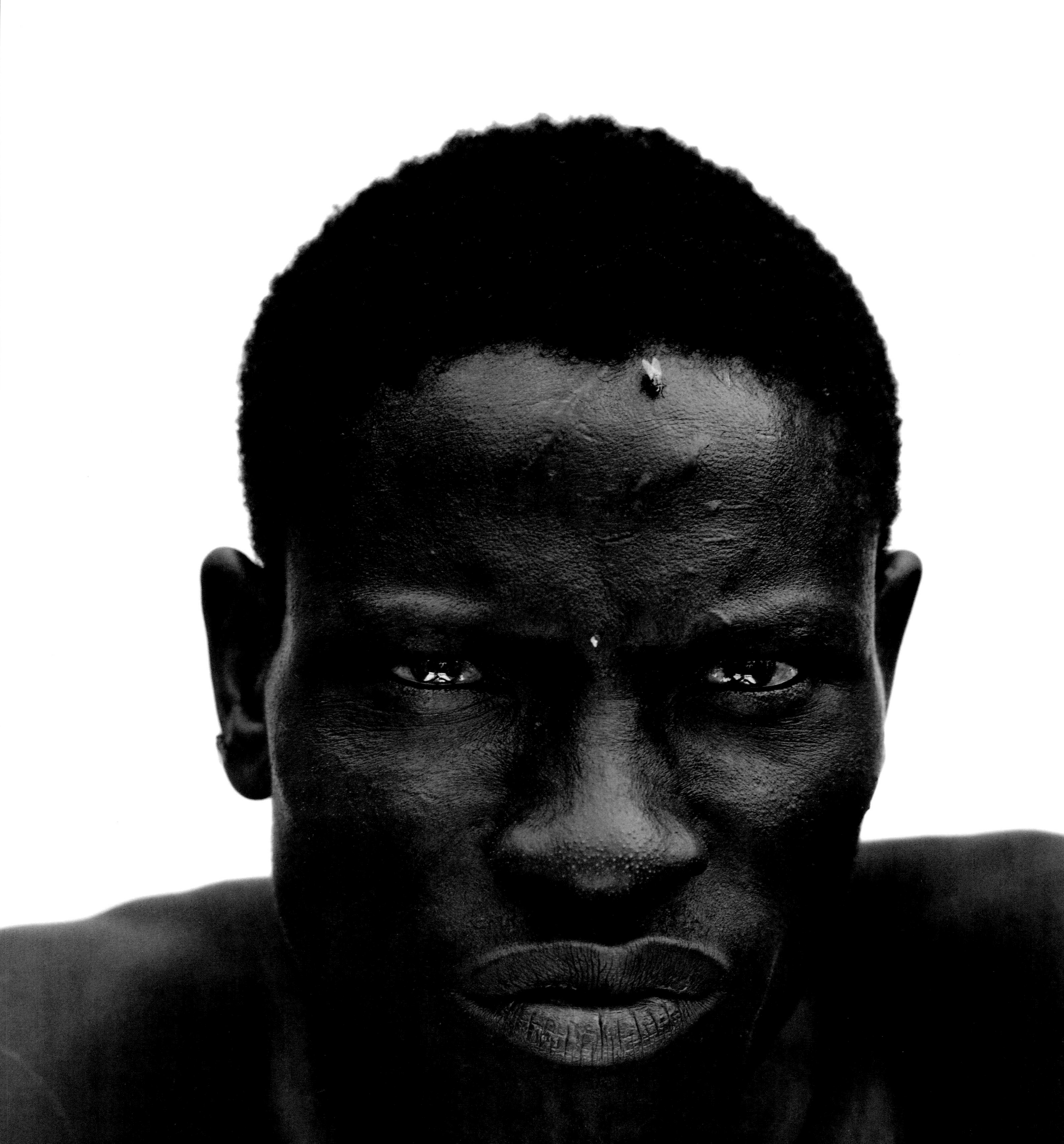

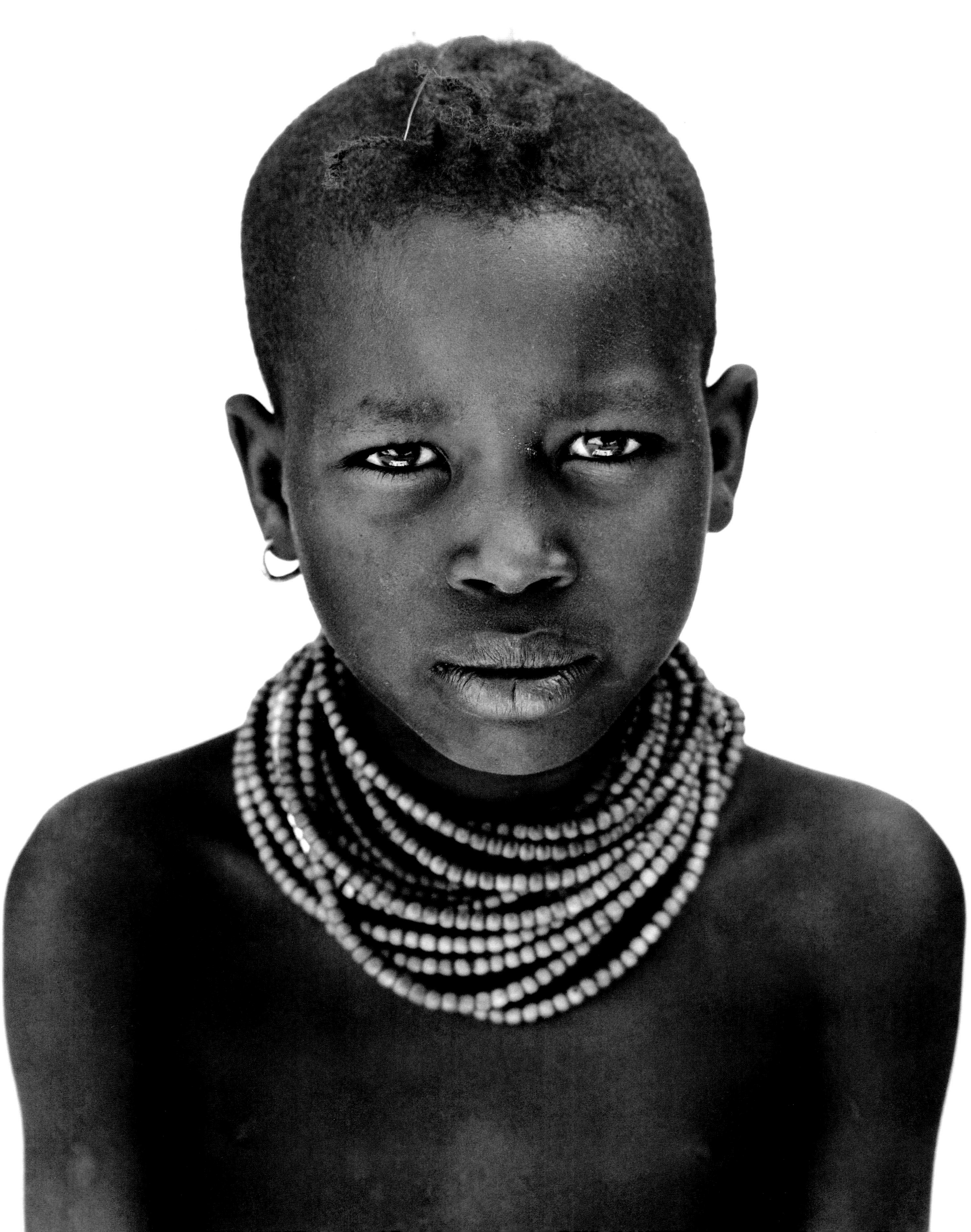

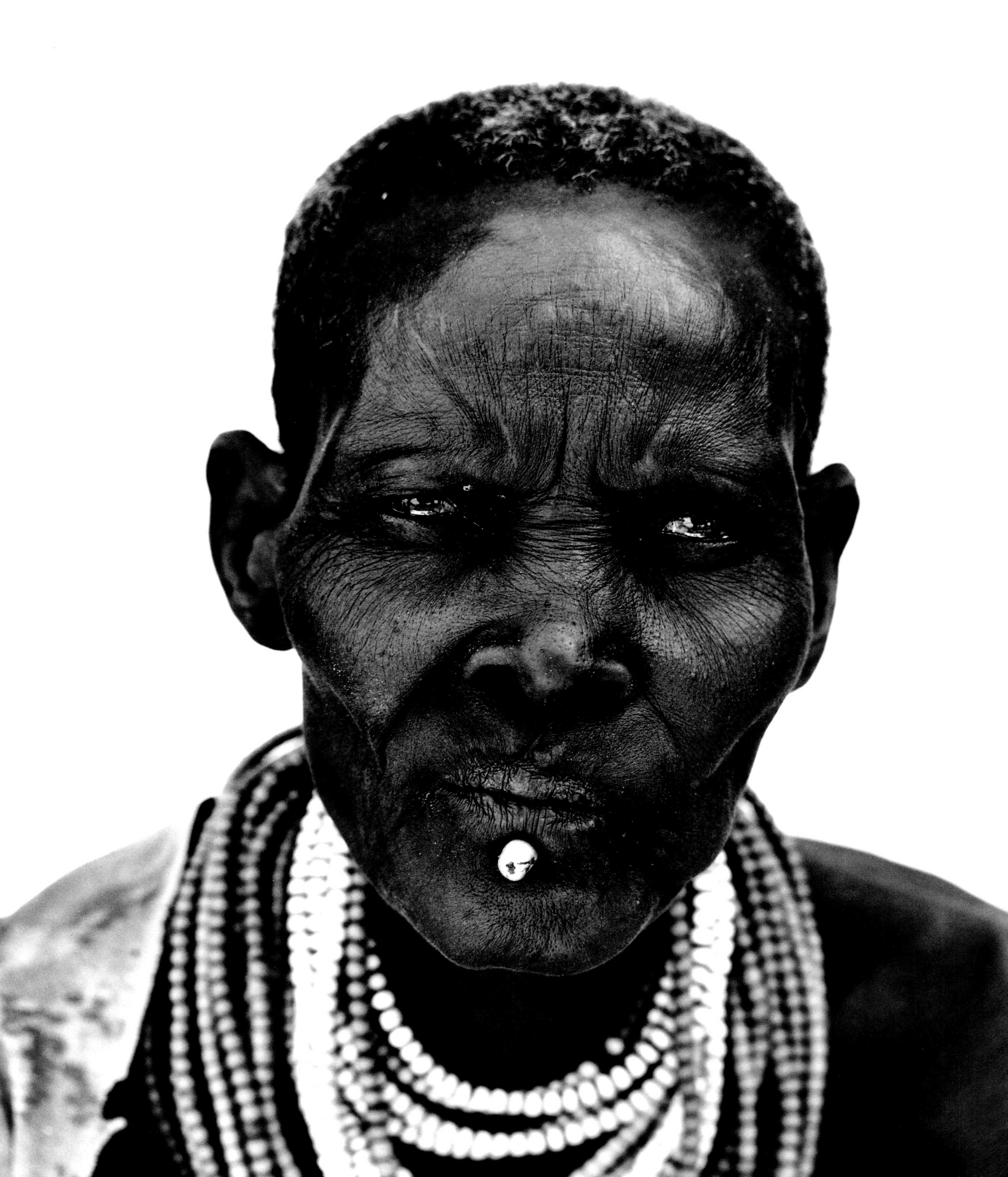

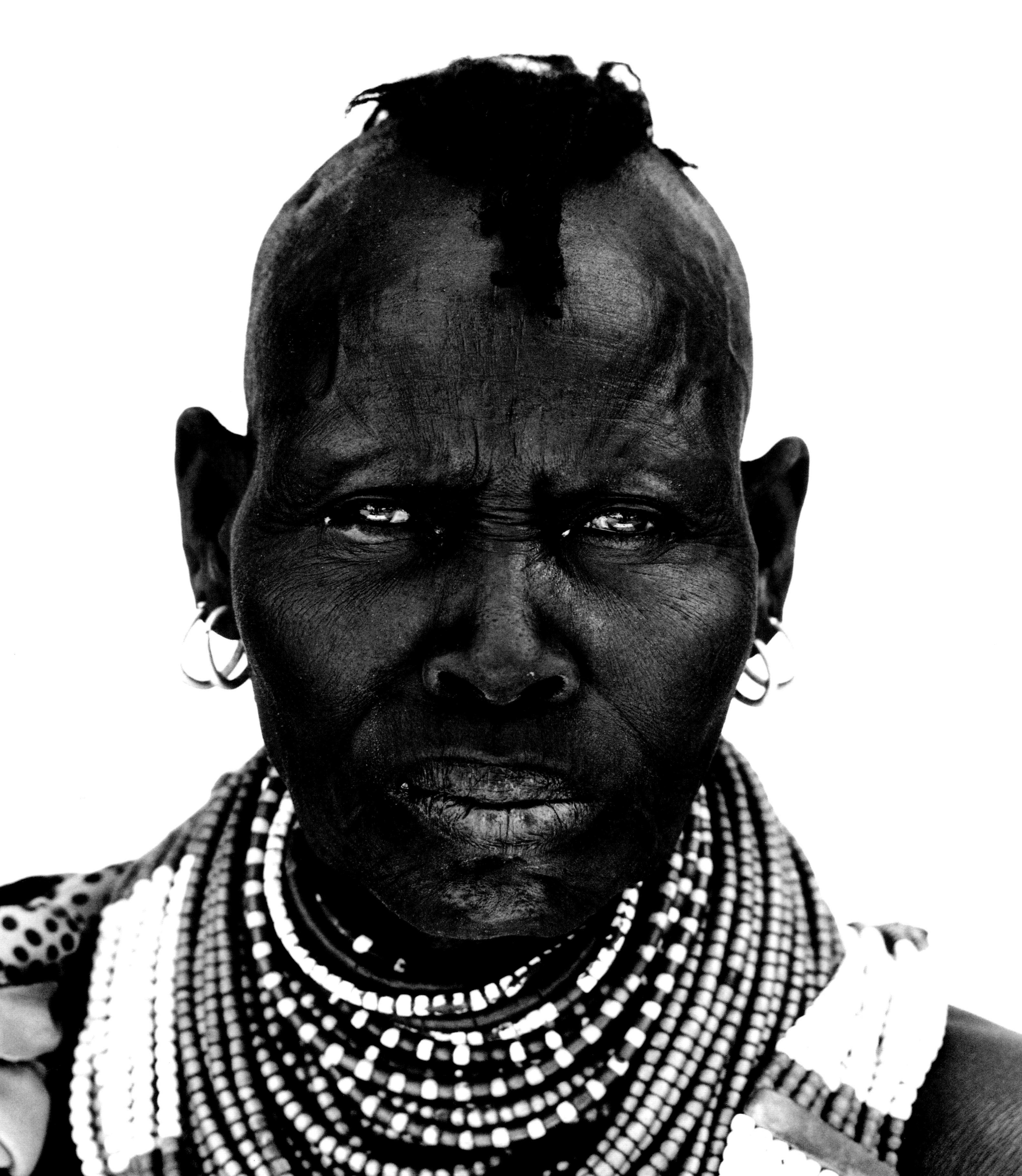

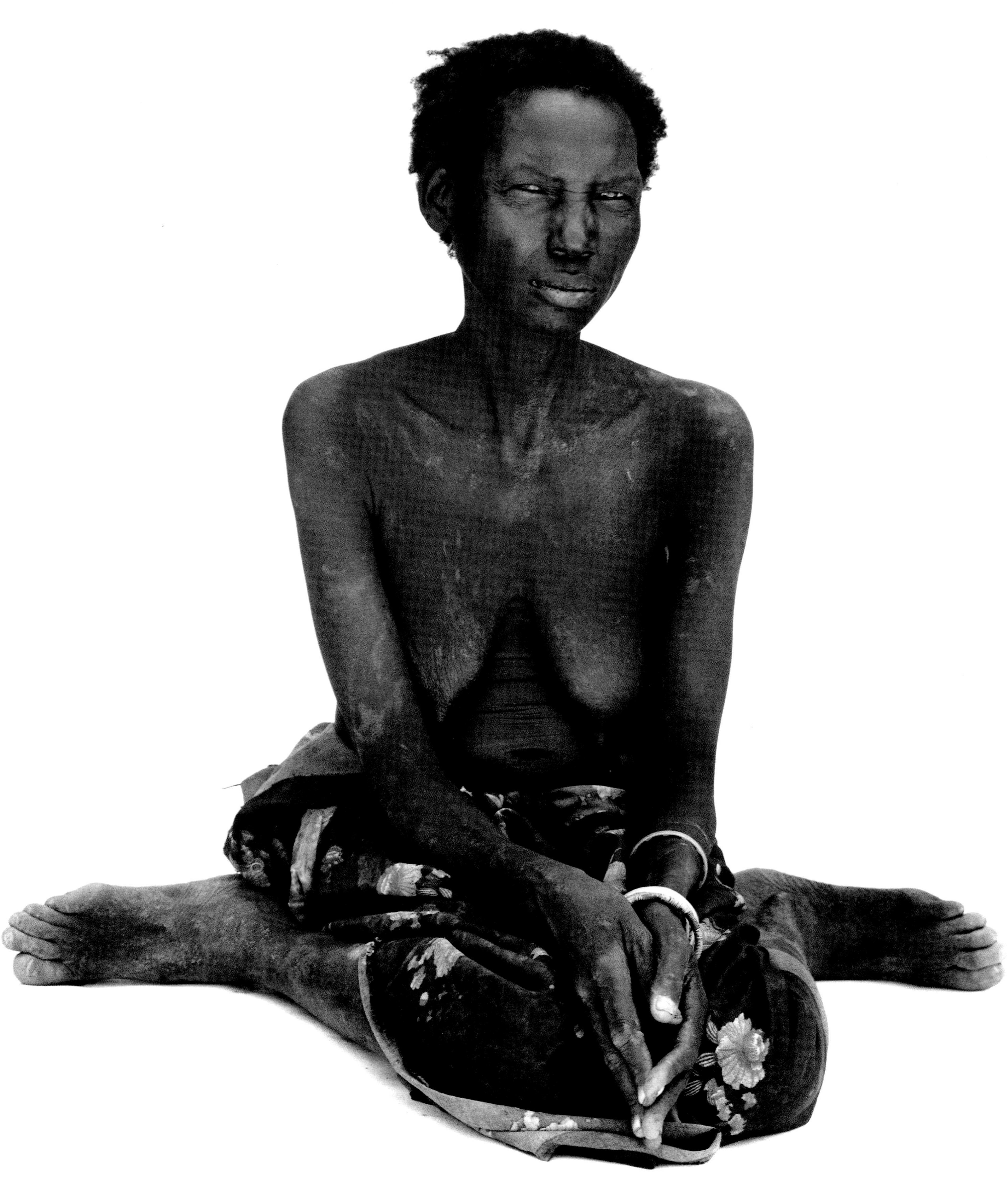

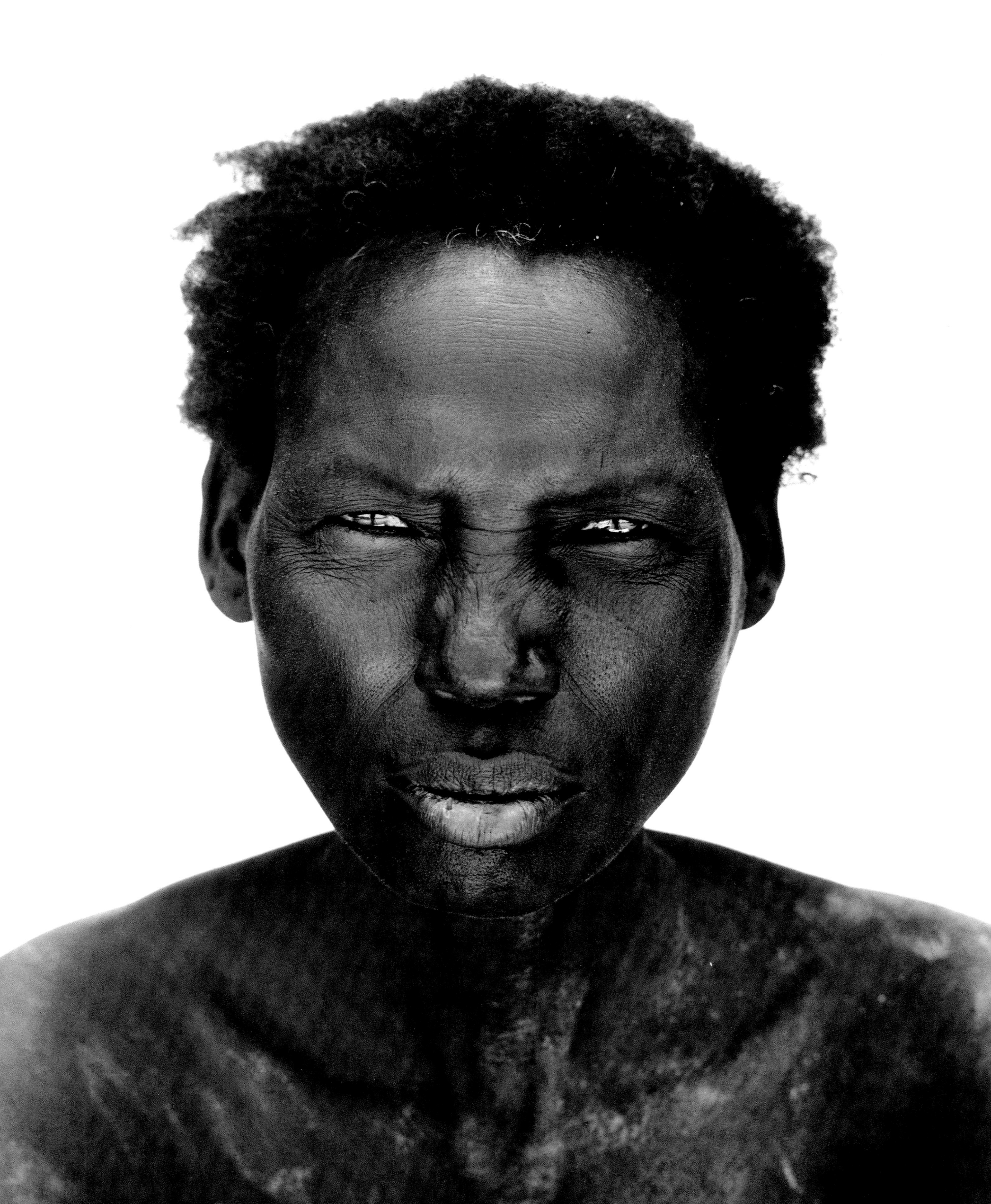

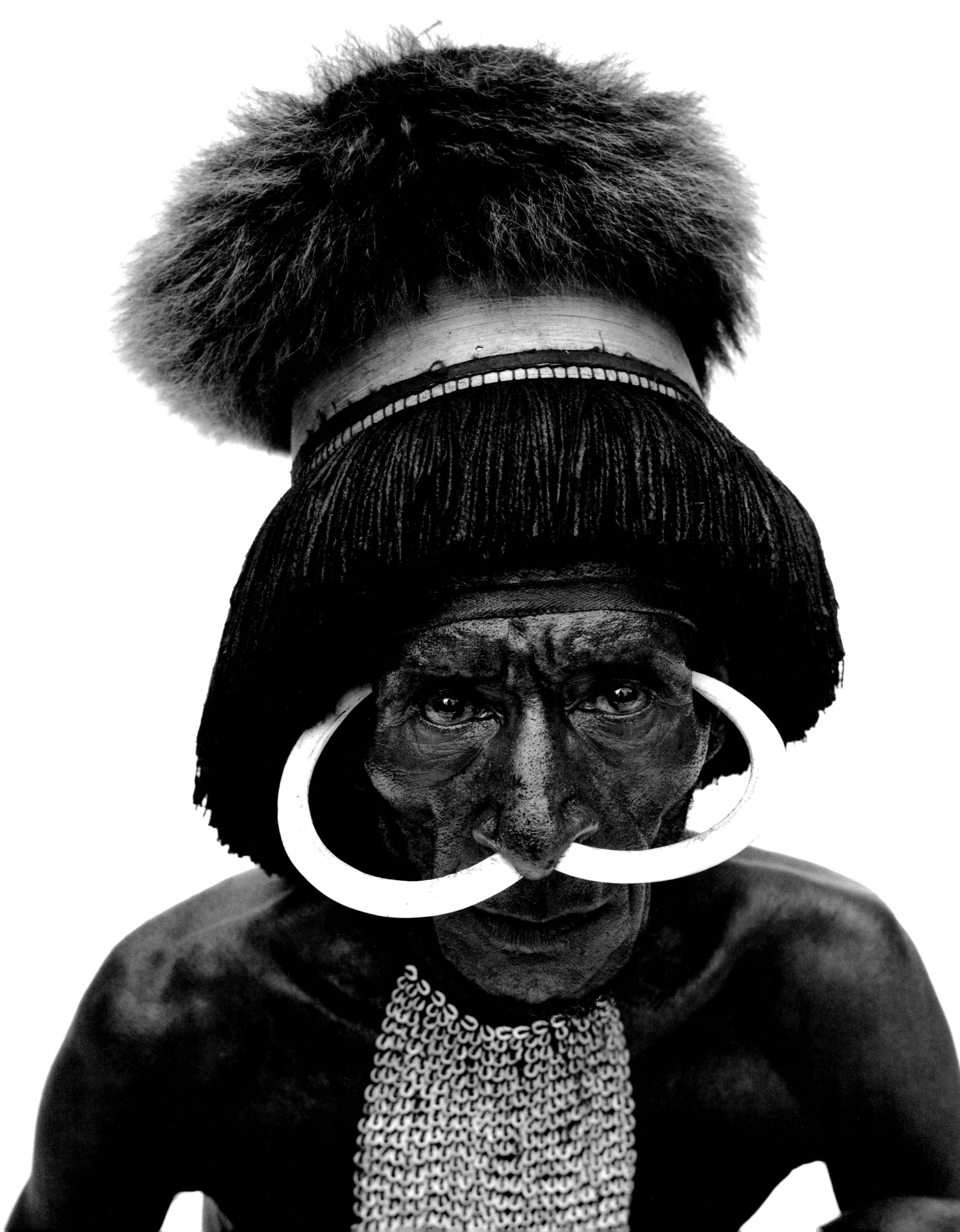

Irian Jaya Dani Tribe

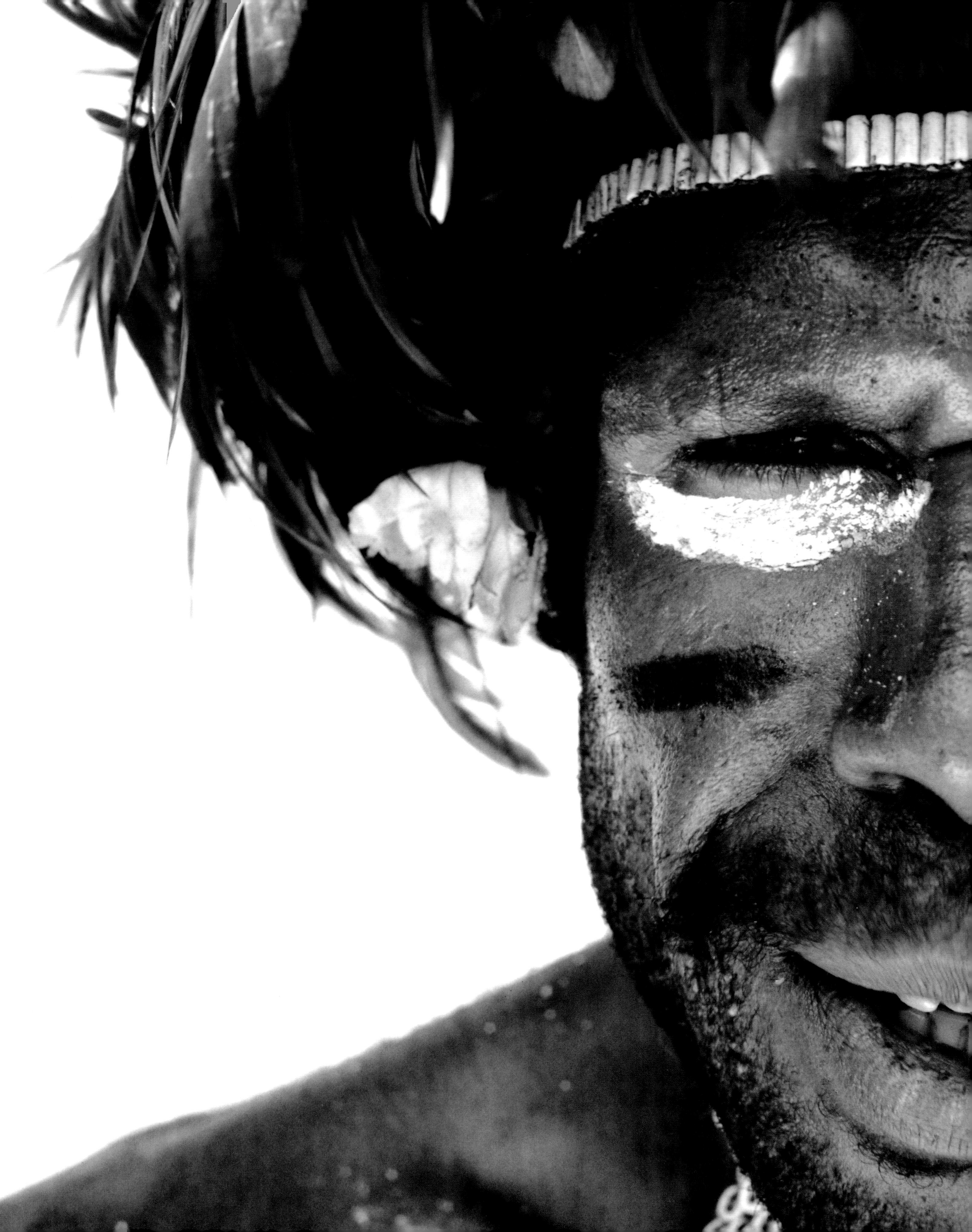

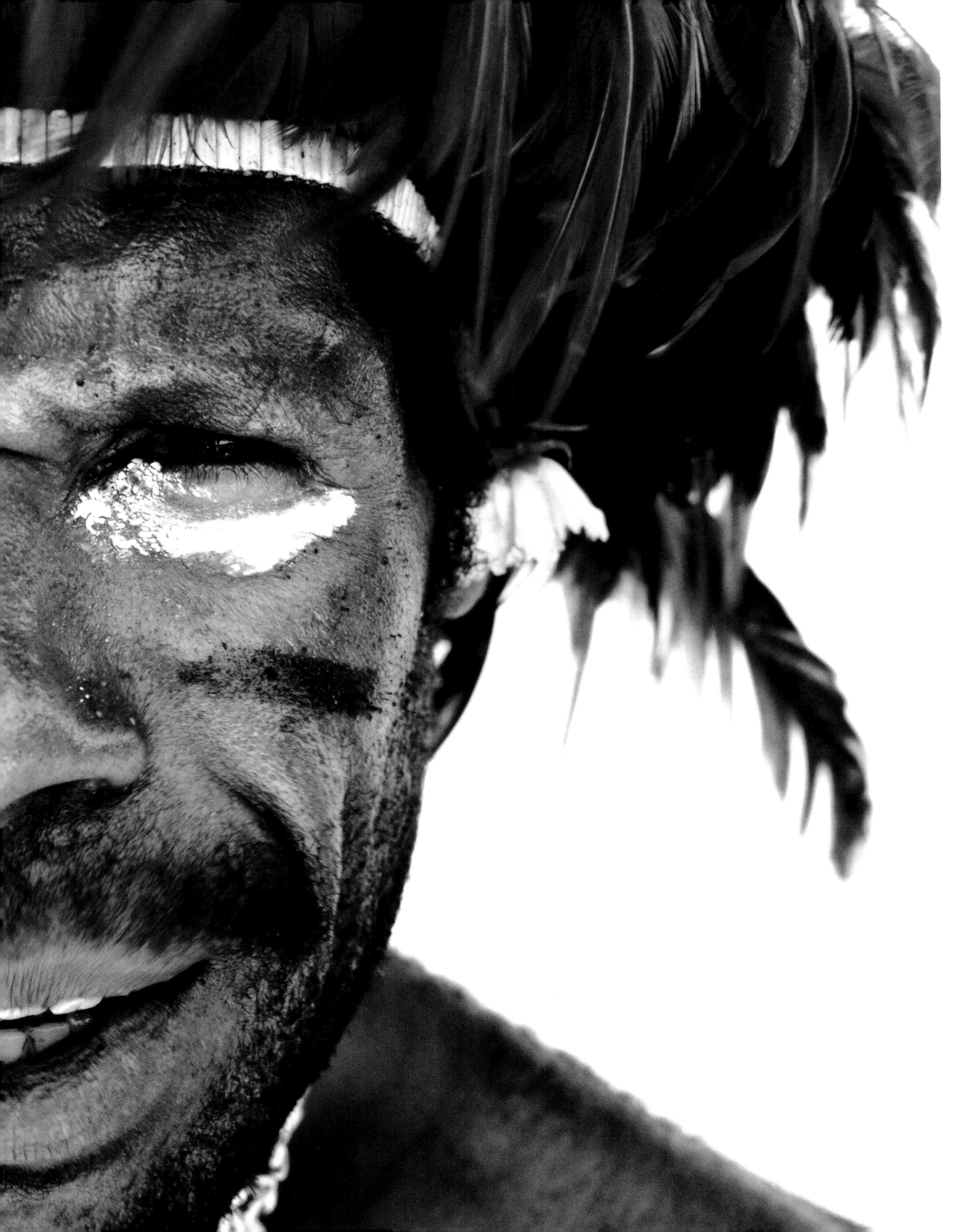

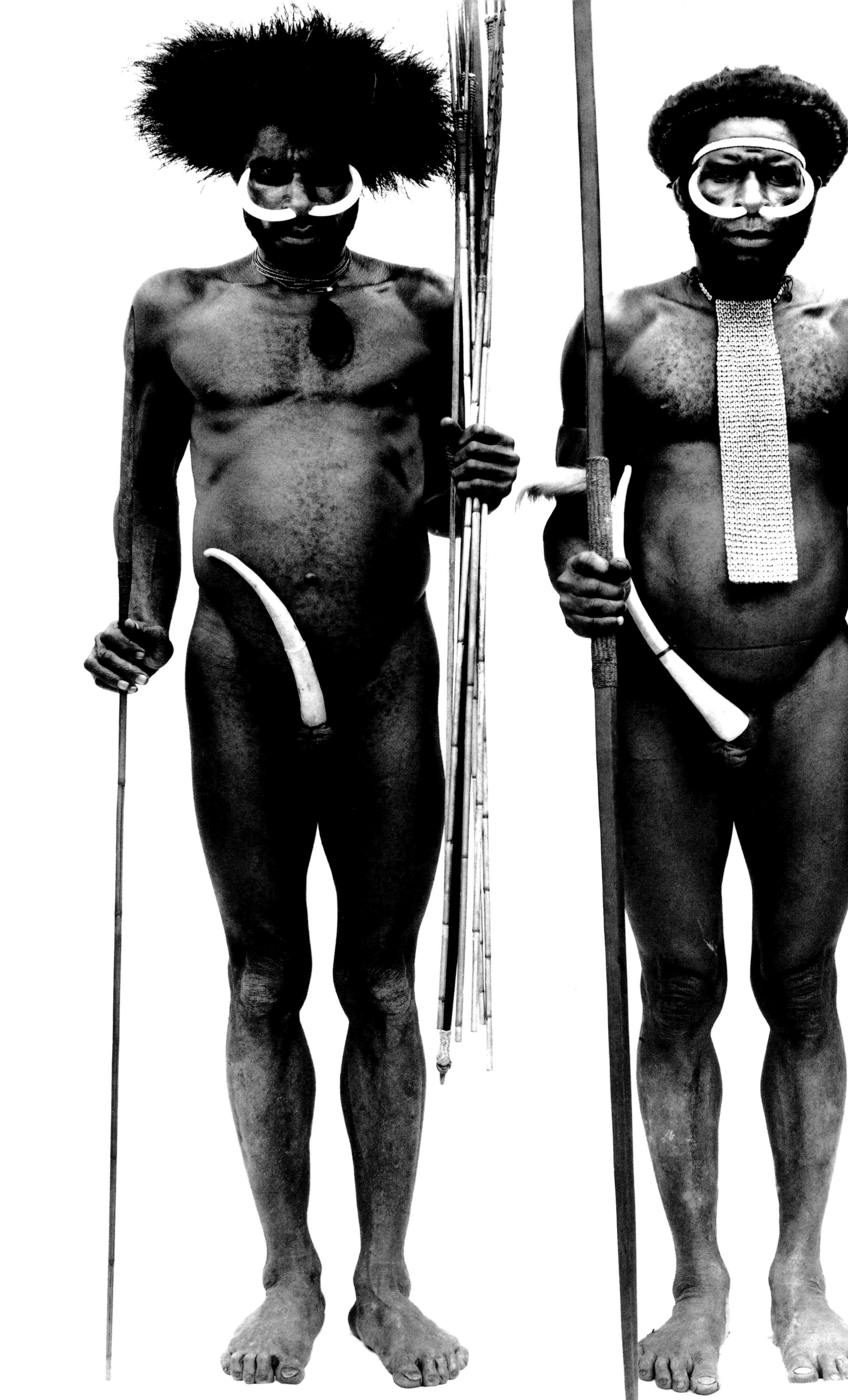

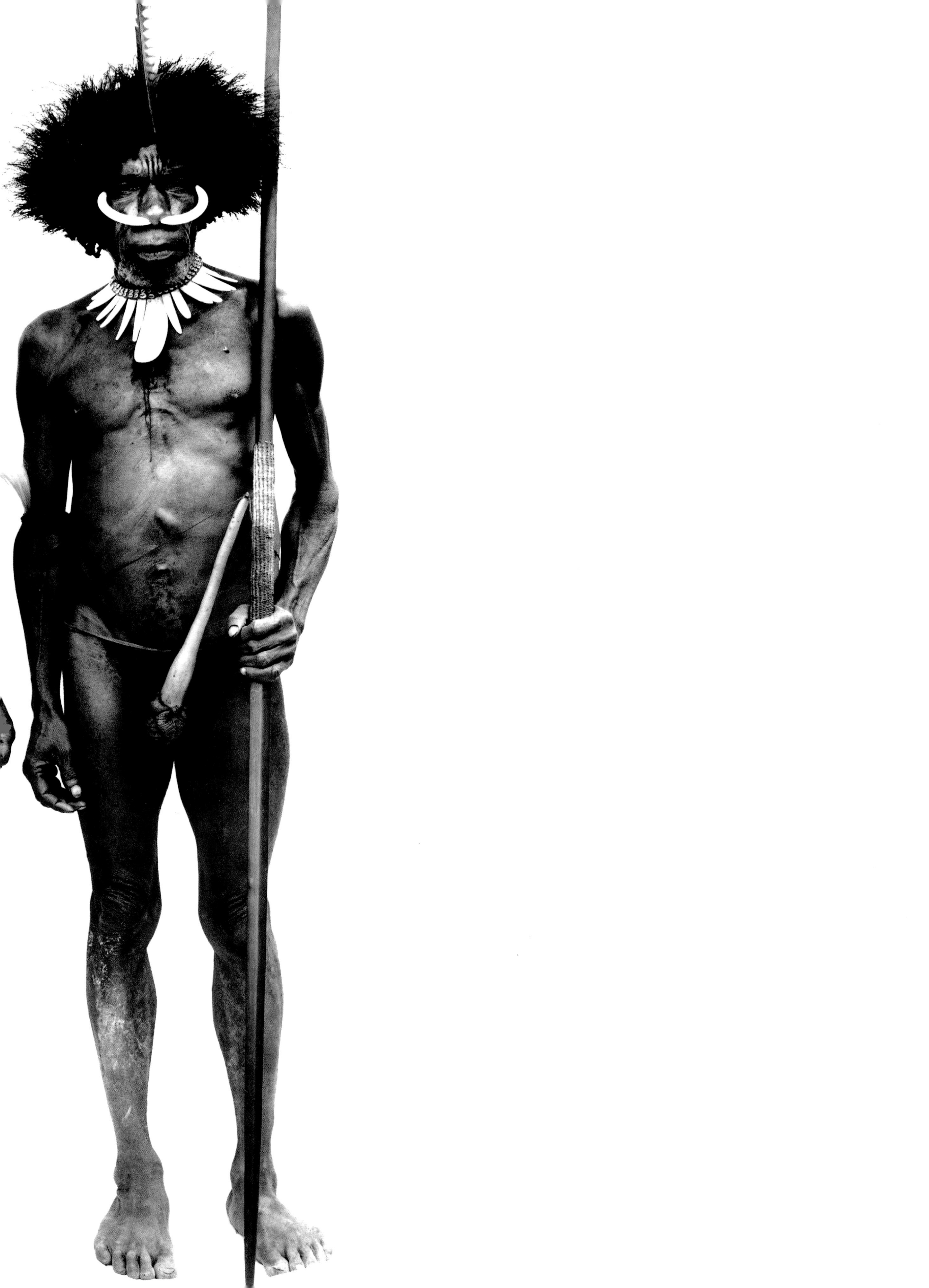

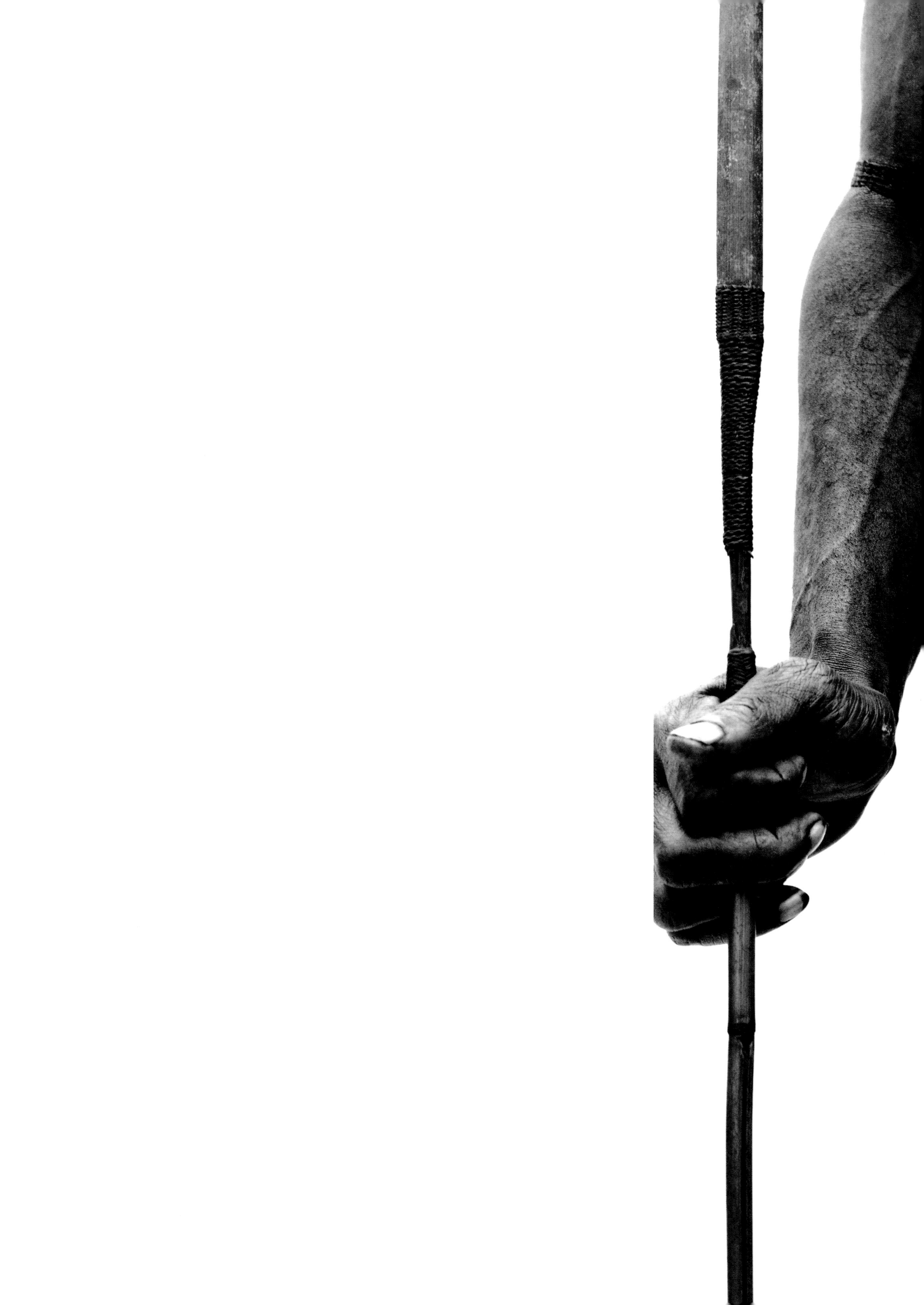

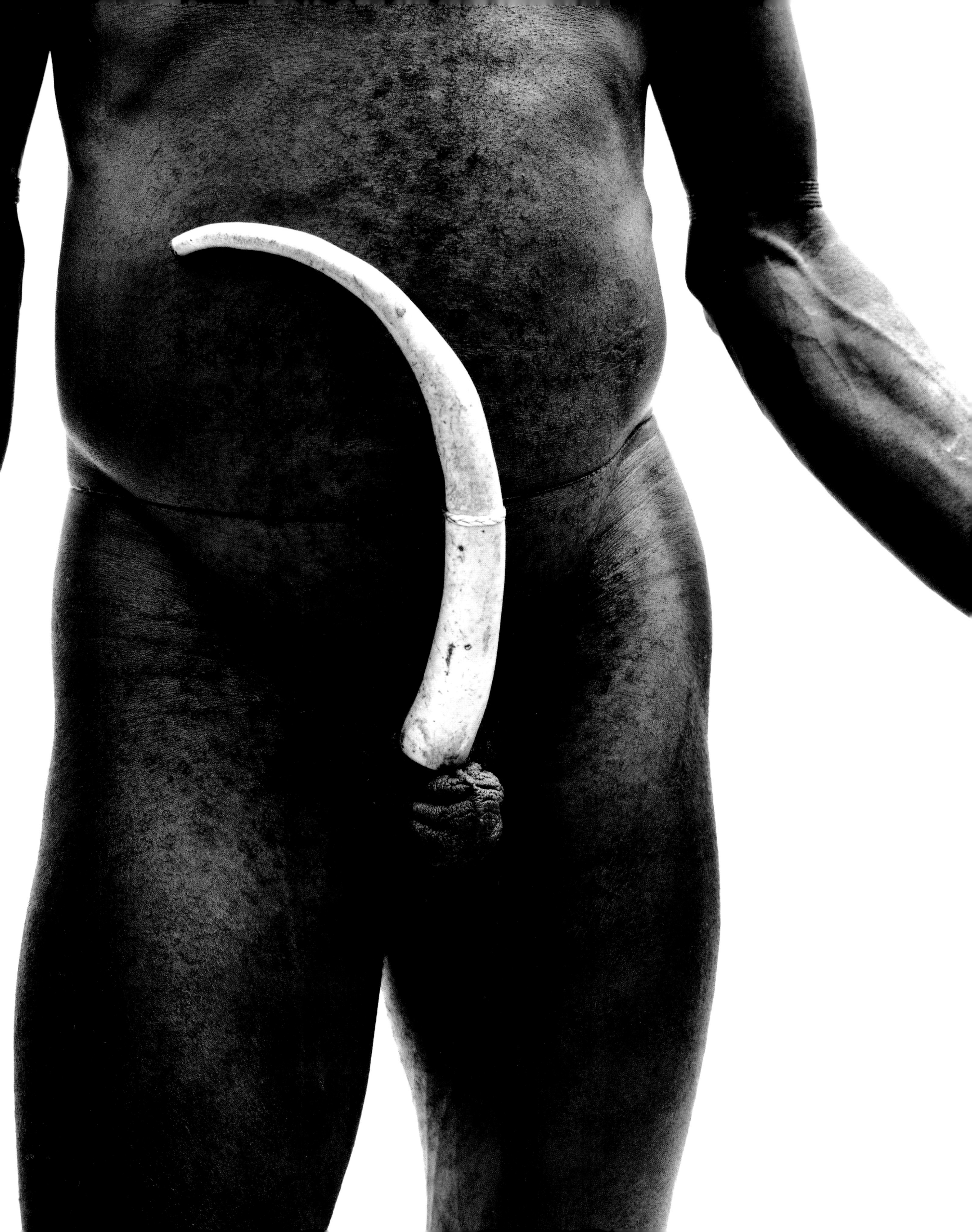

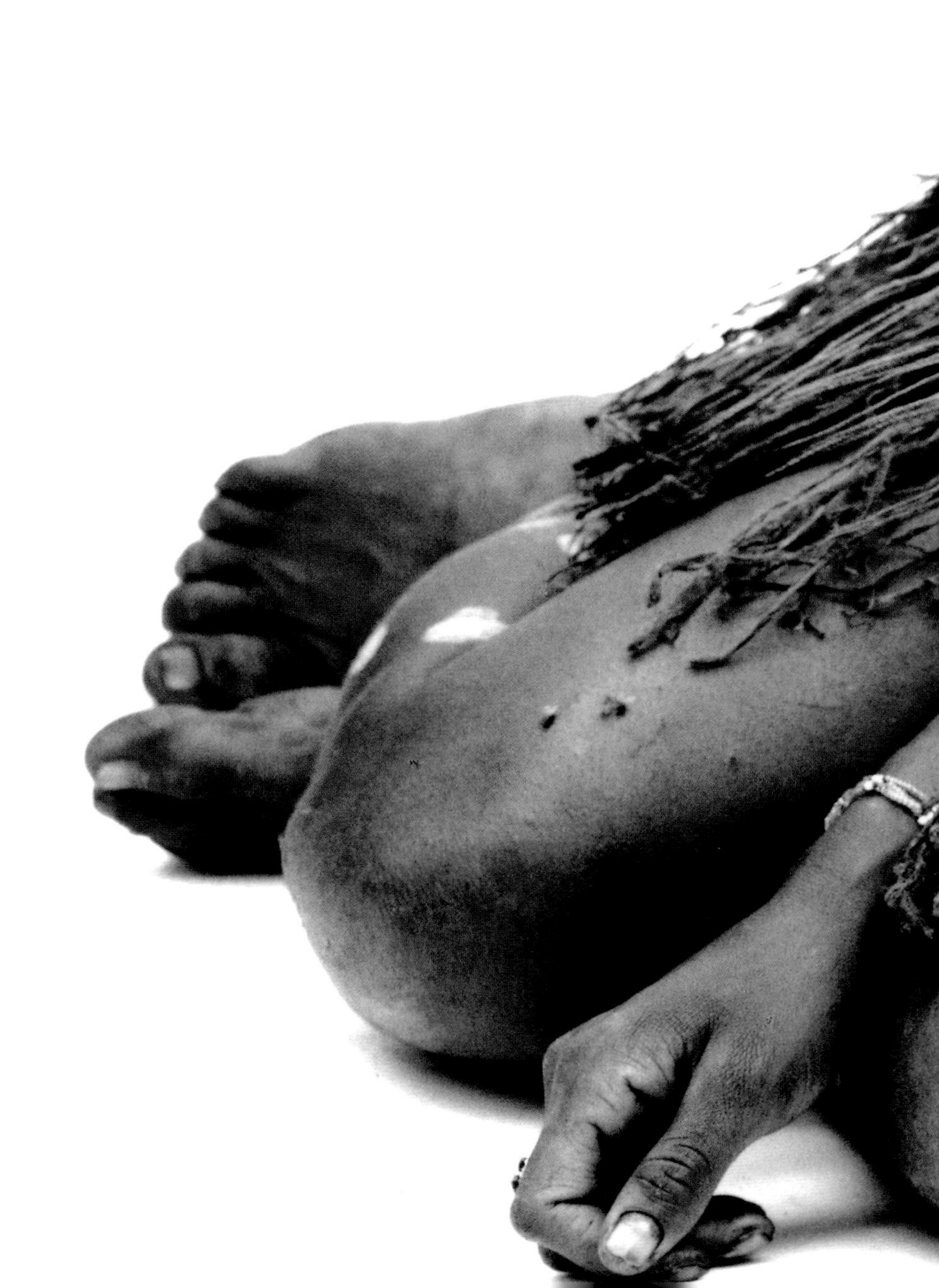

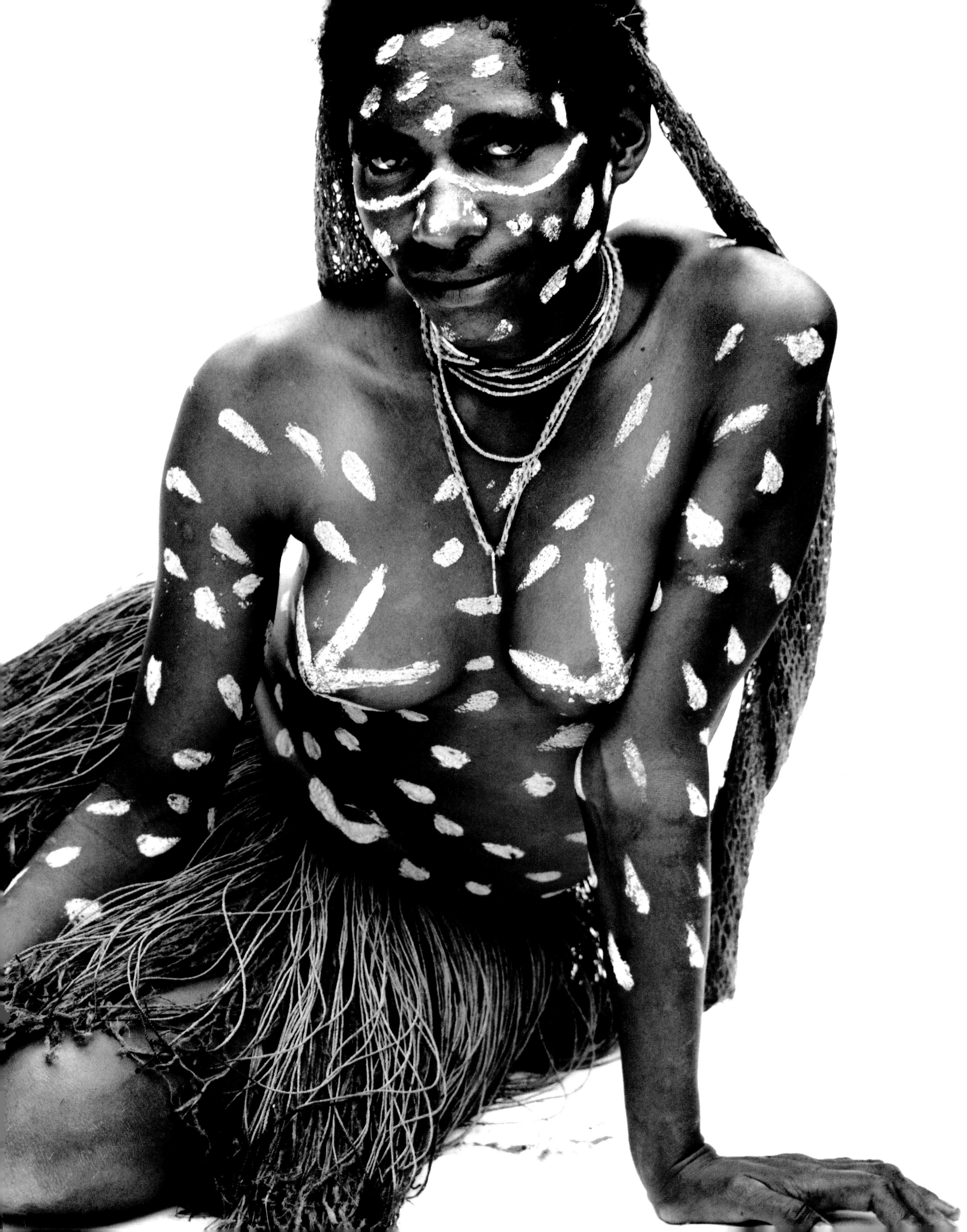

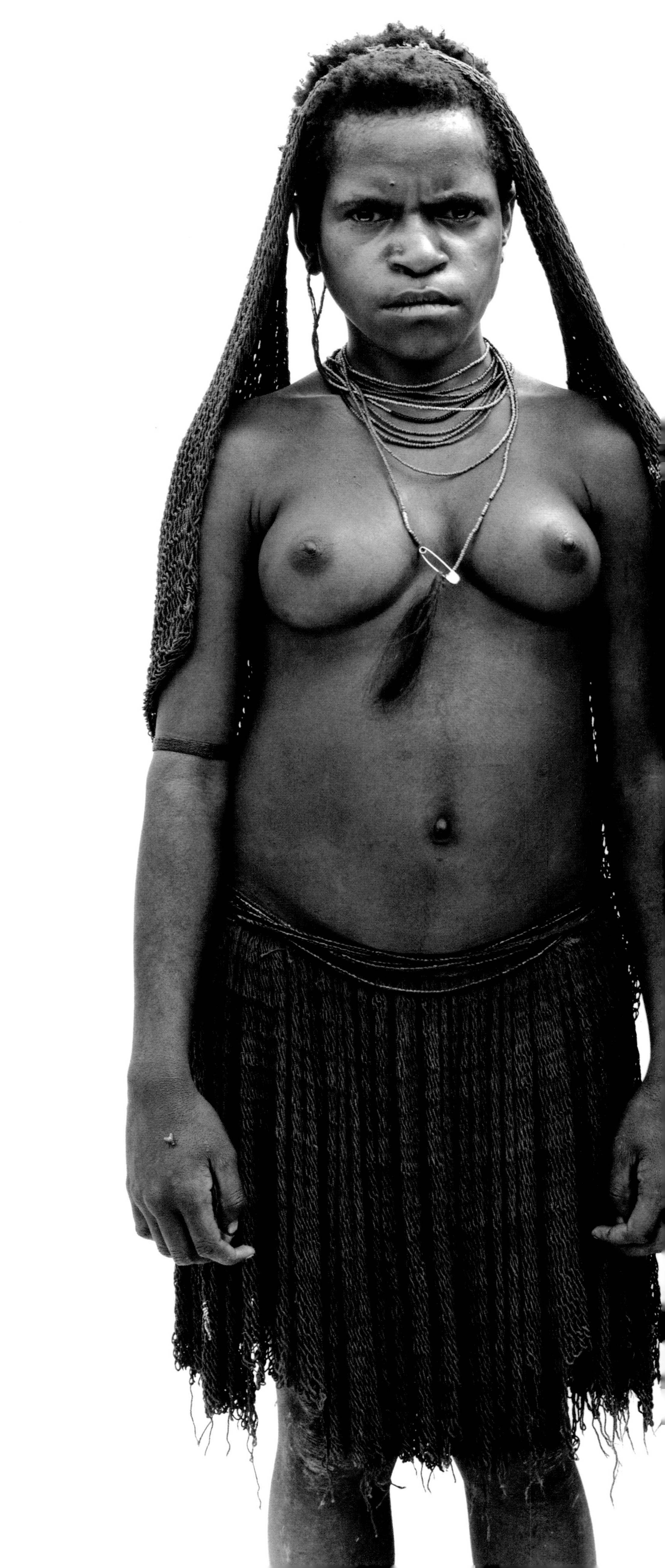

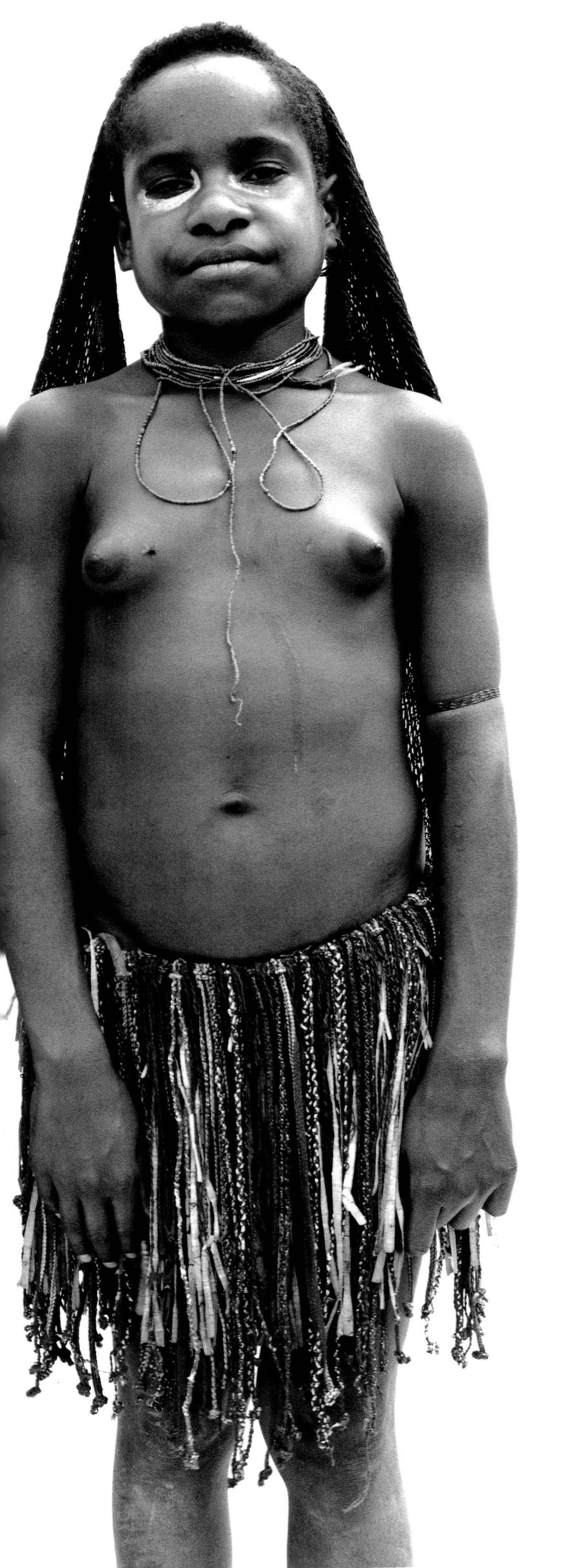

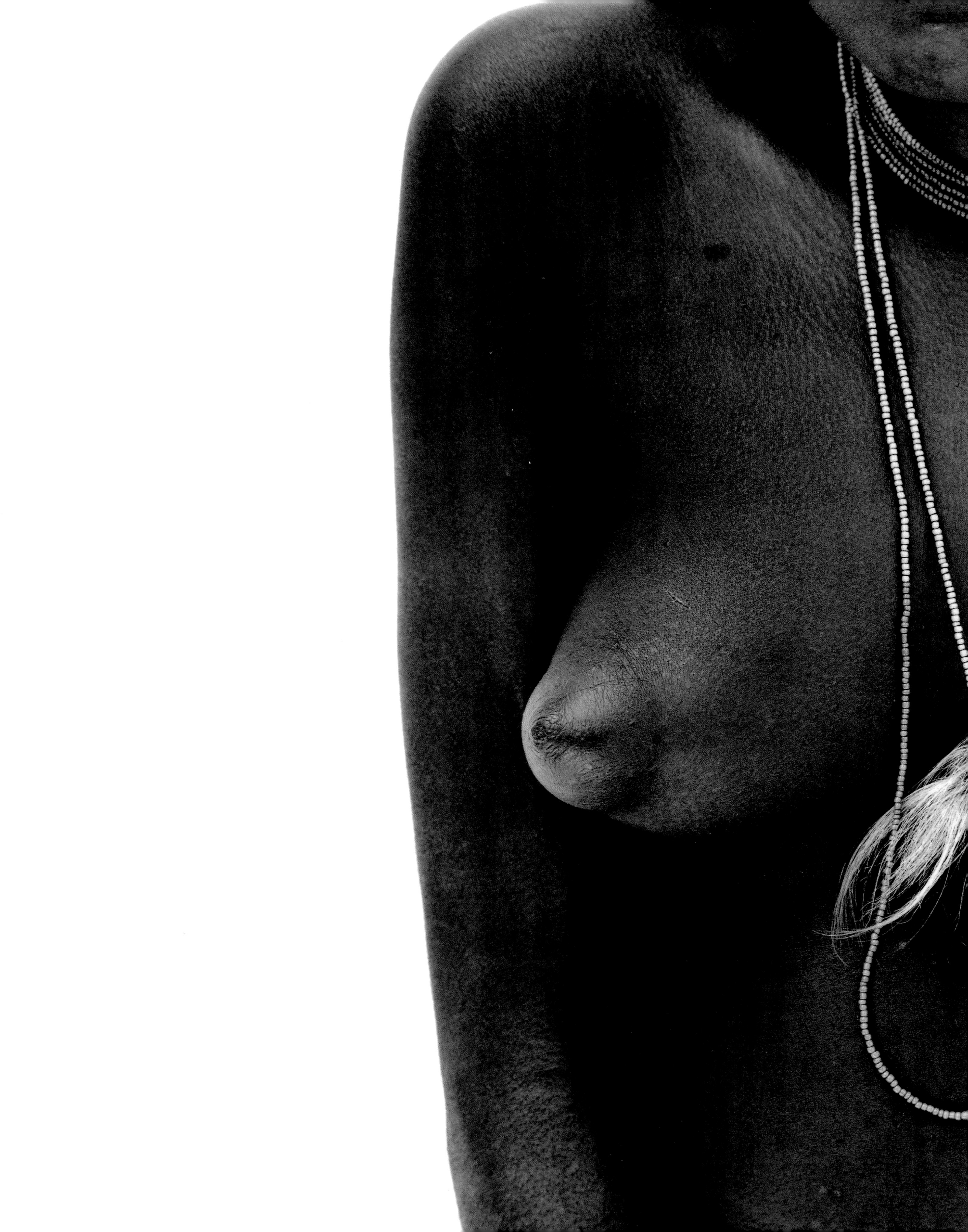

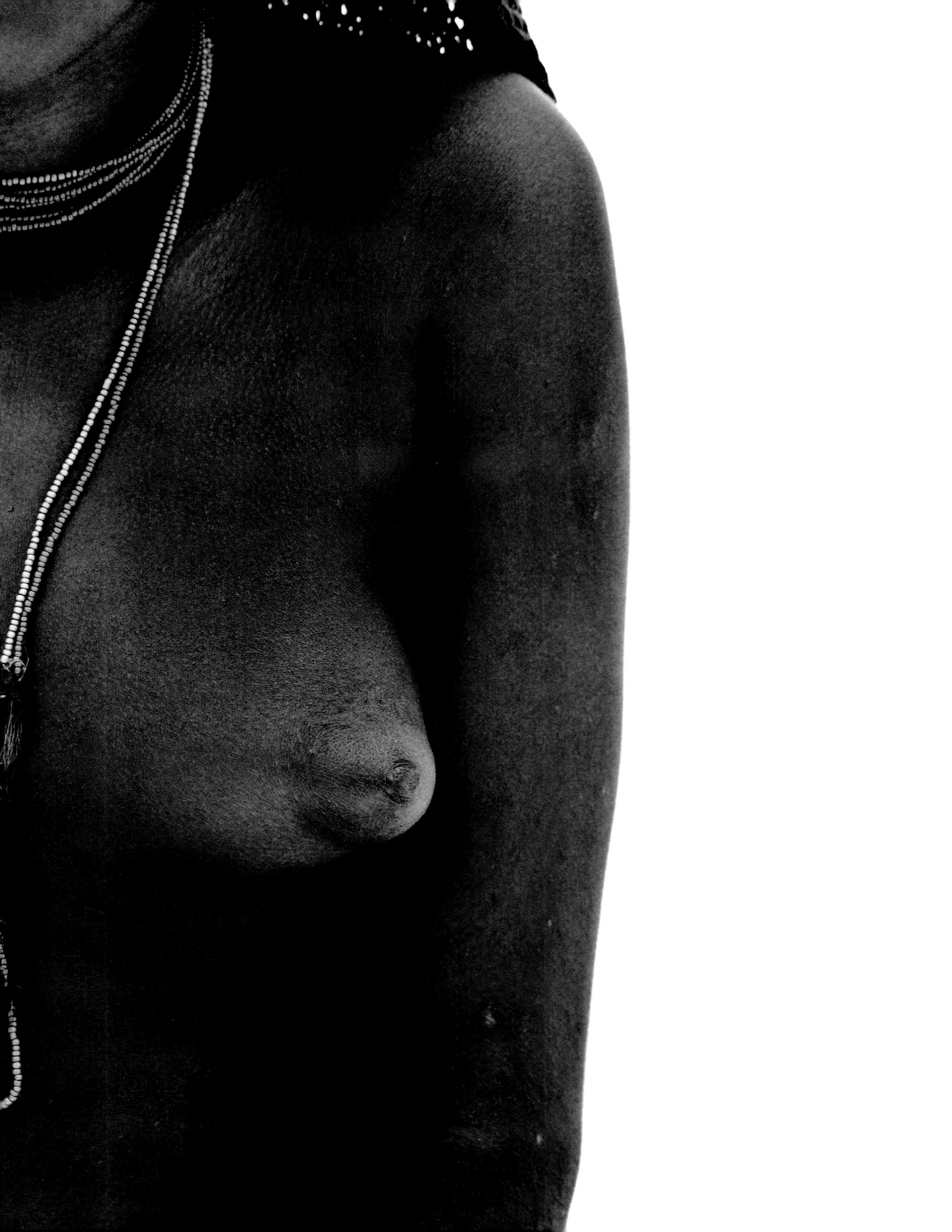

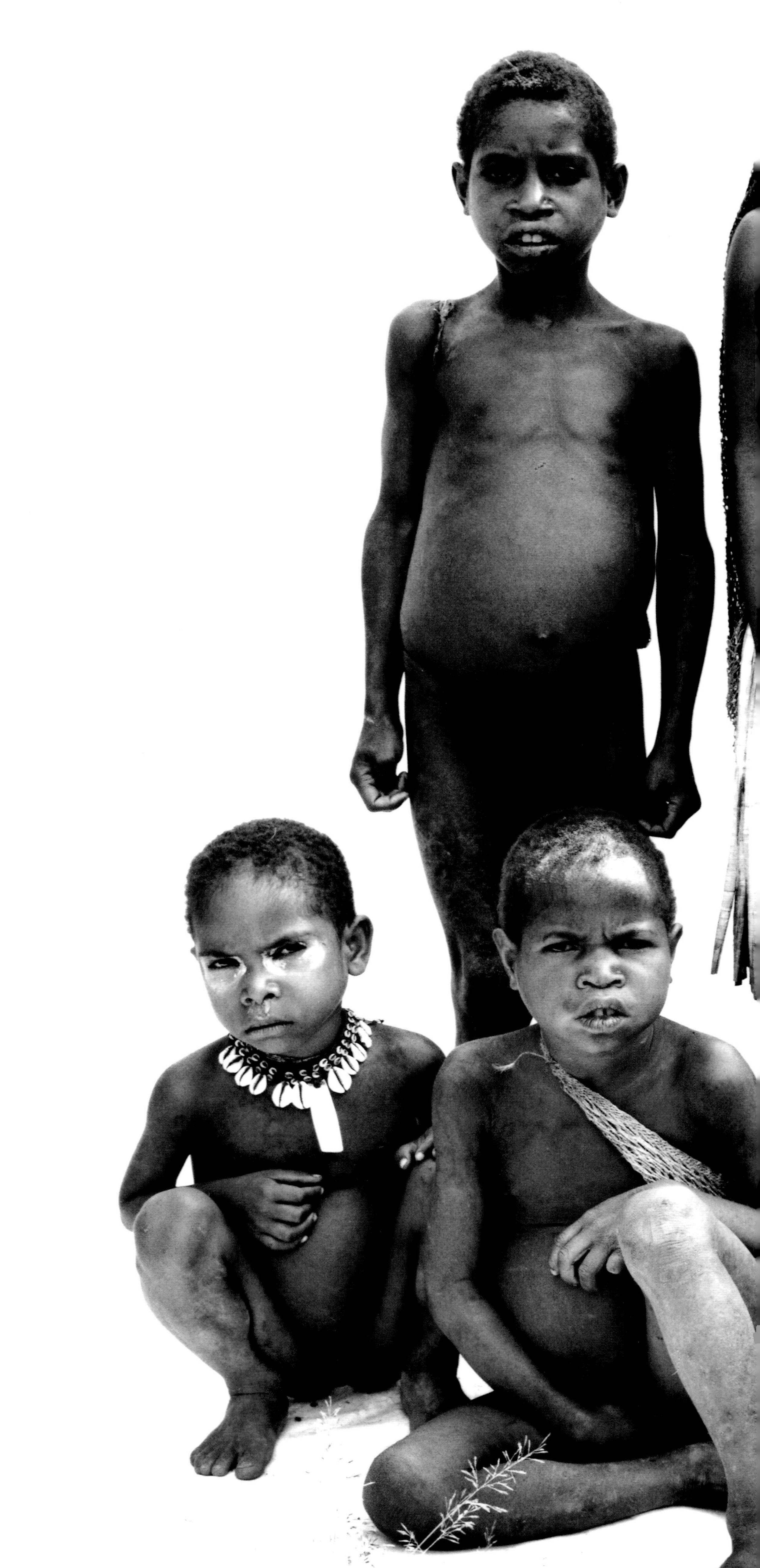

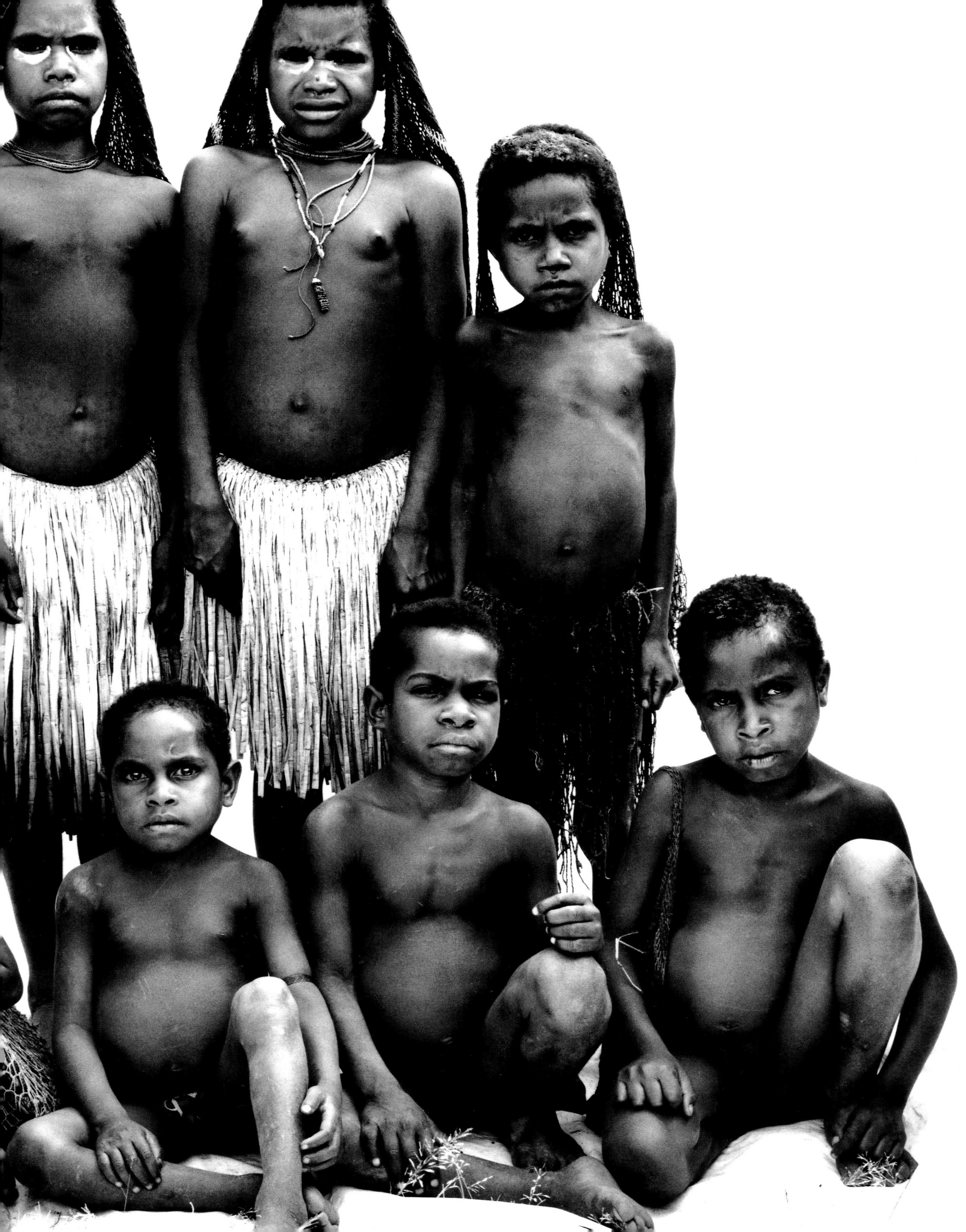

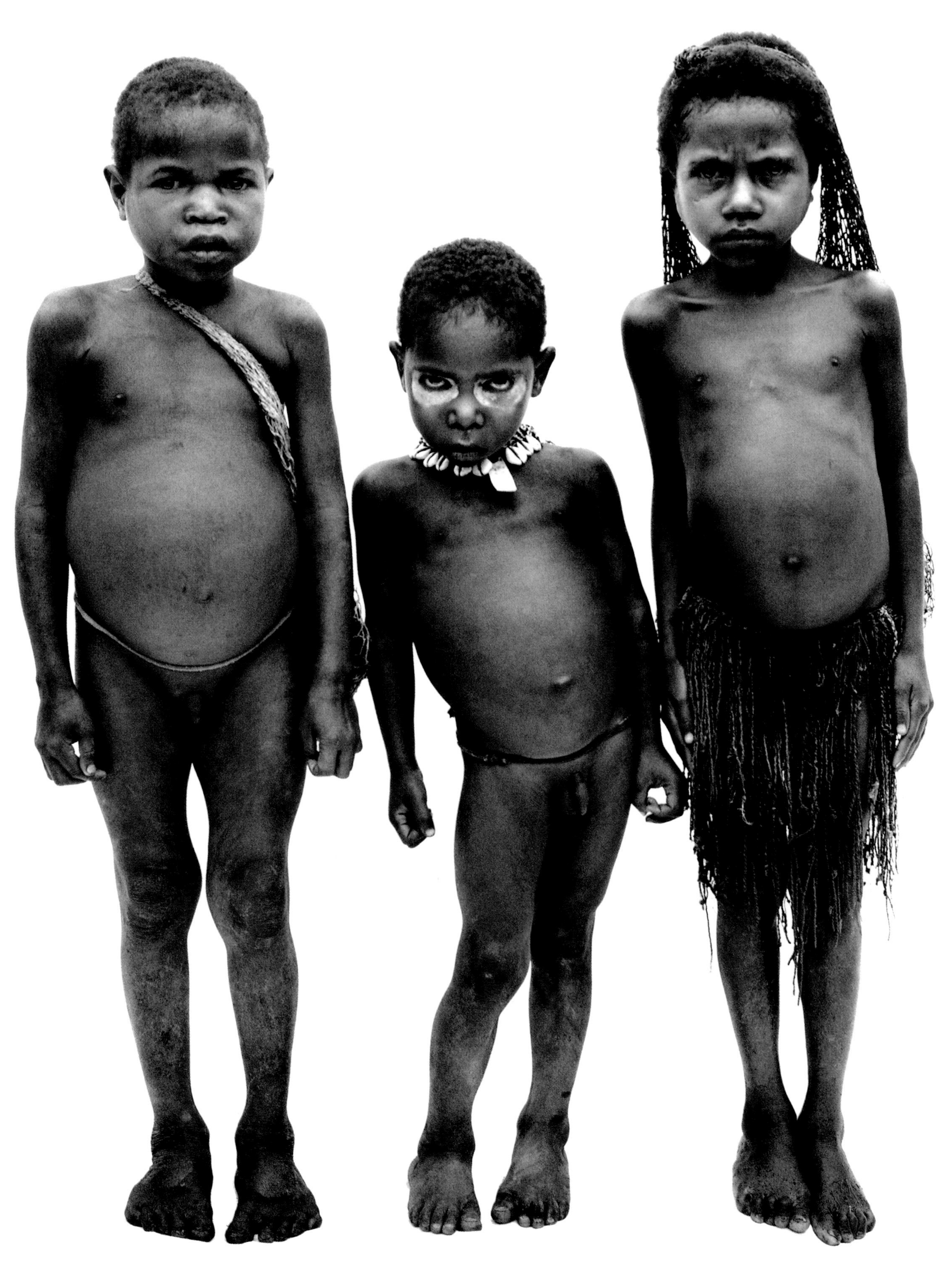

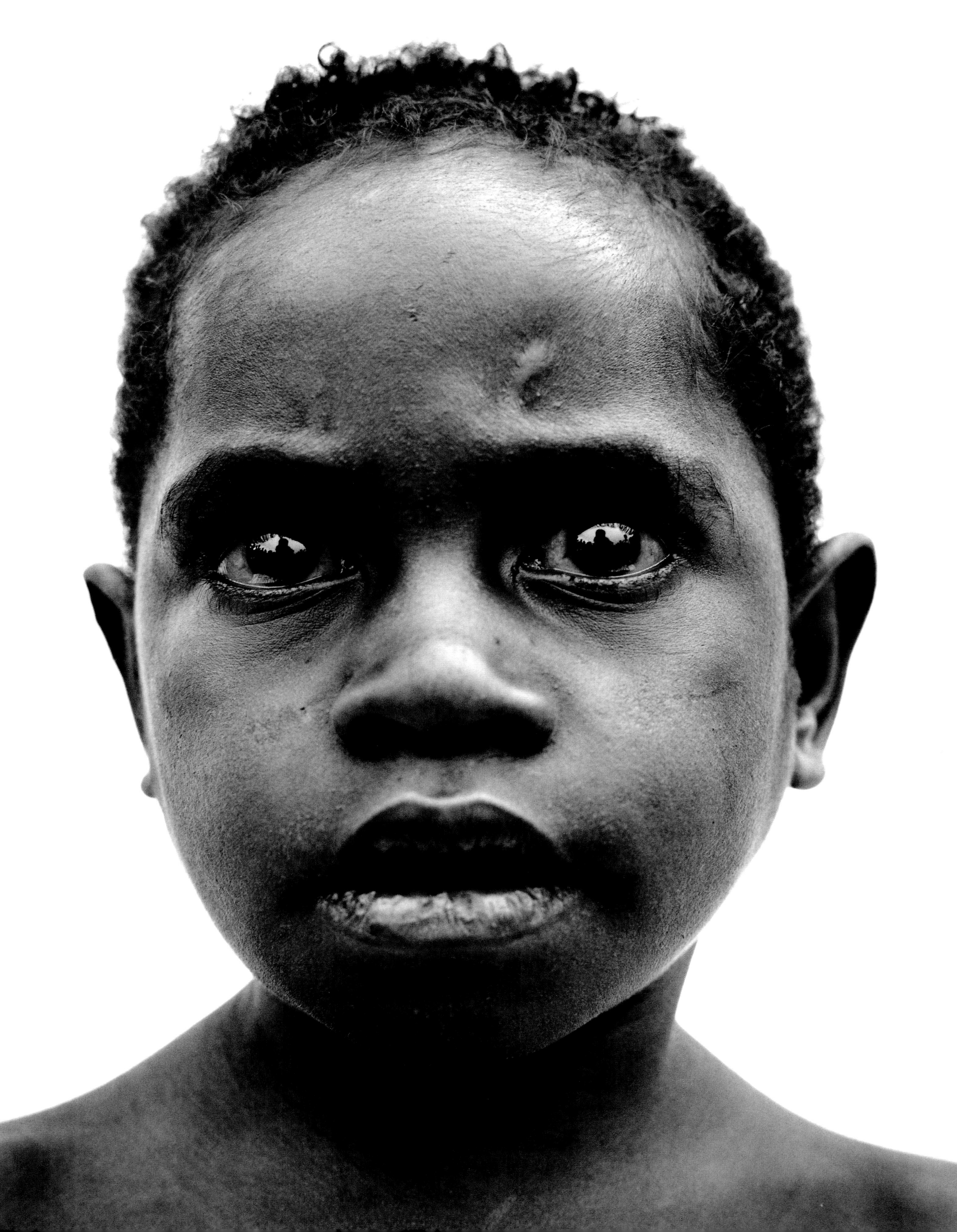

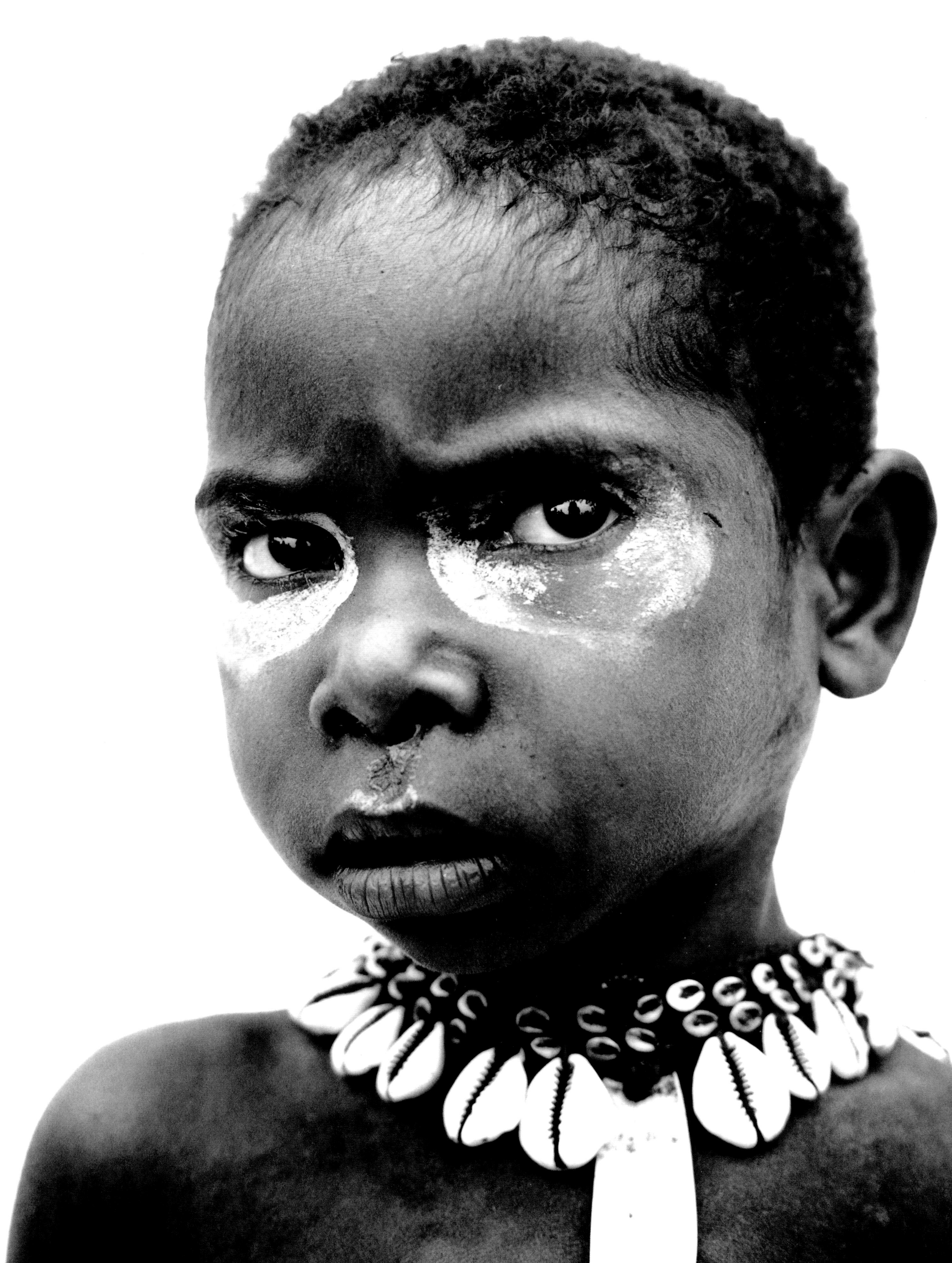

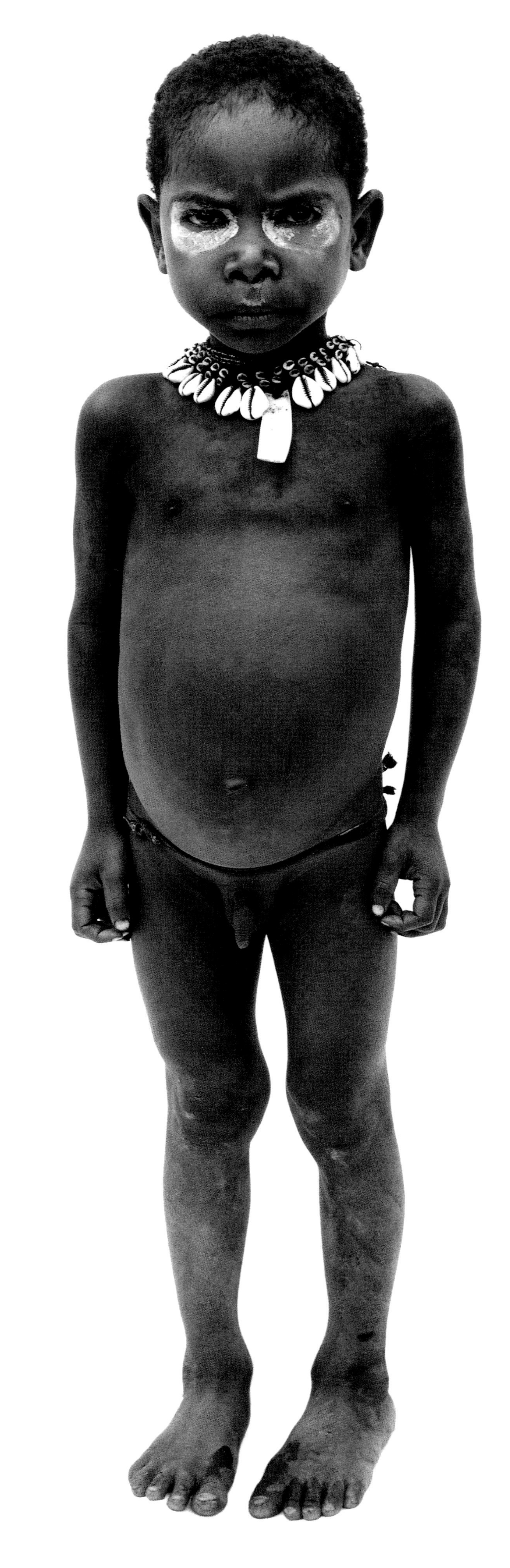

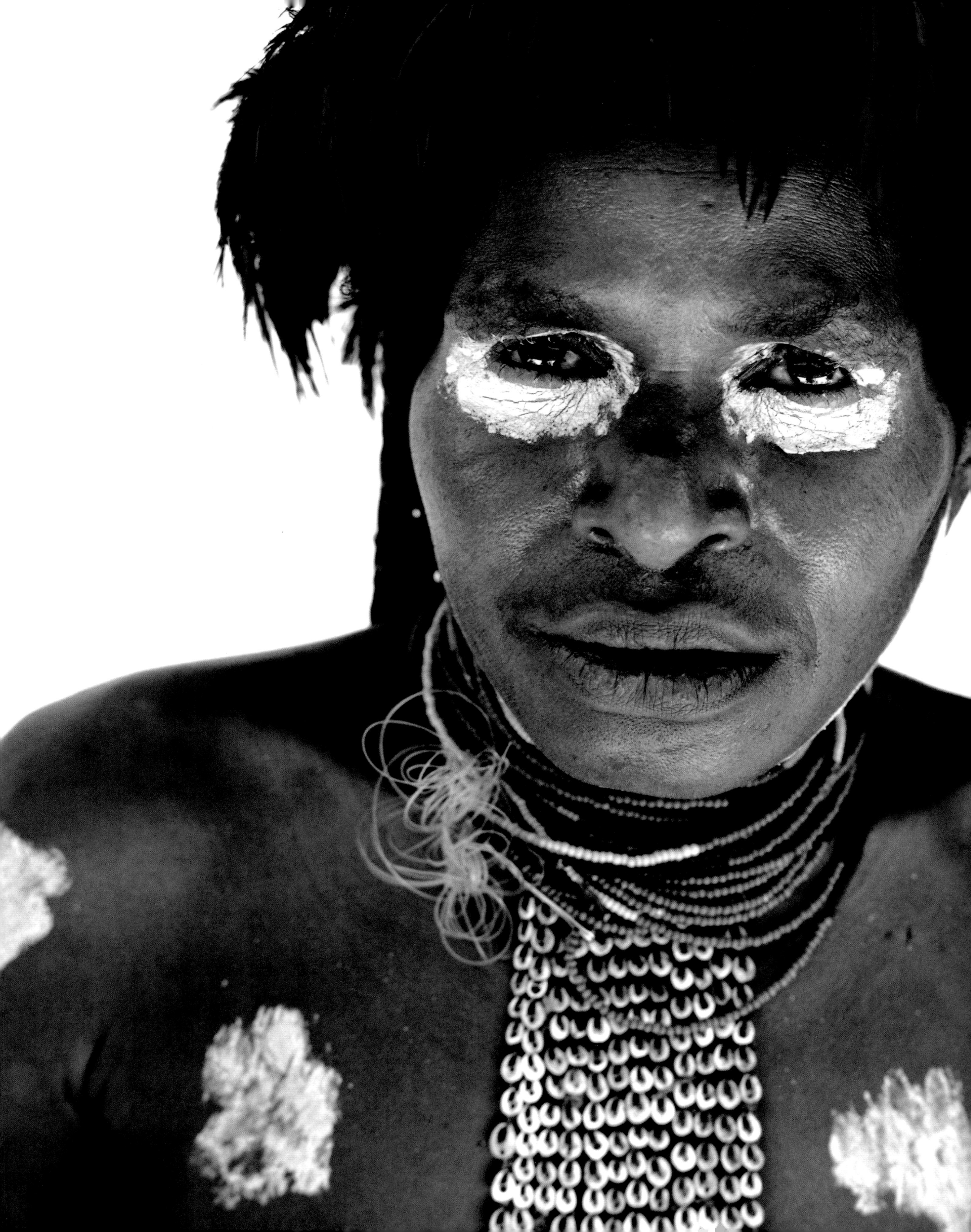

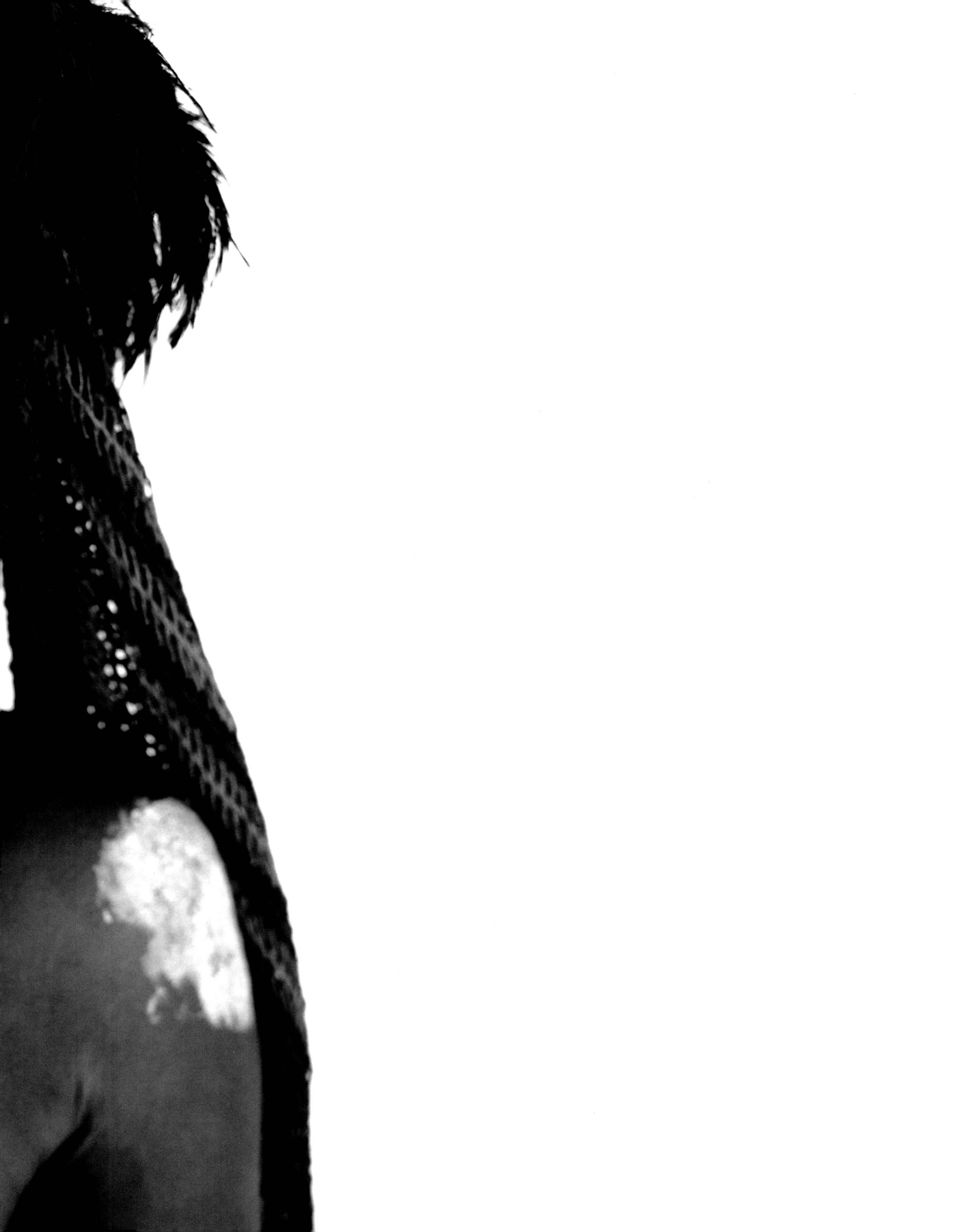

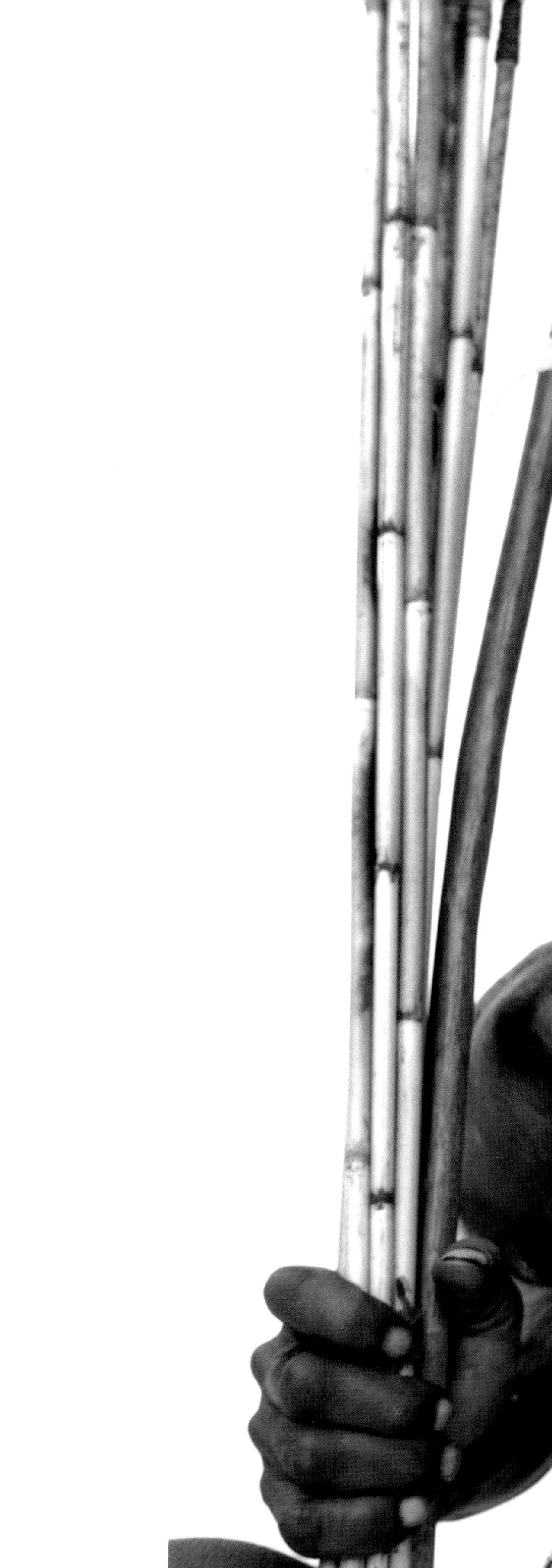

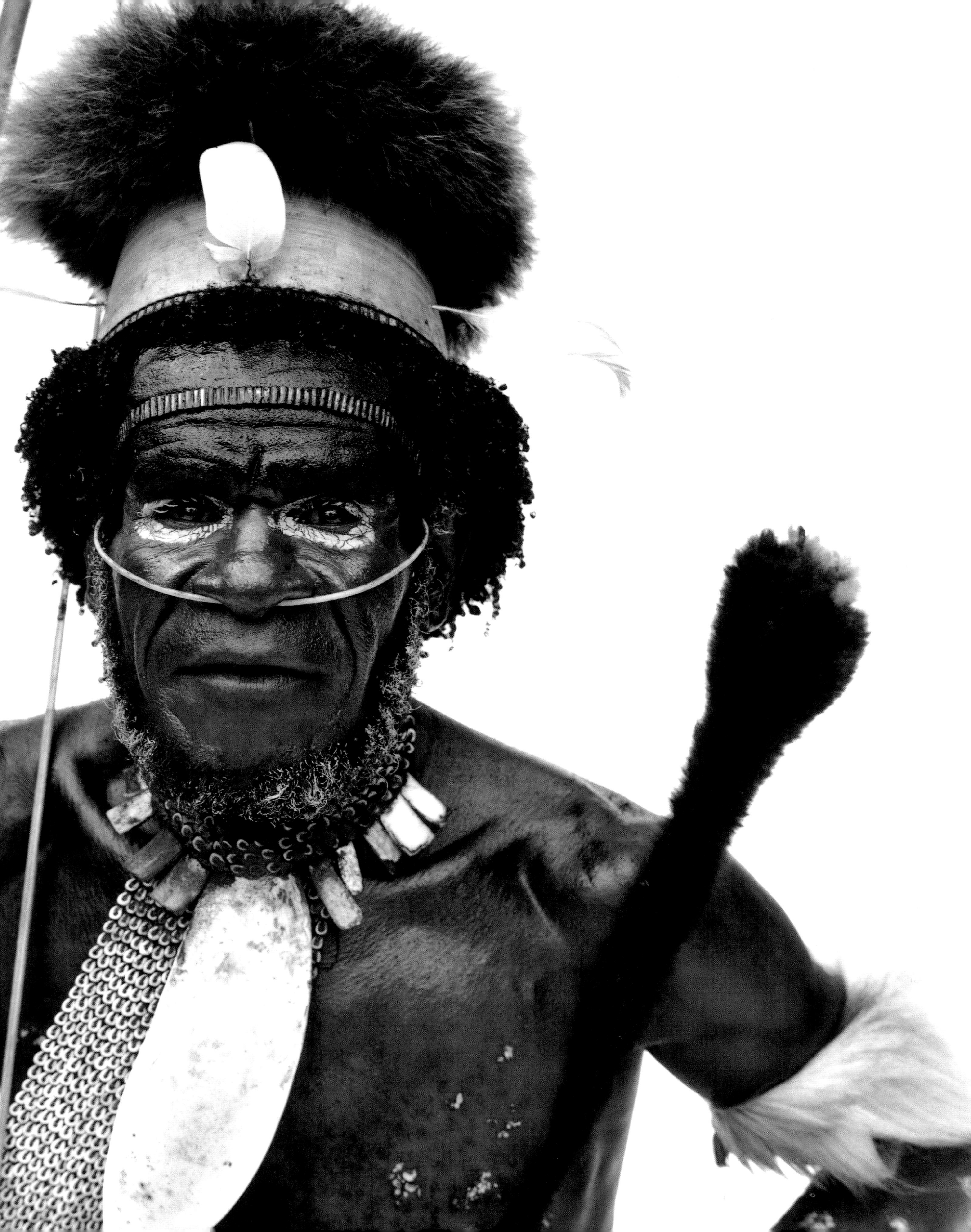

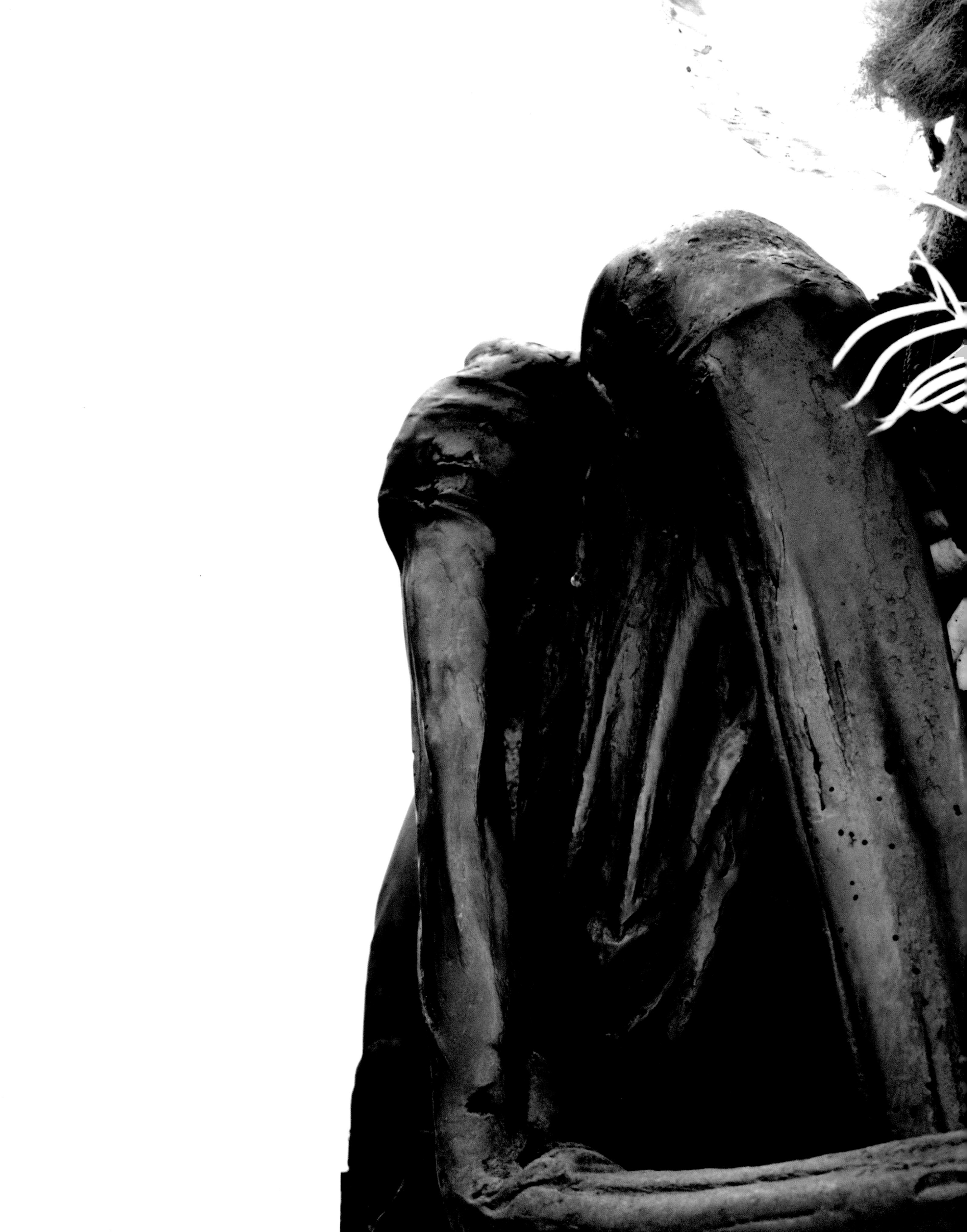

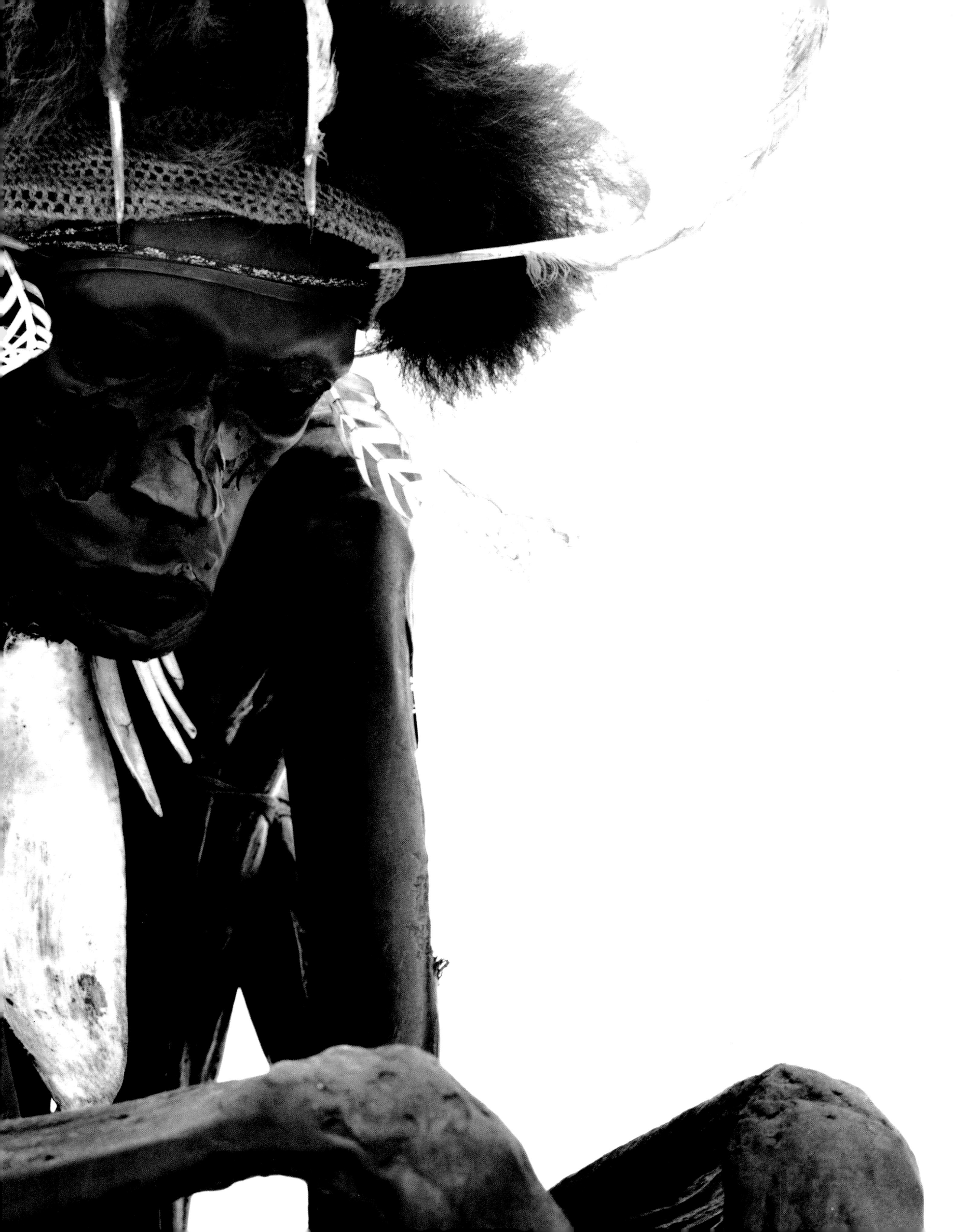

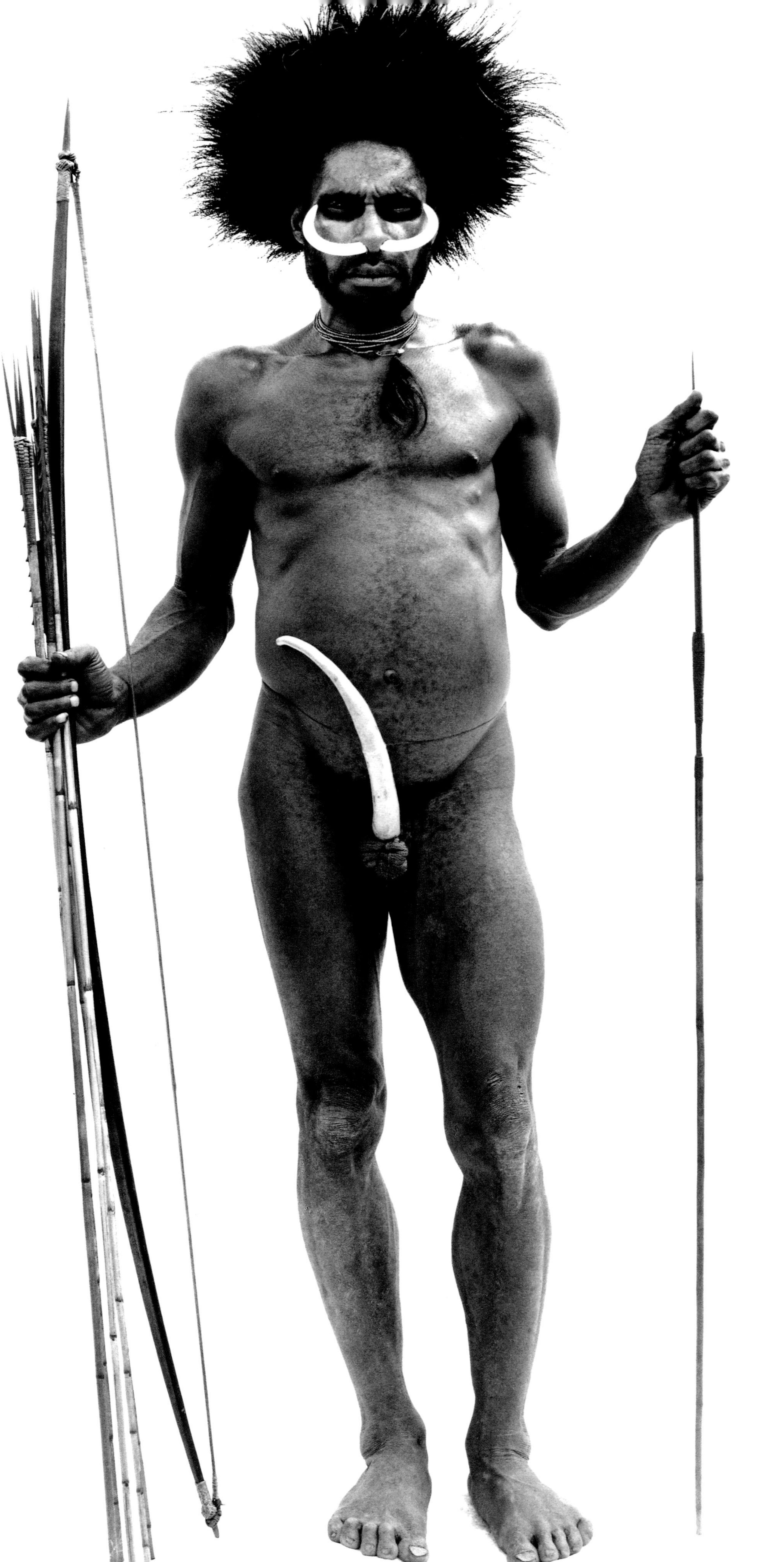

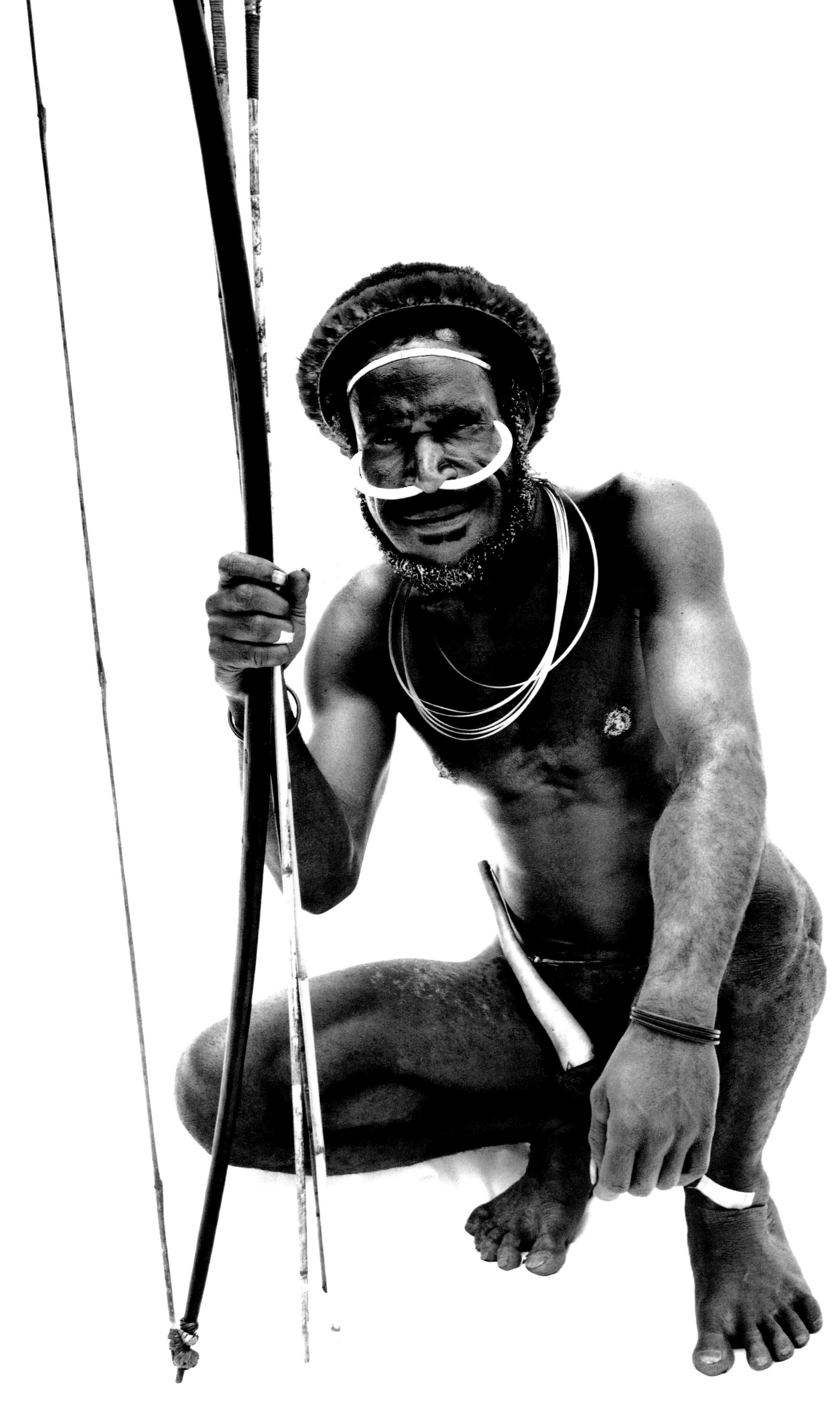

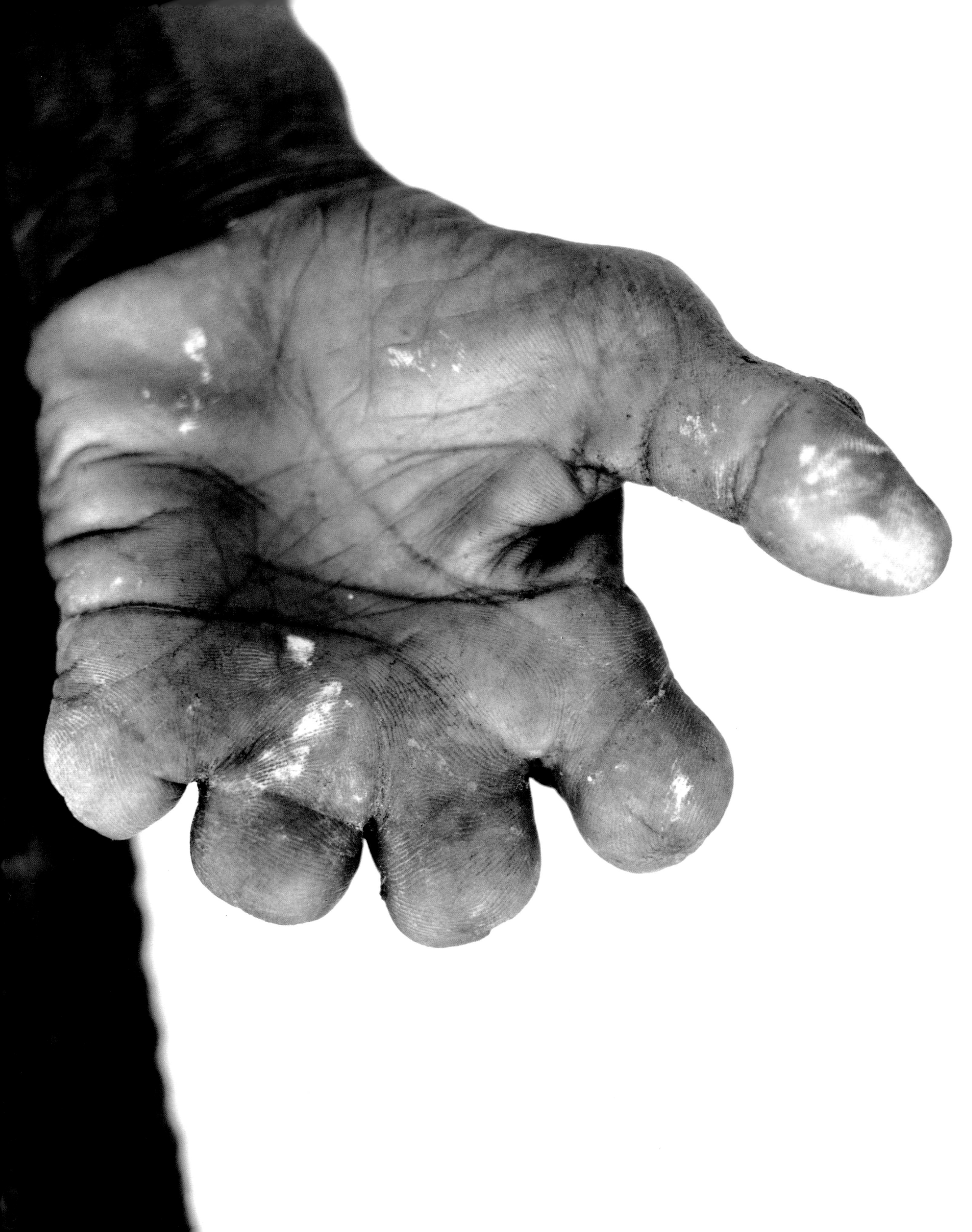

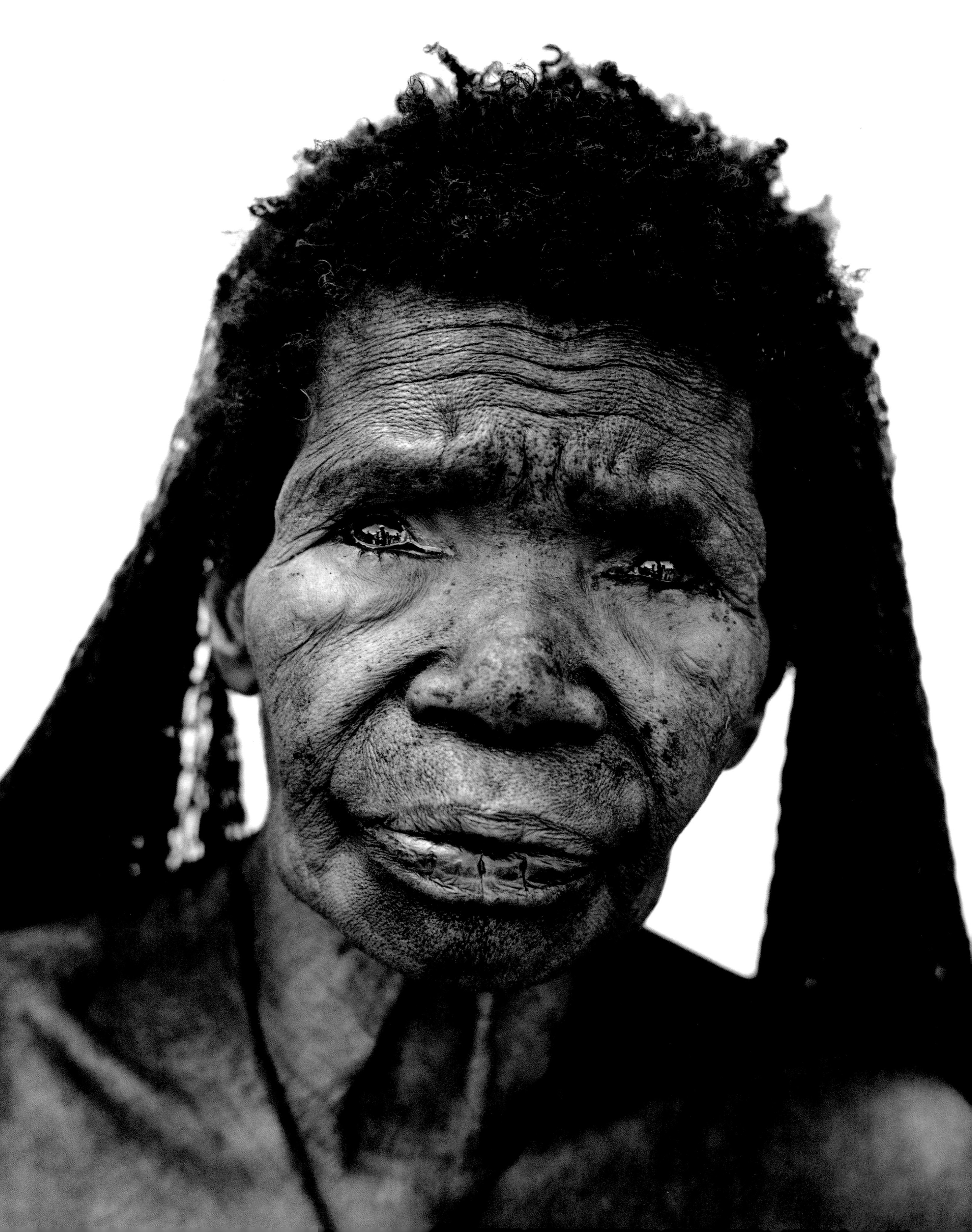

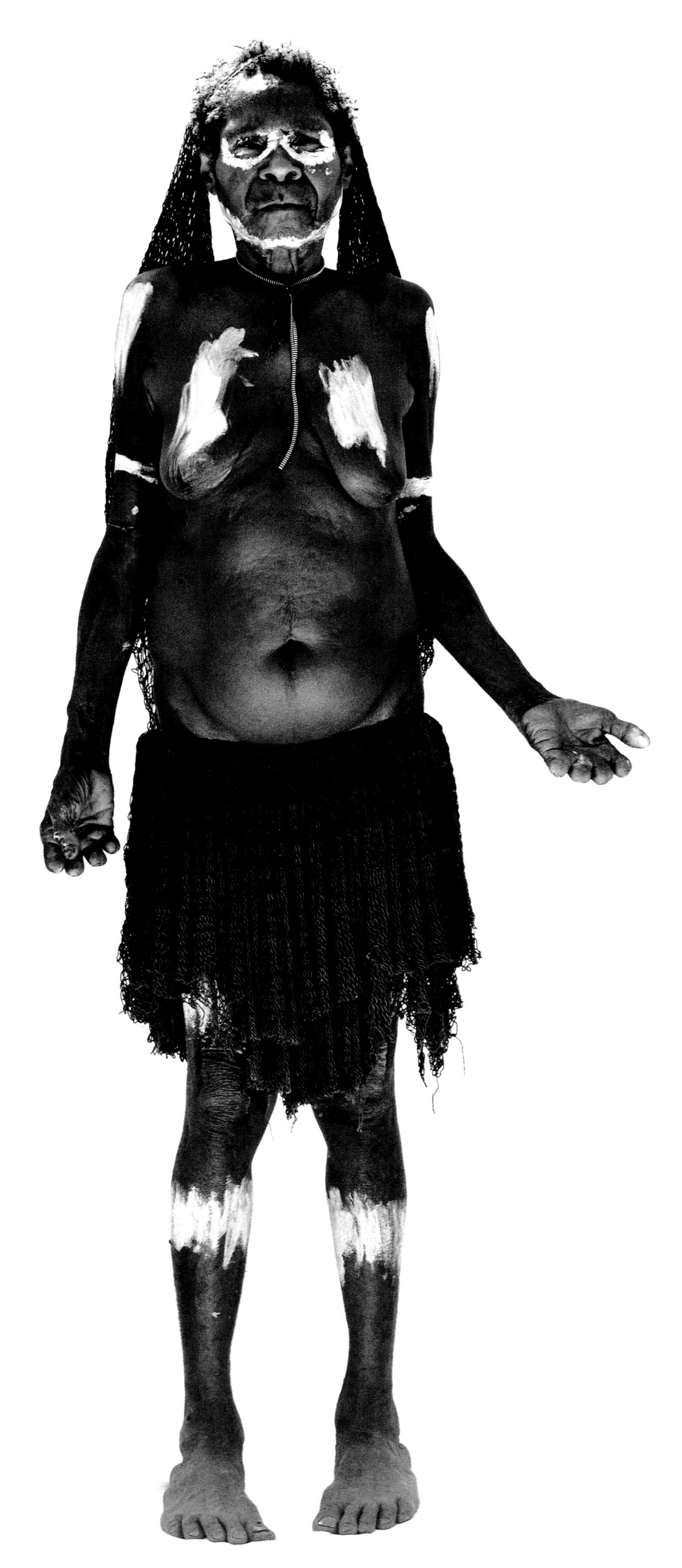

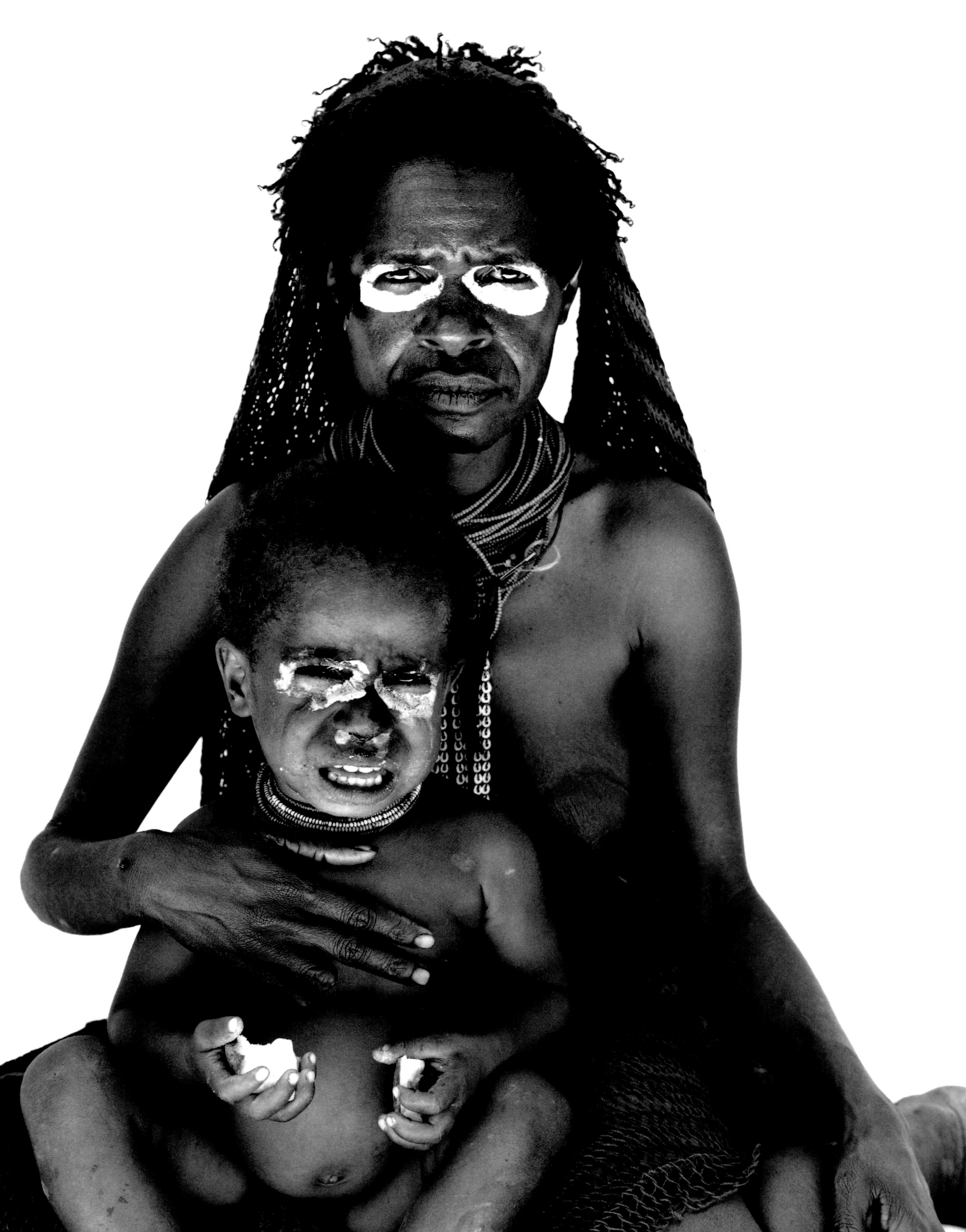

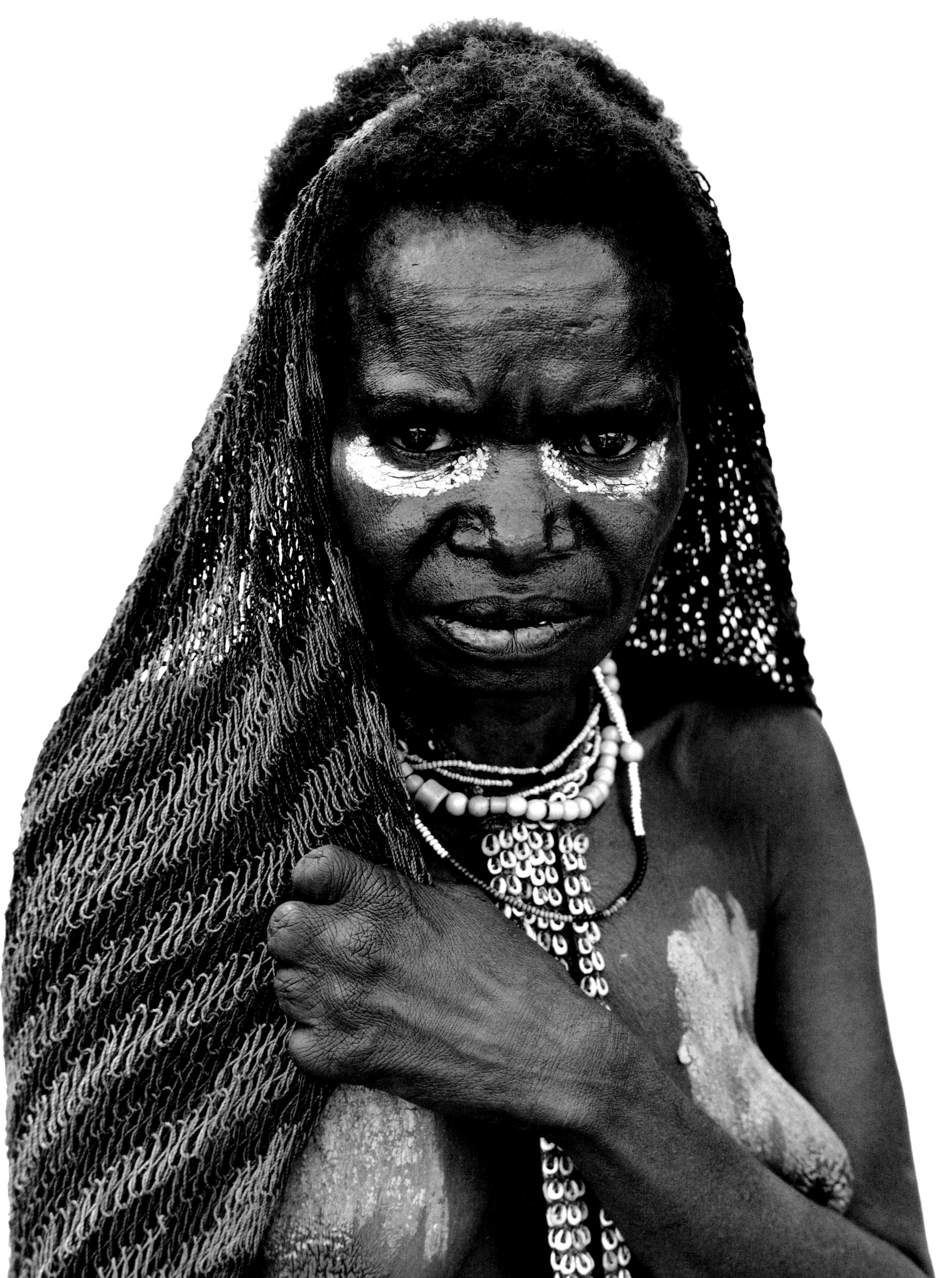

Ethiopia Amhara Tribe

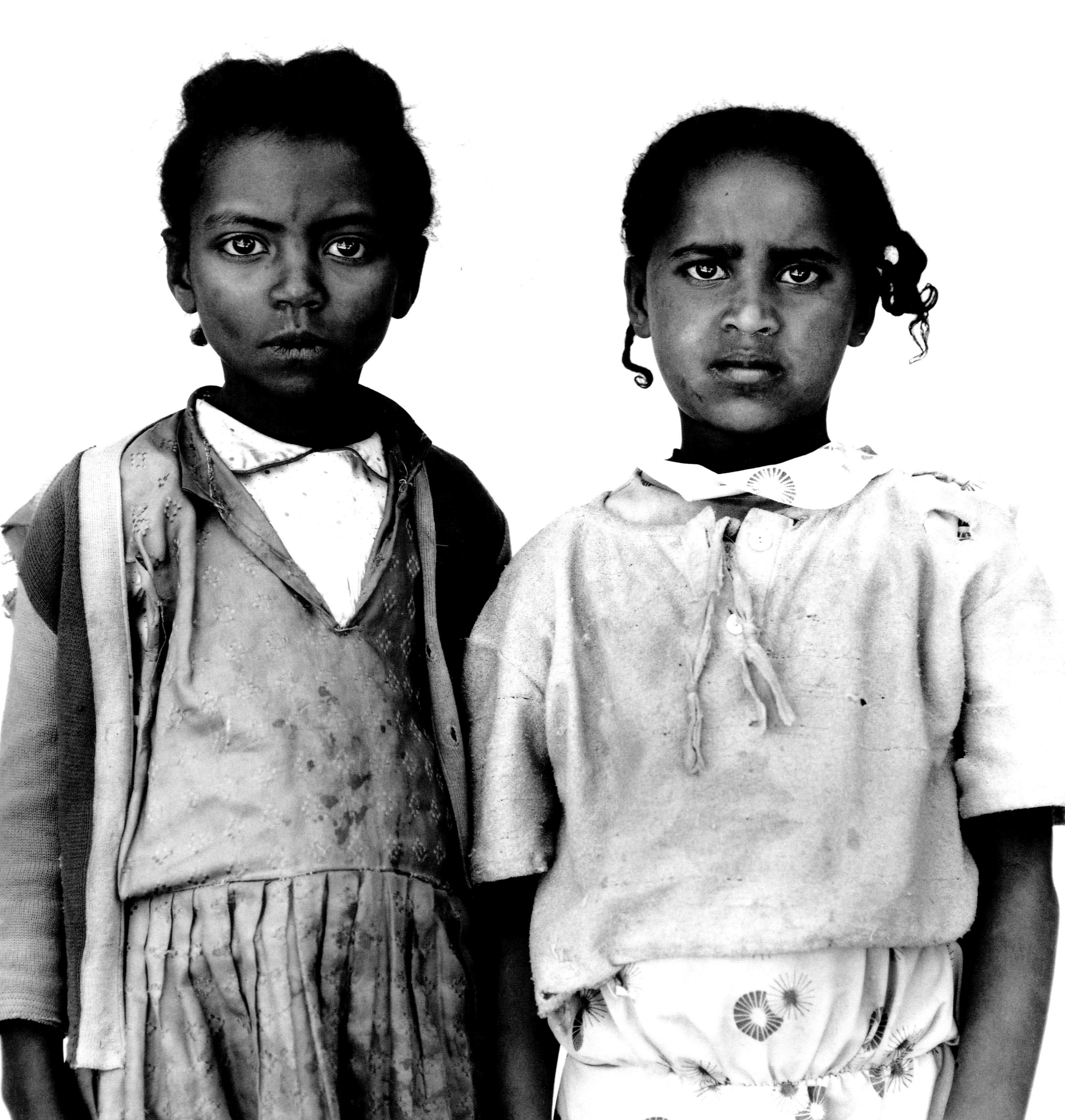

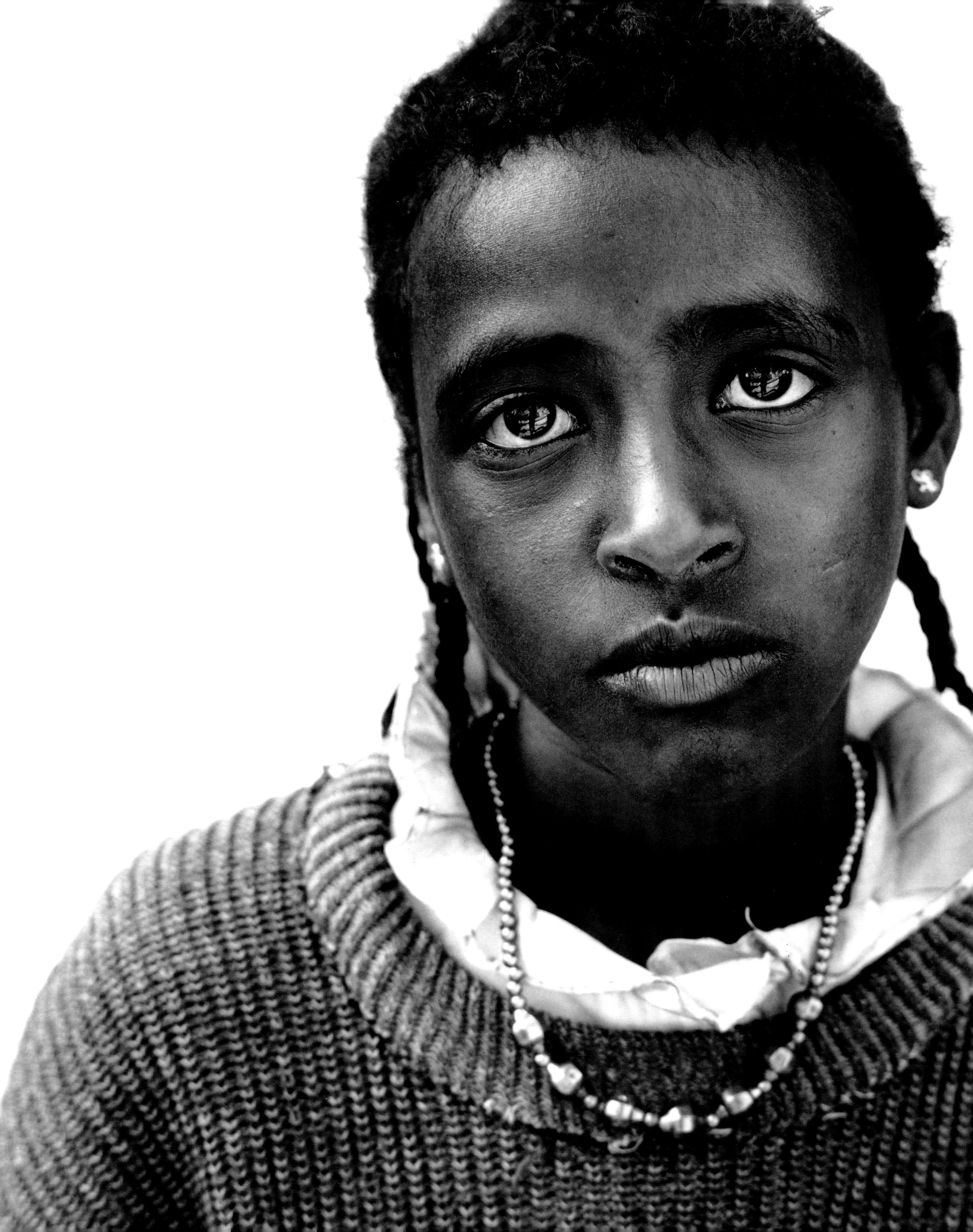

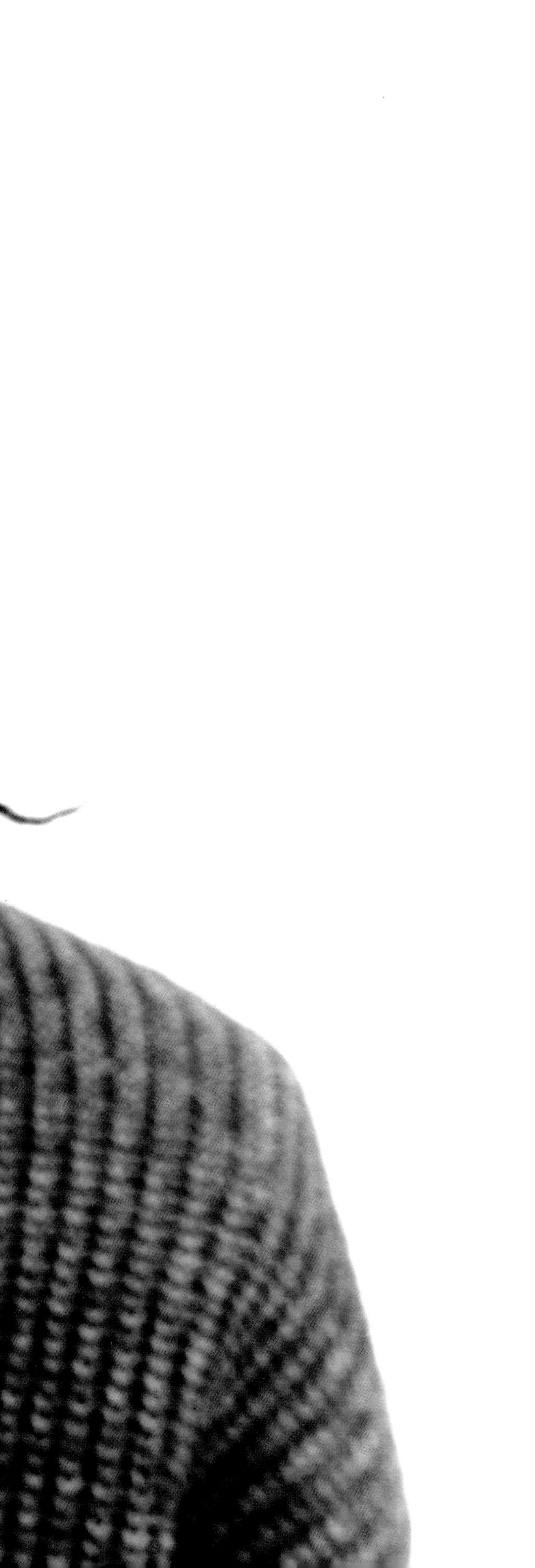

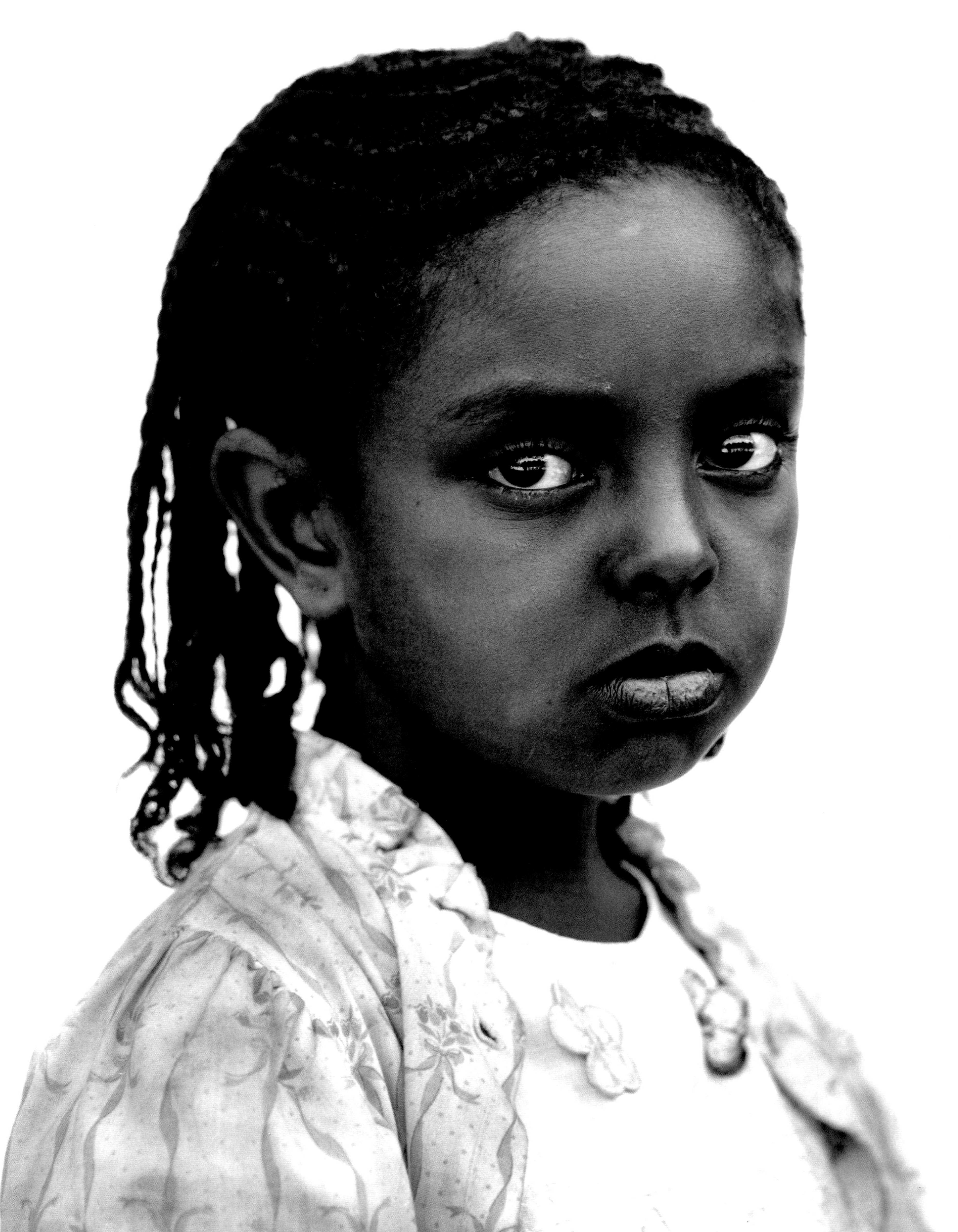

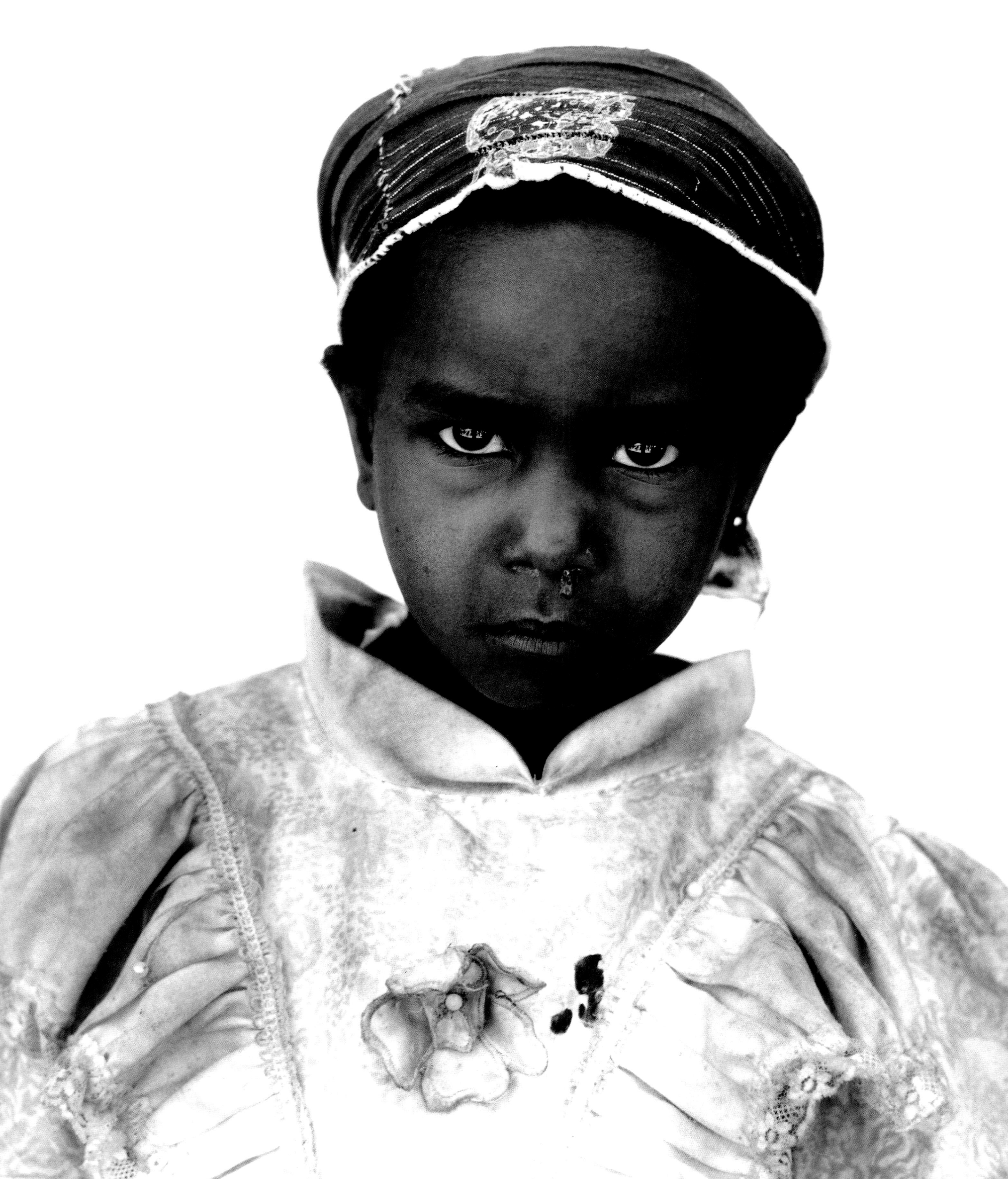

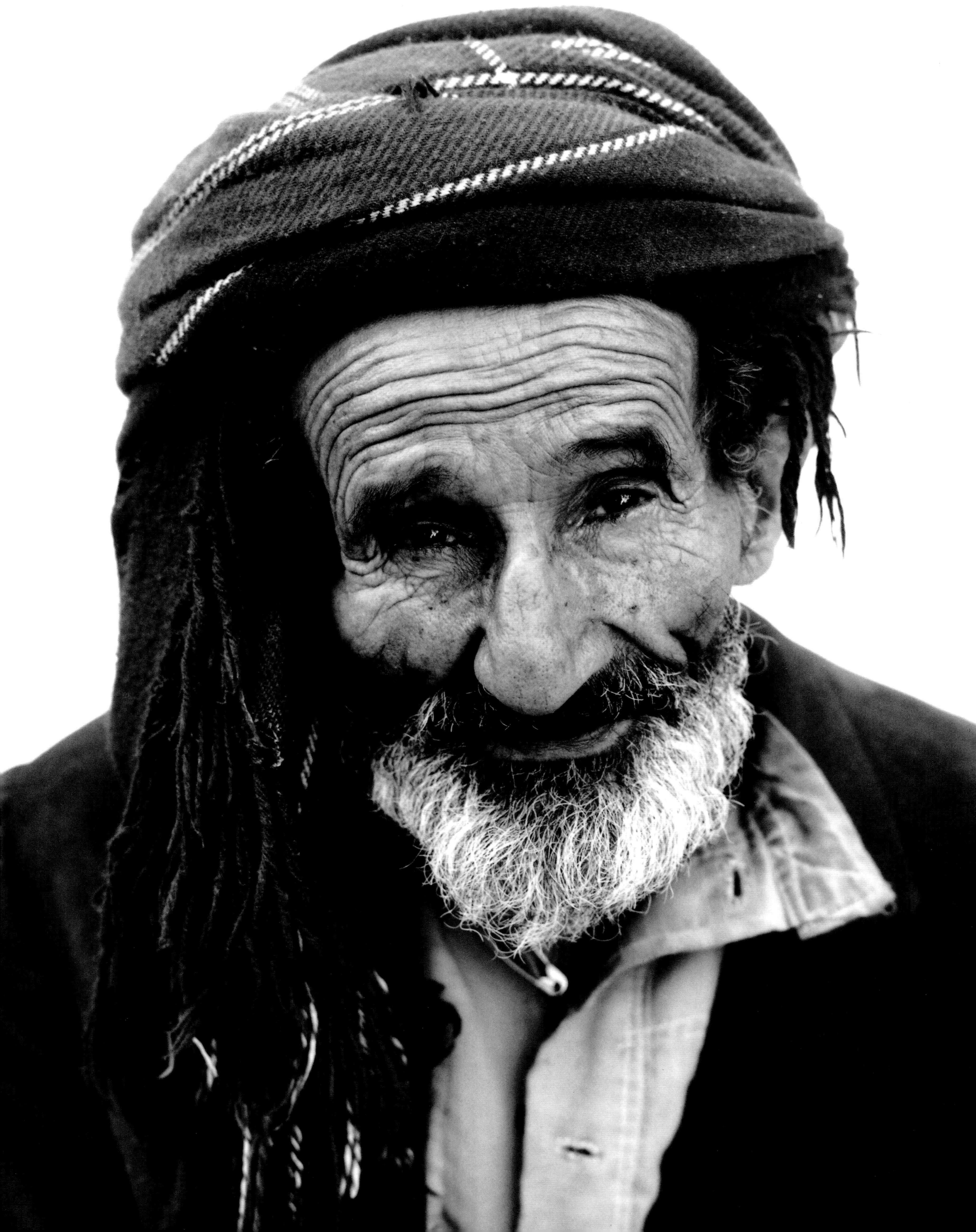

Yemen Beni Husheich Tribe

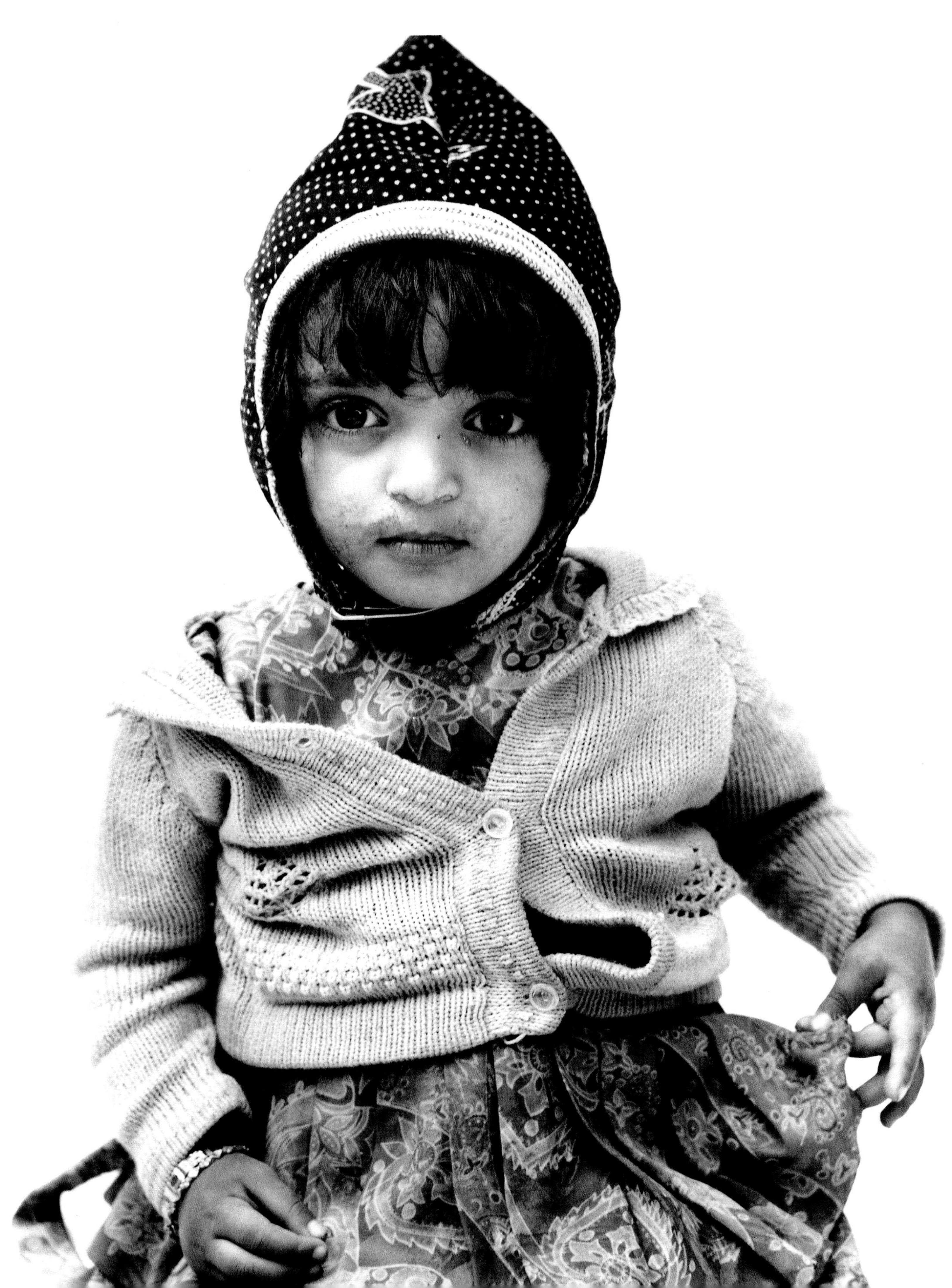

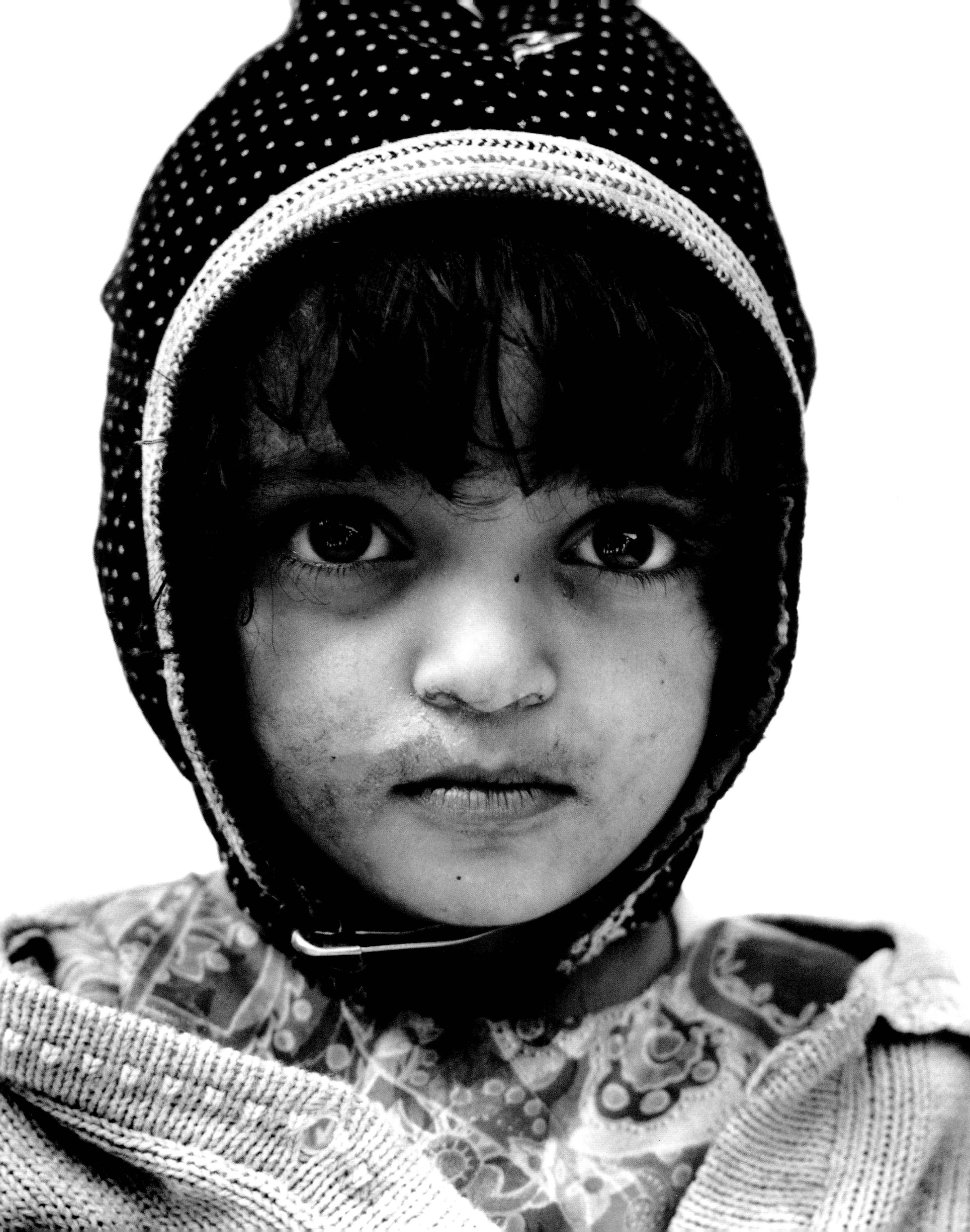

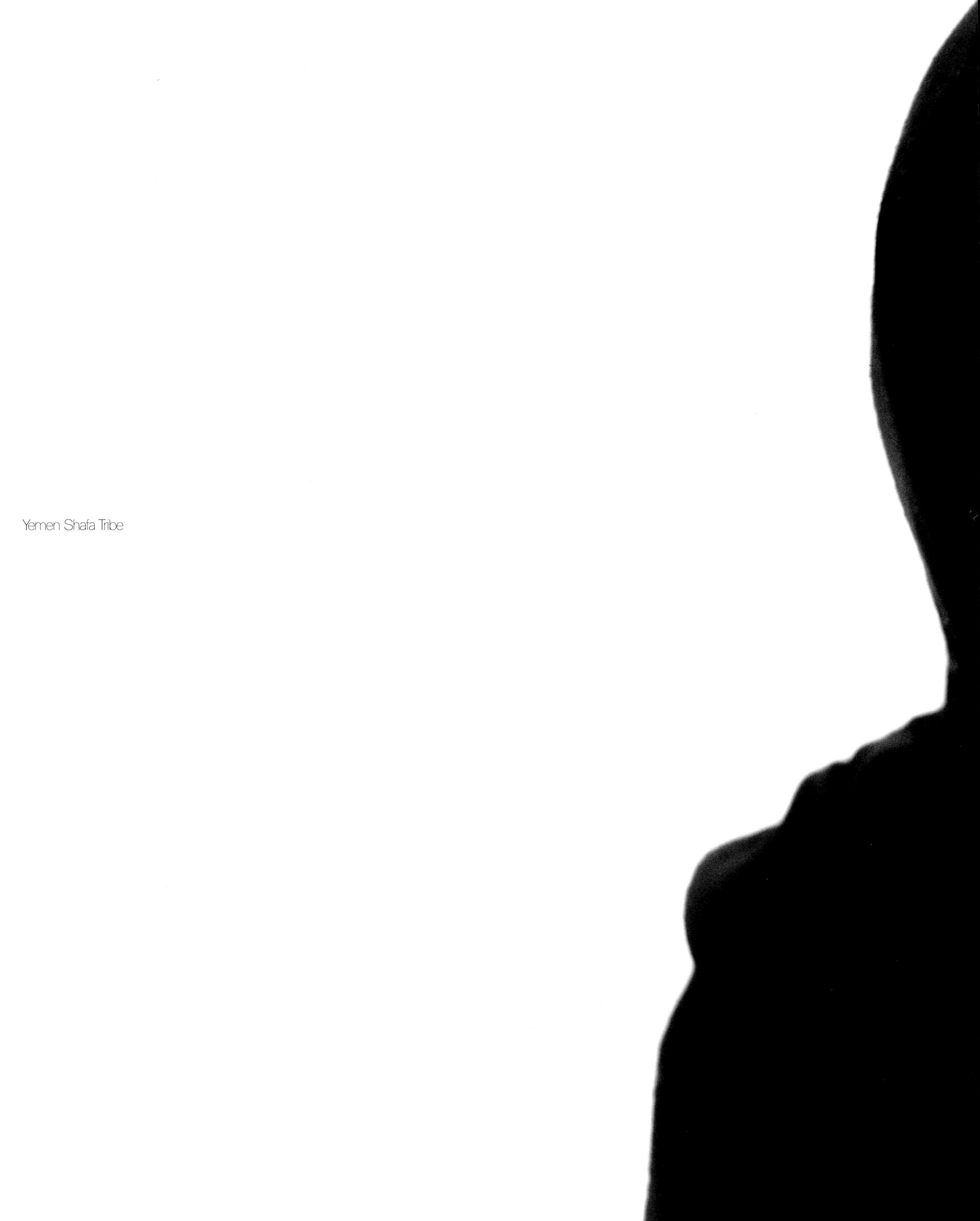

Yemen Shafa Tribe

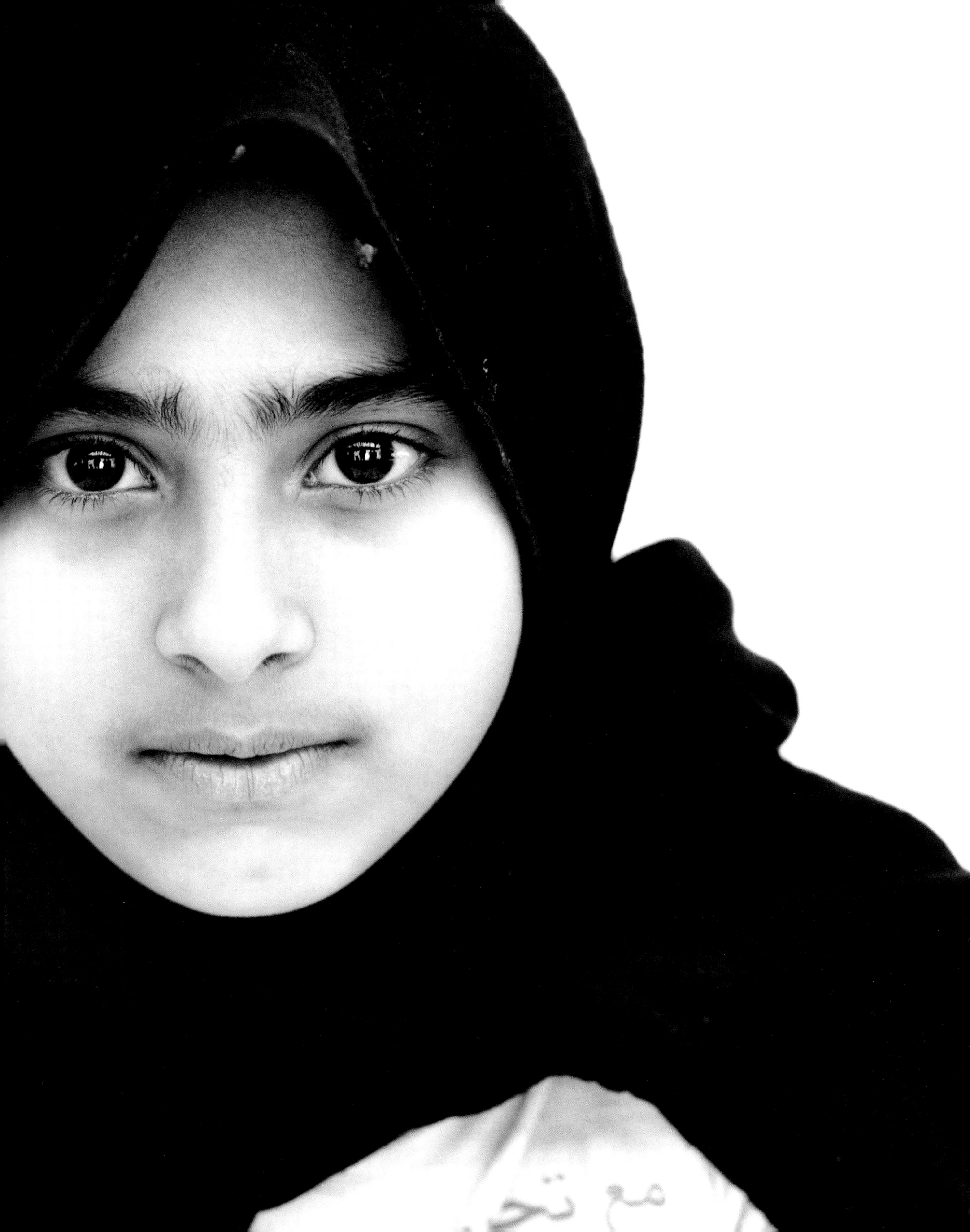

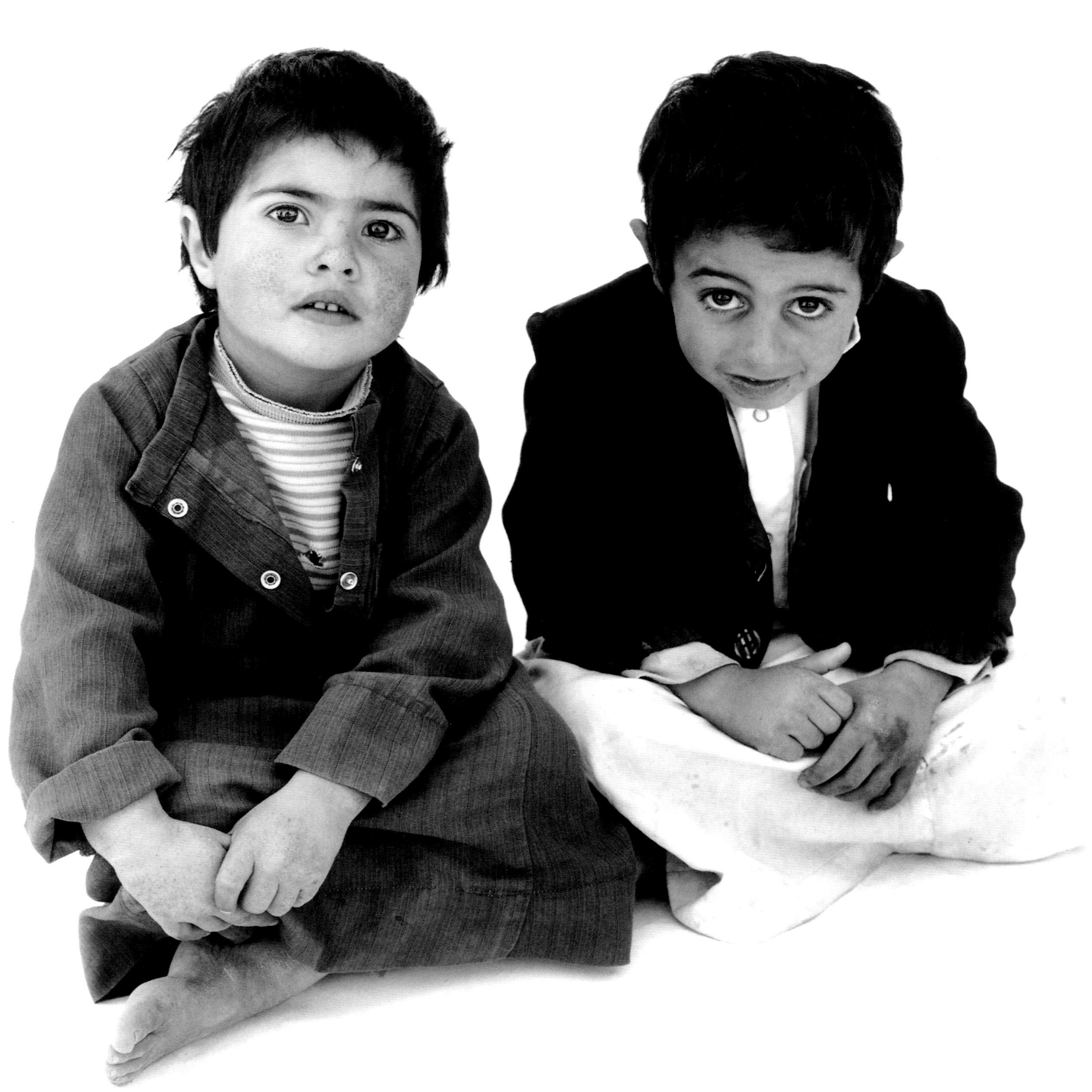

Yemen Beni Suraym Tribe

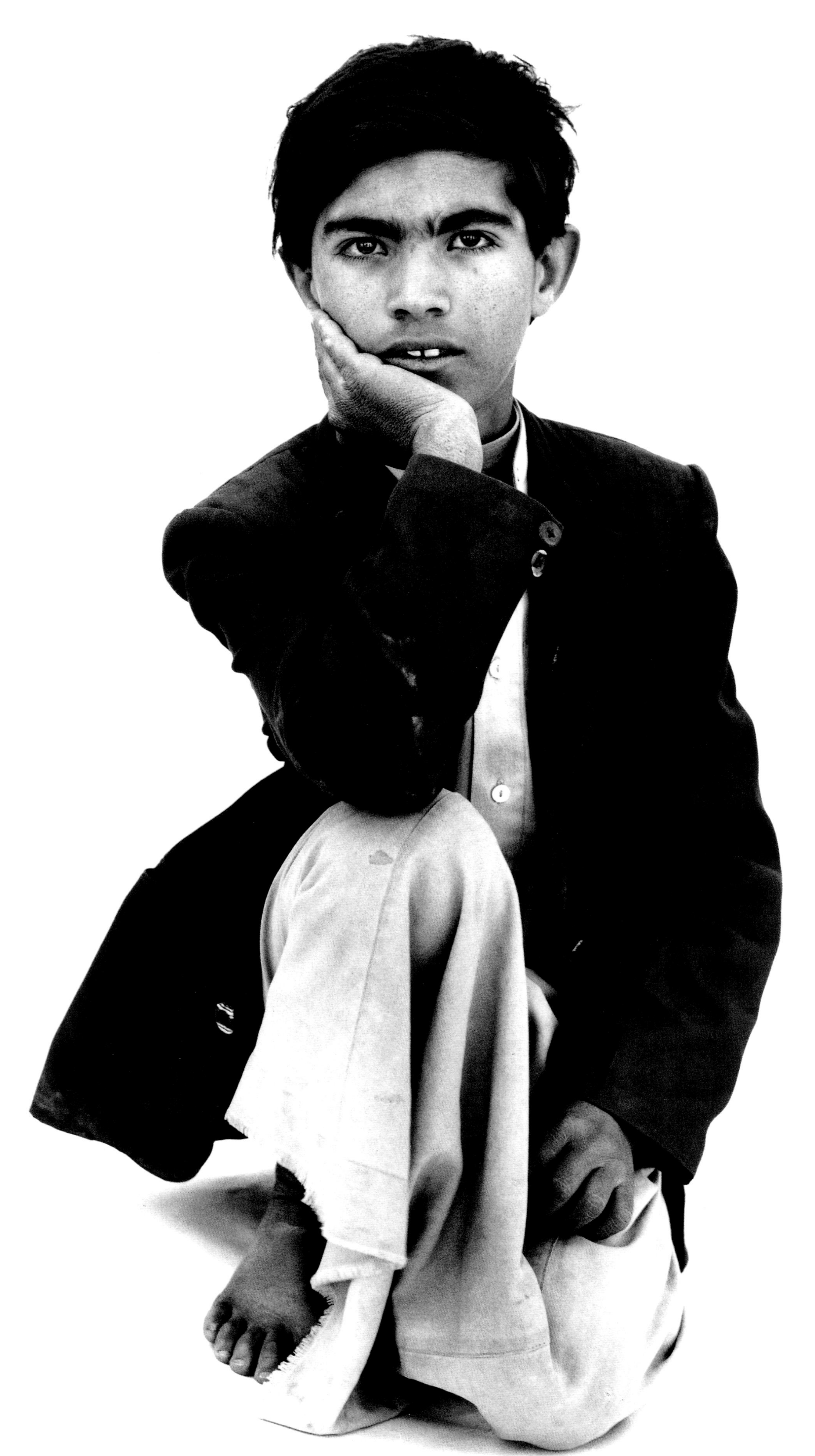

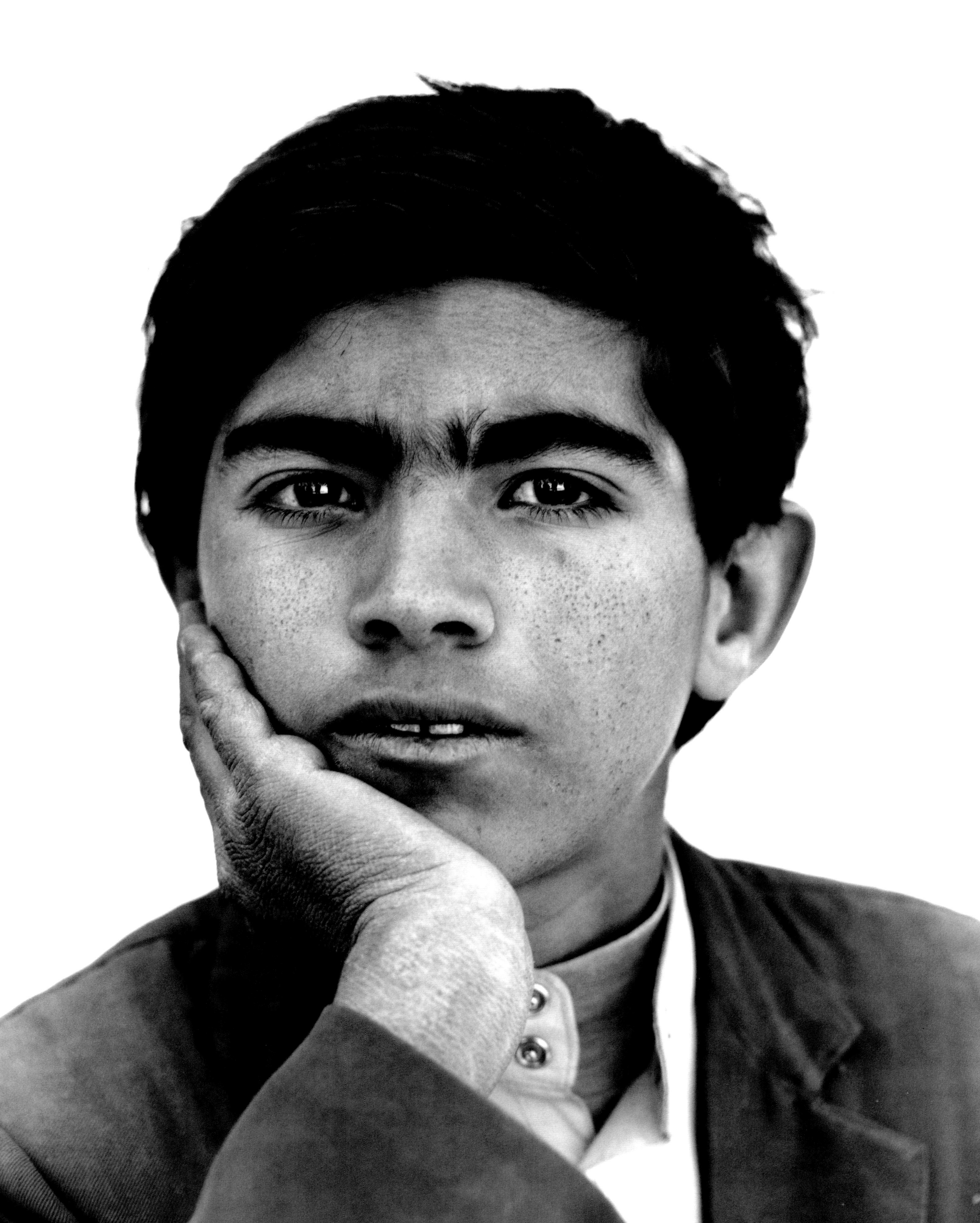

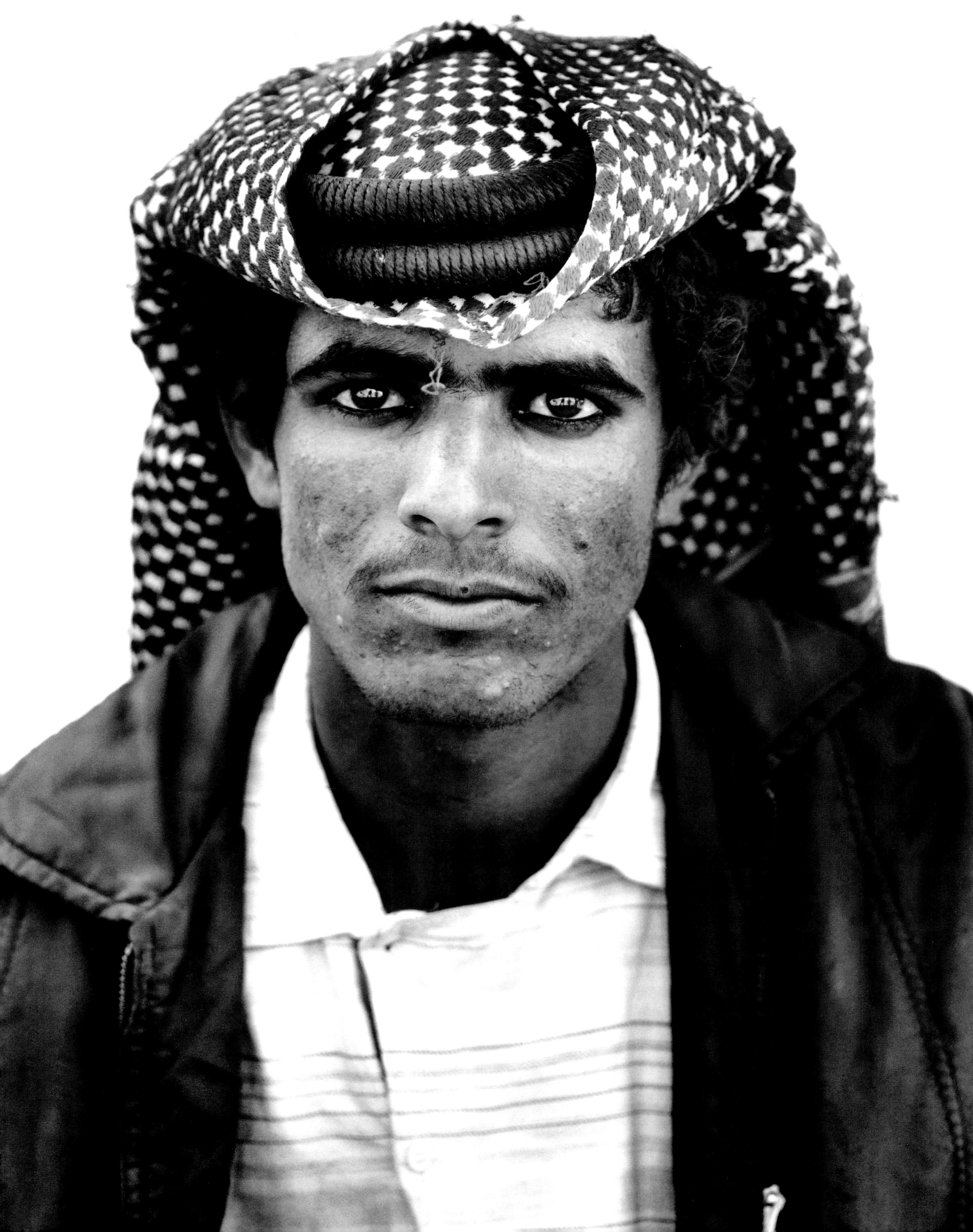

Jordan Beduin Tribe

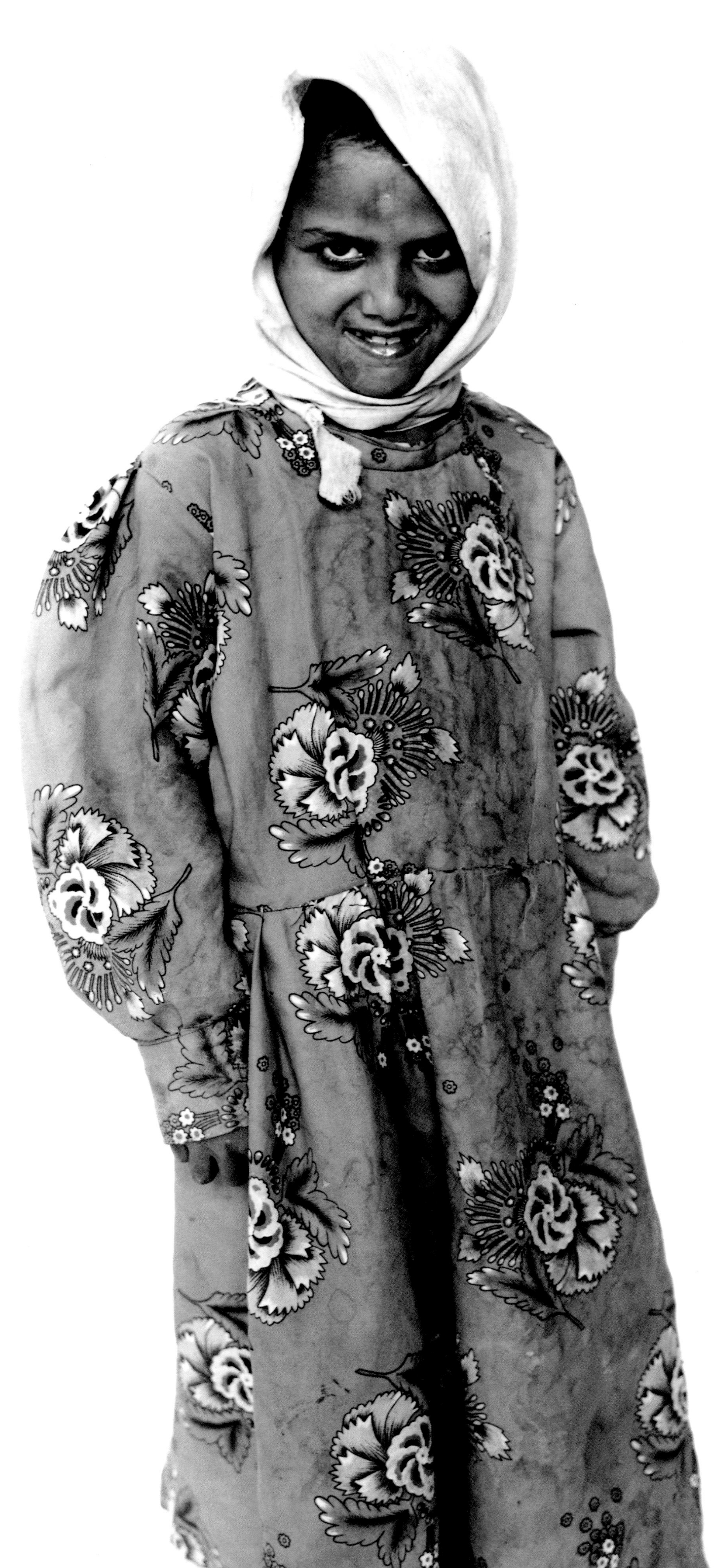

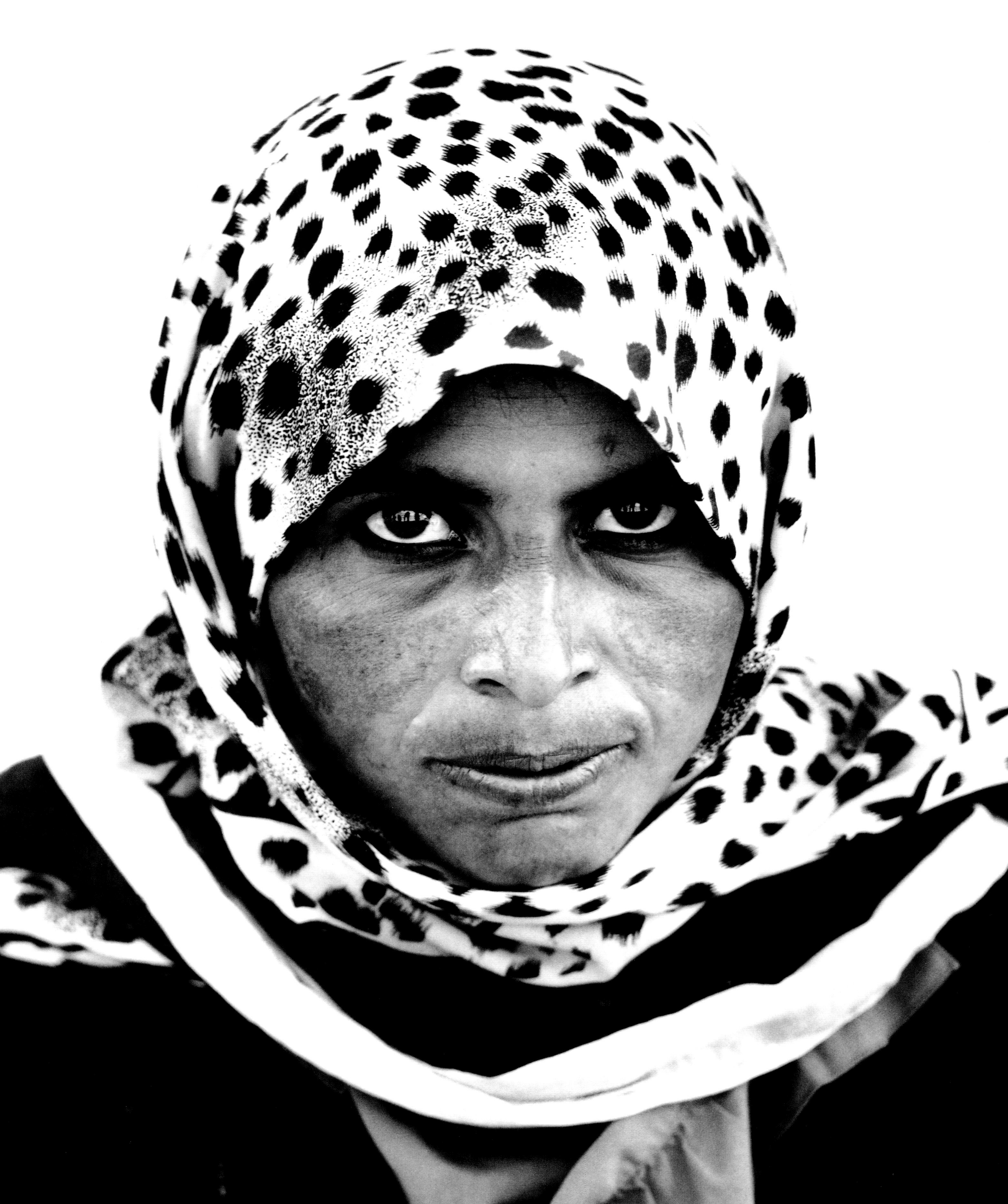

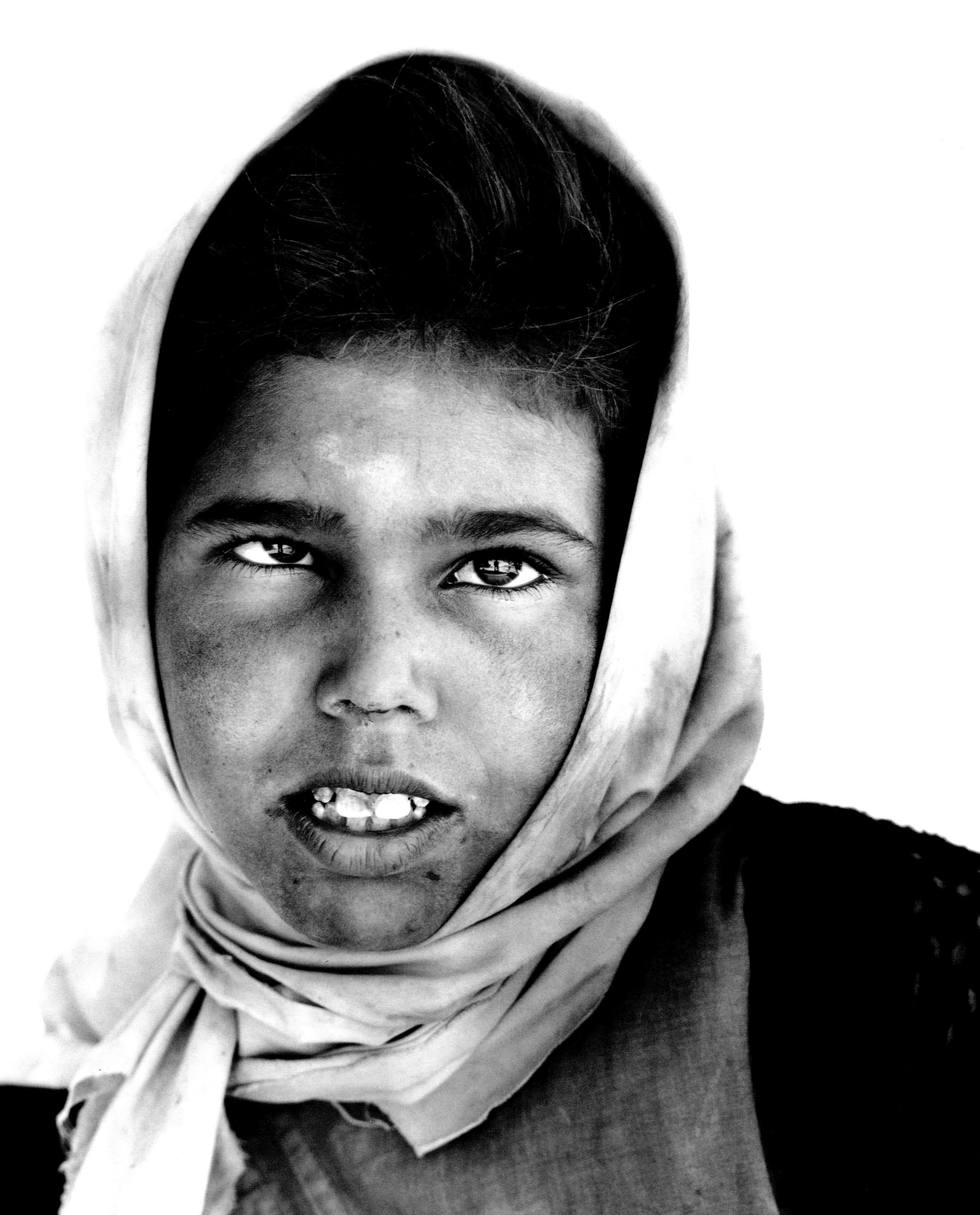

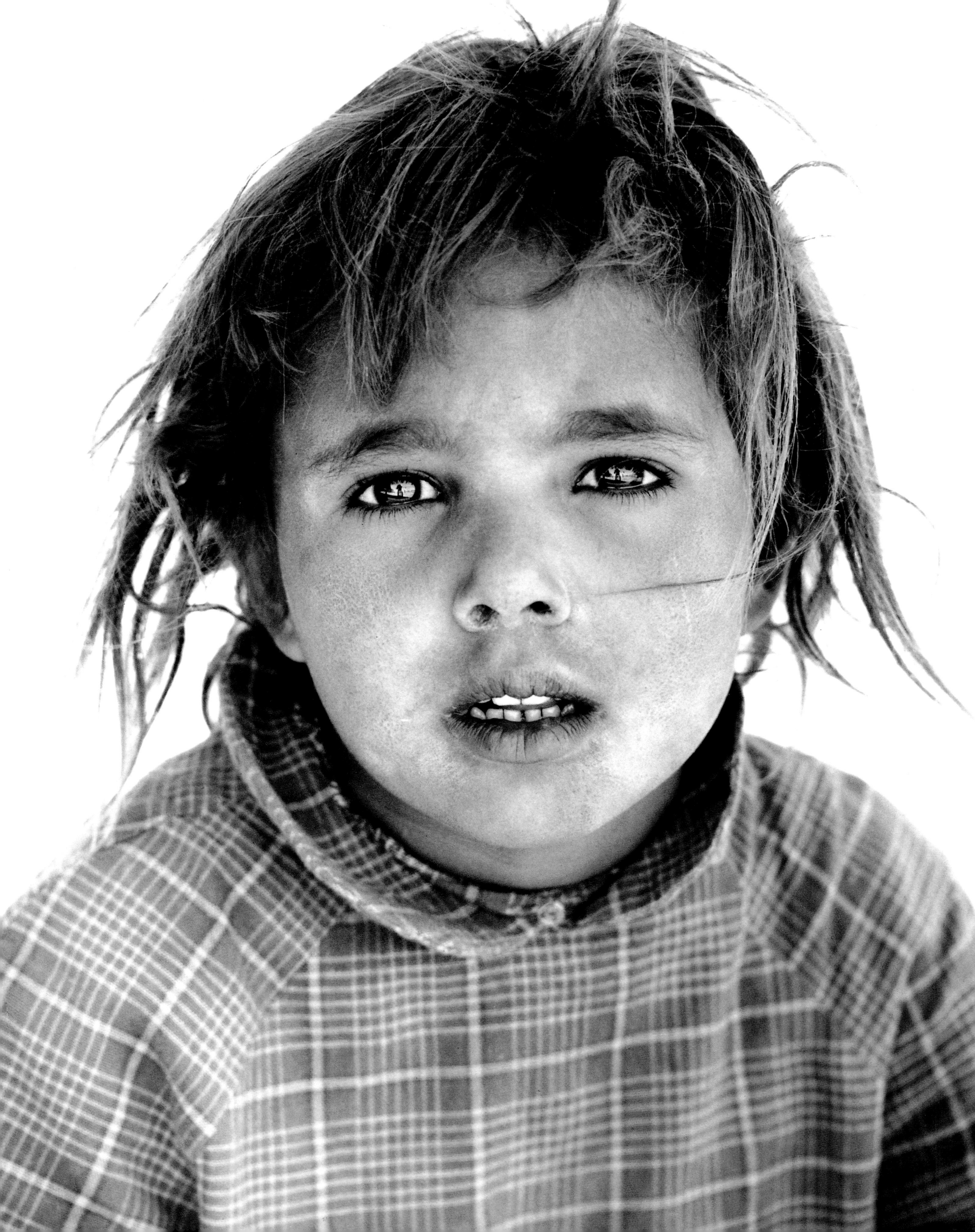

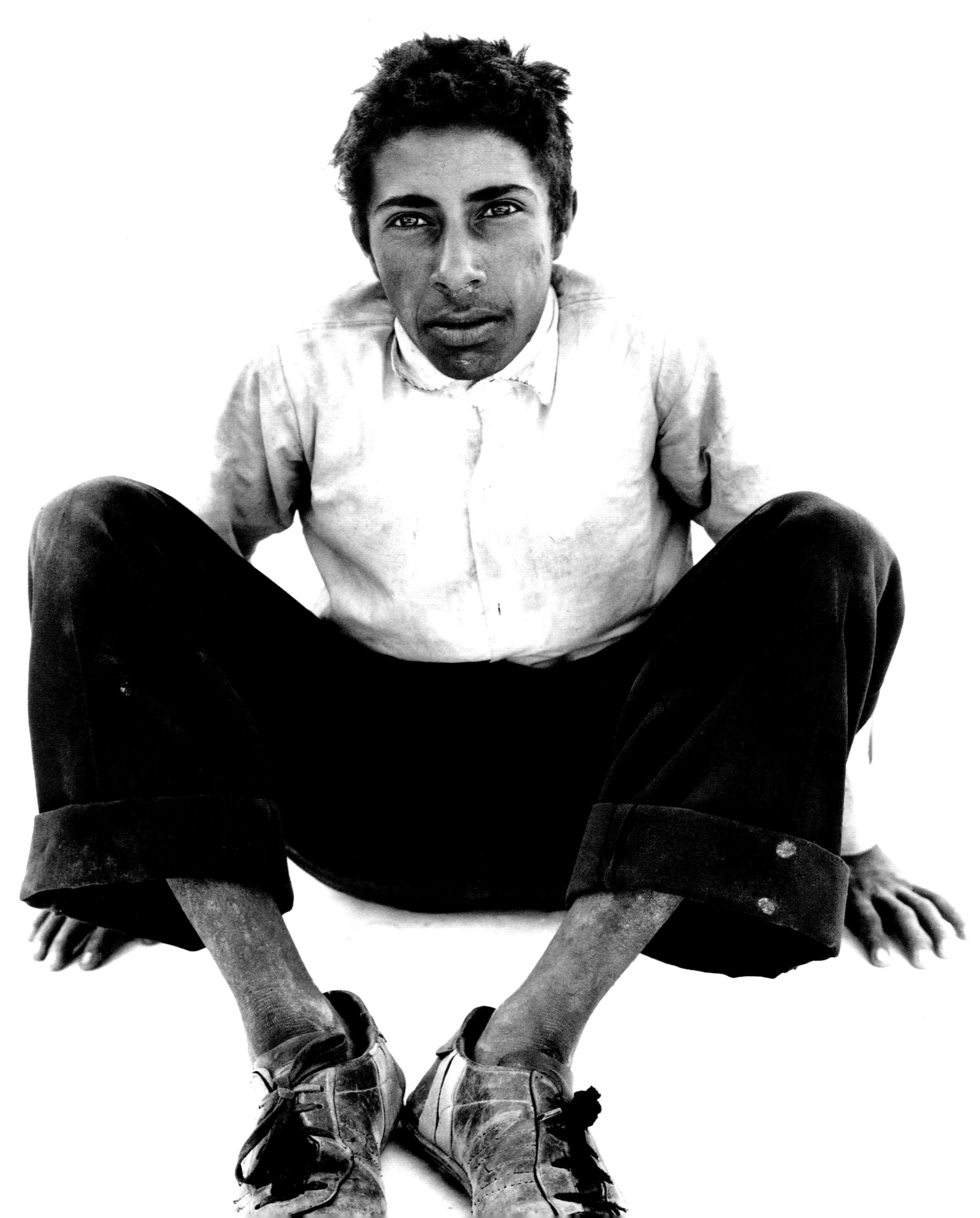

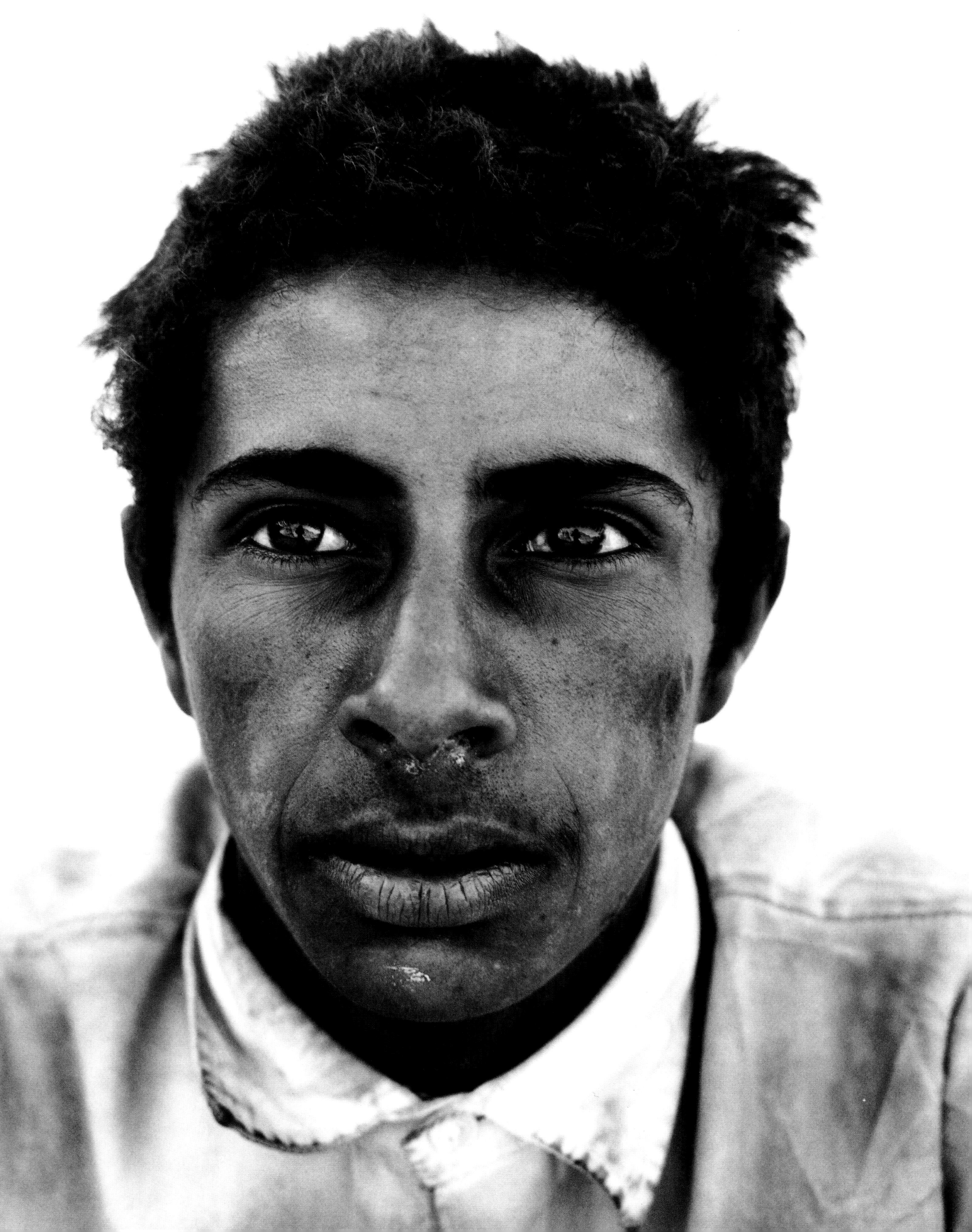

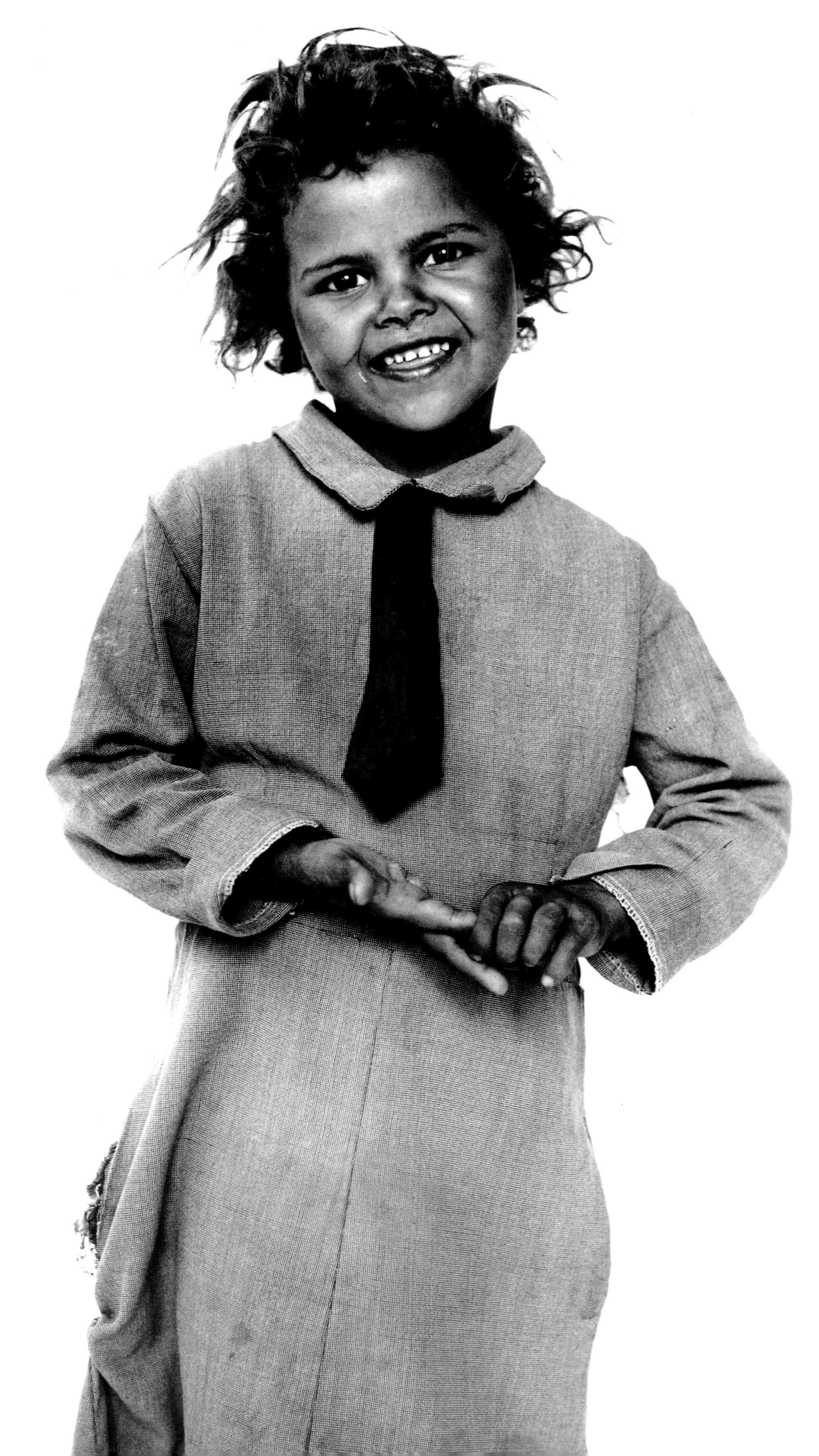

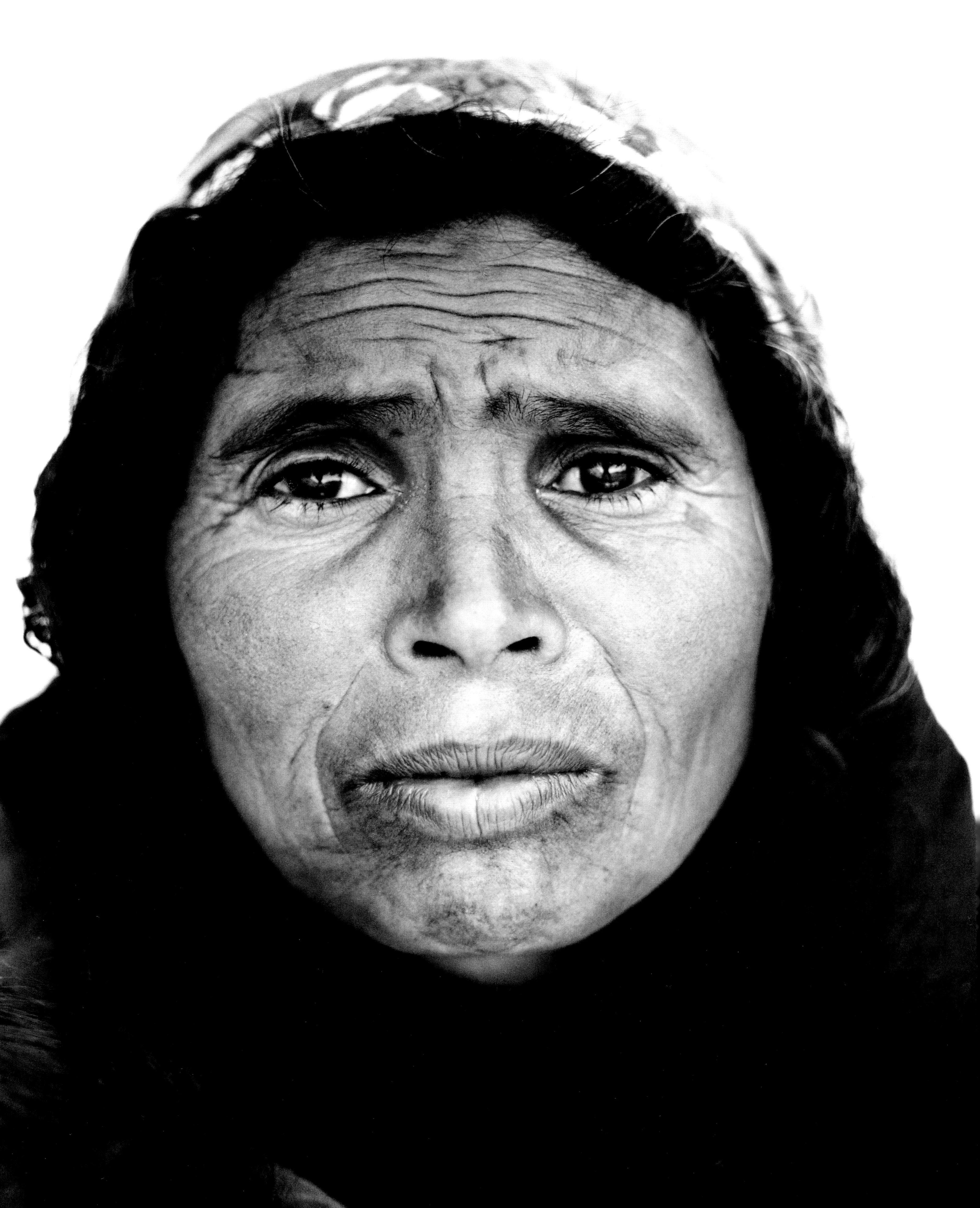

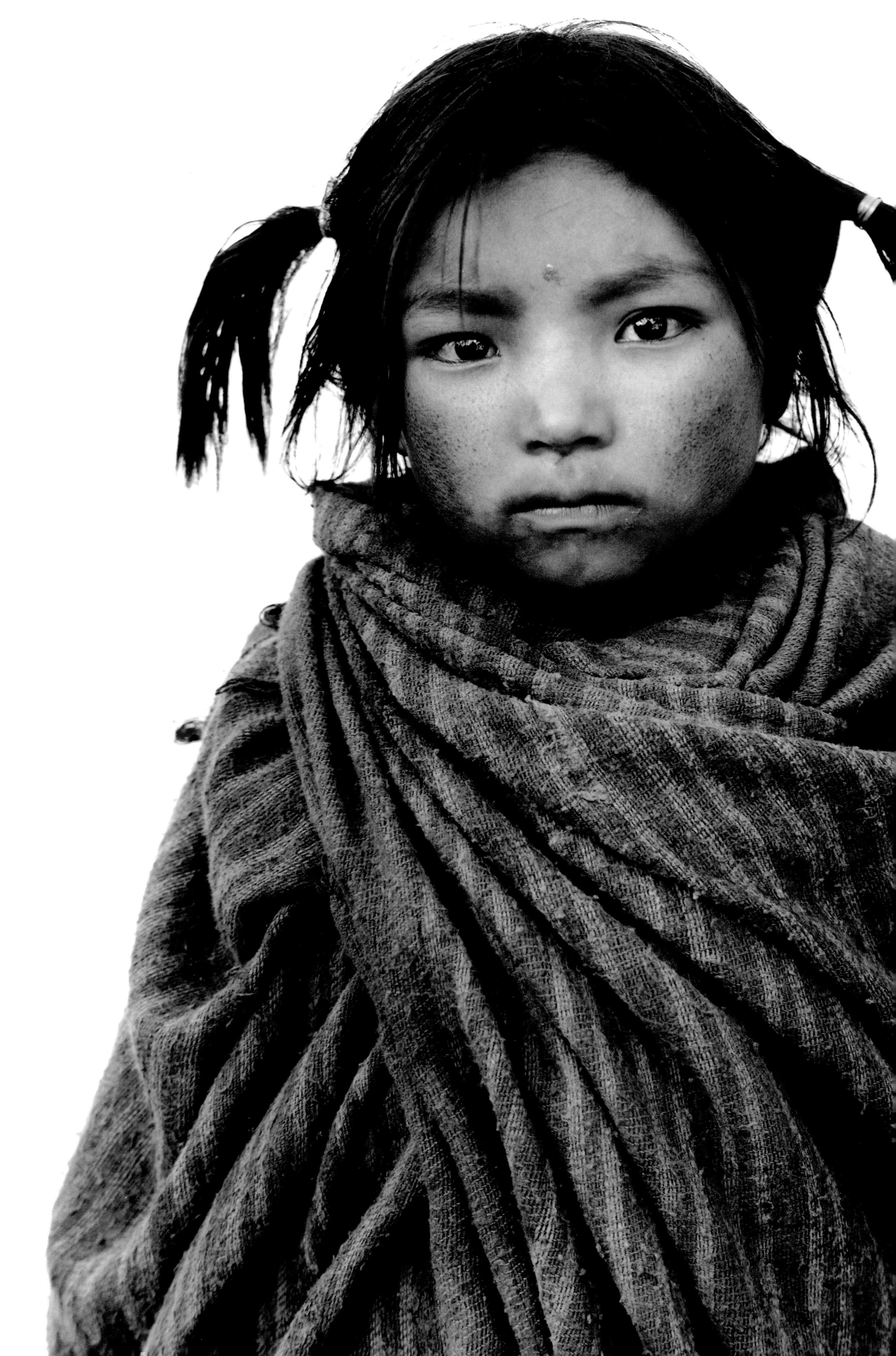

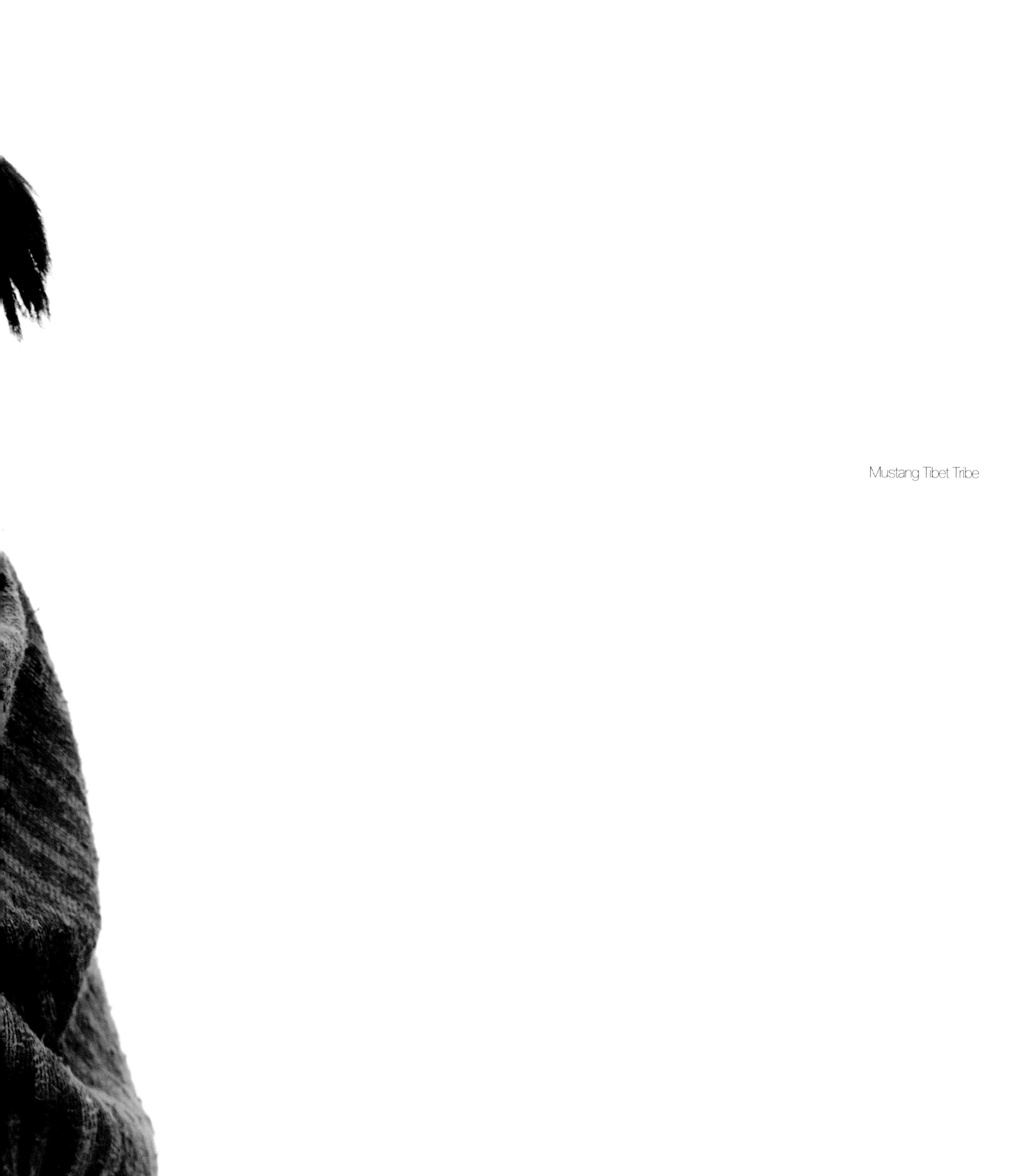

Mustang Tibet Tribe

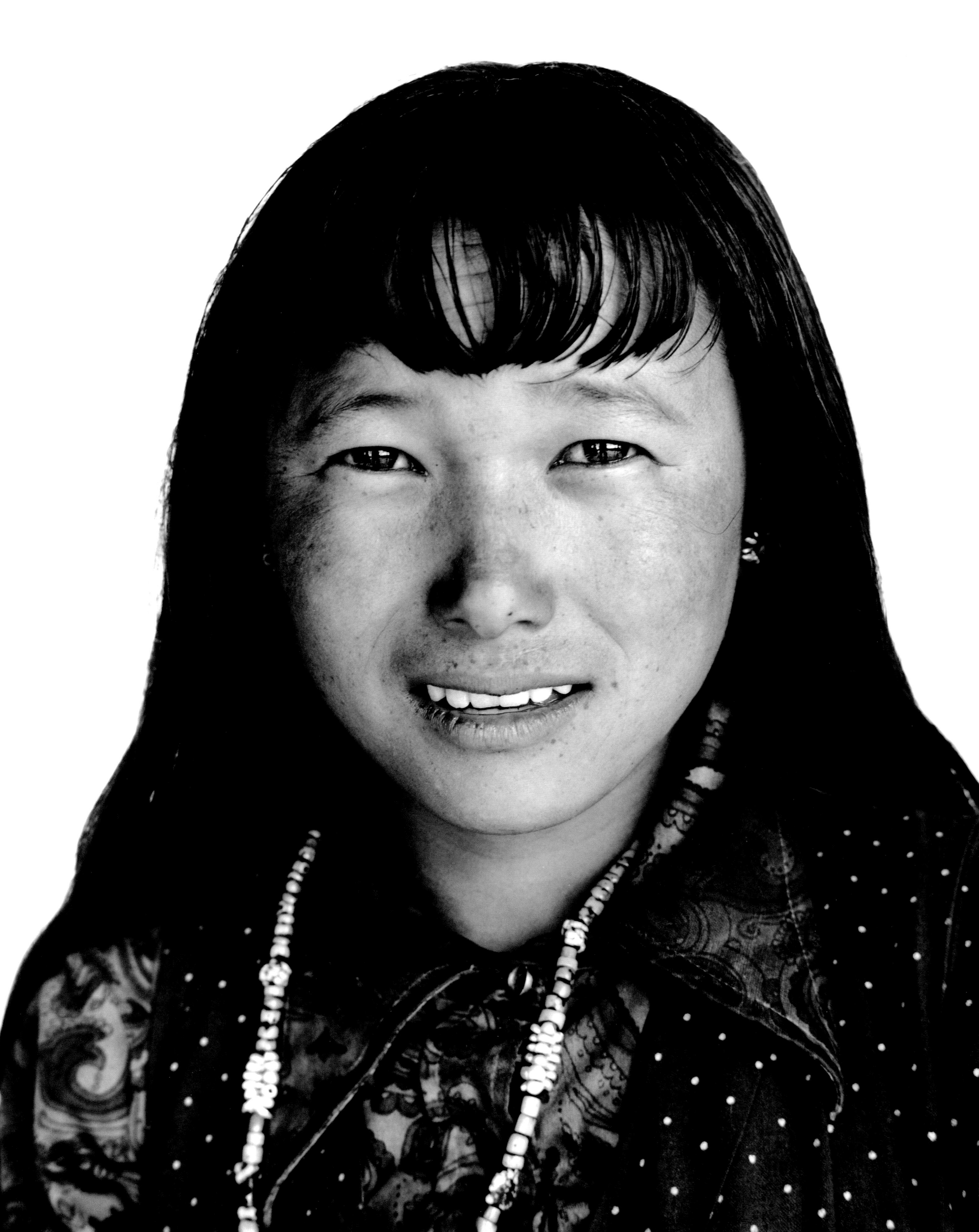

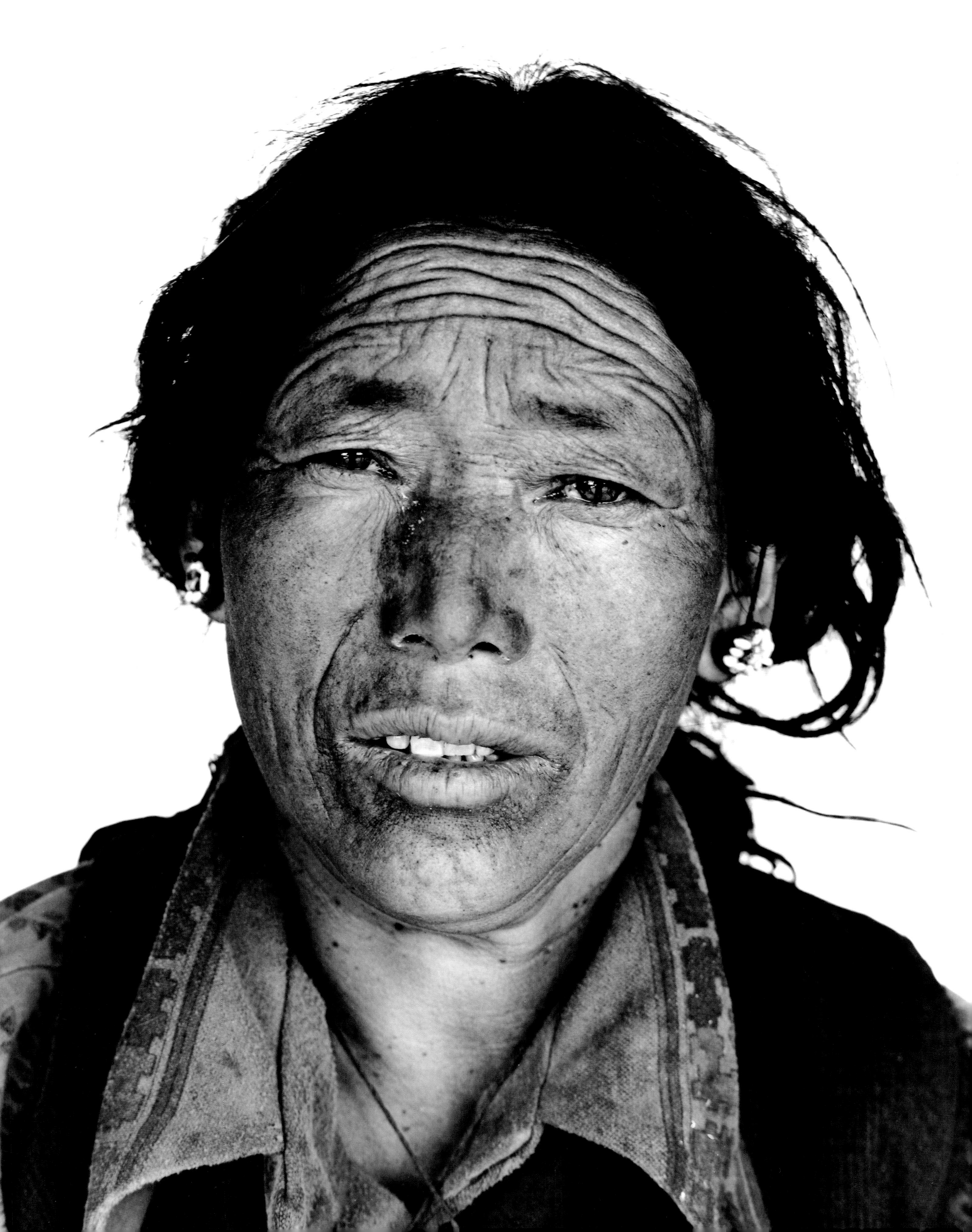

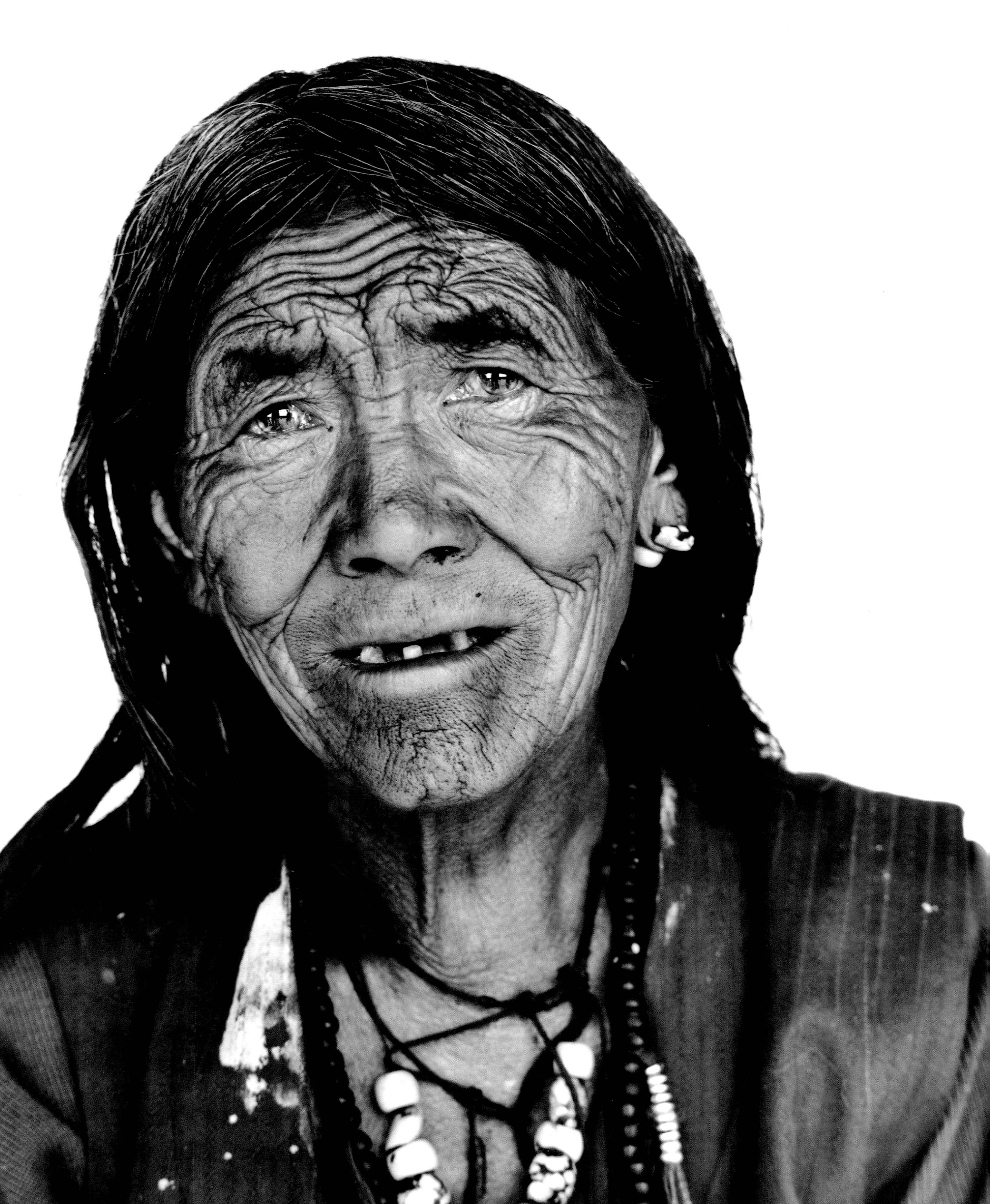

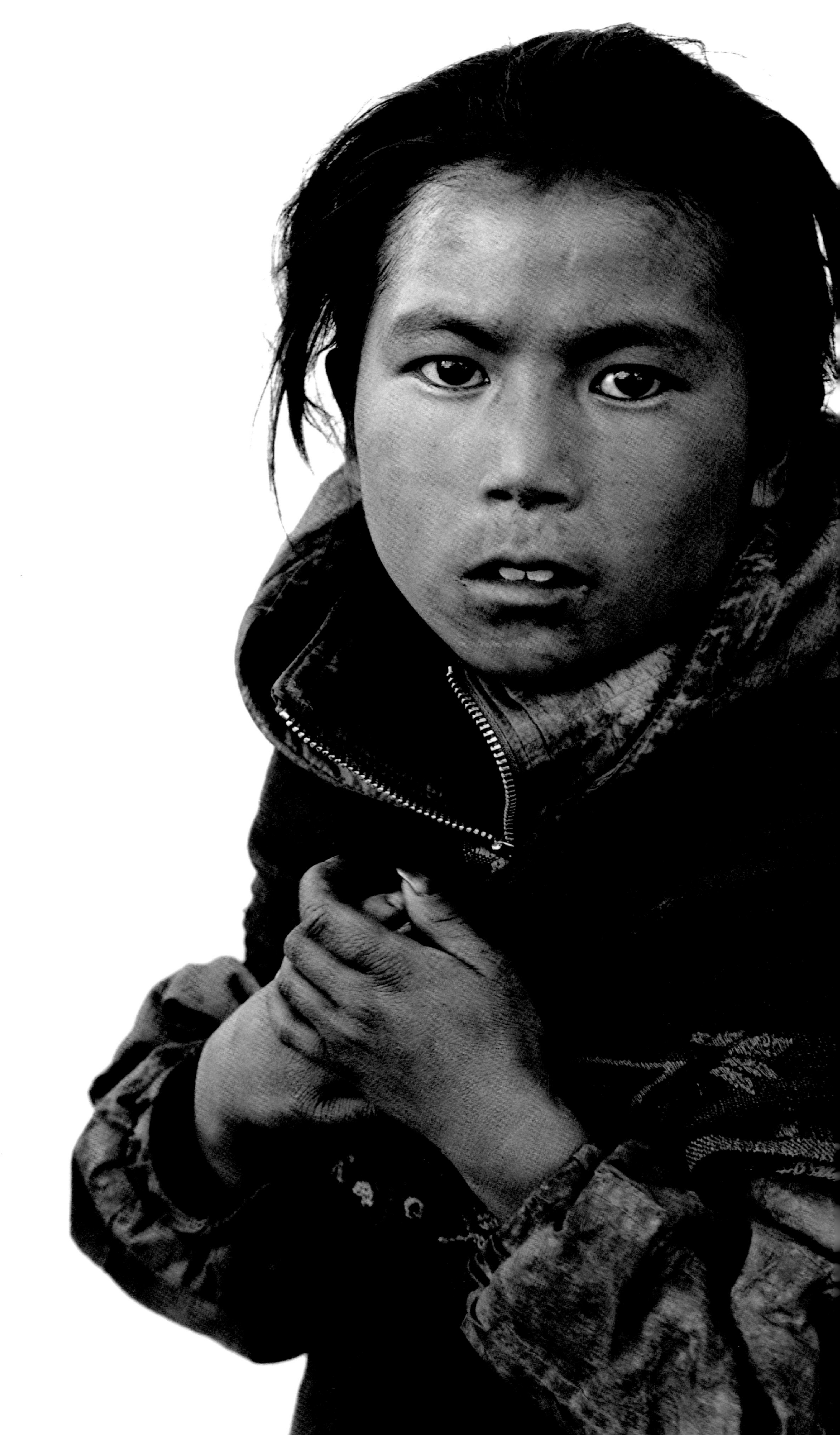

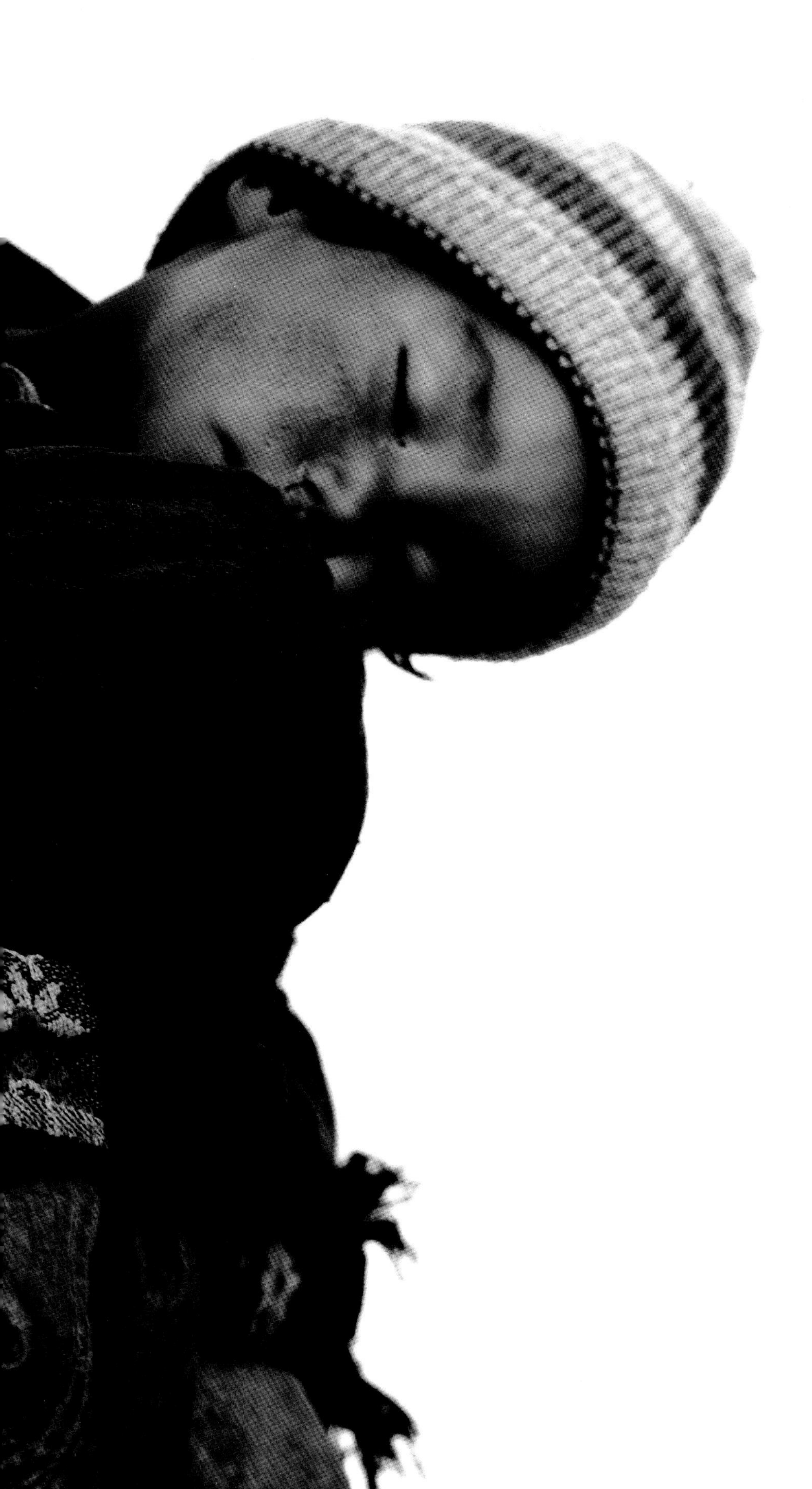

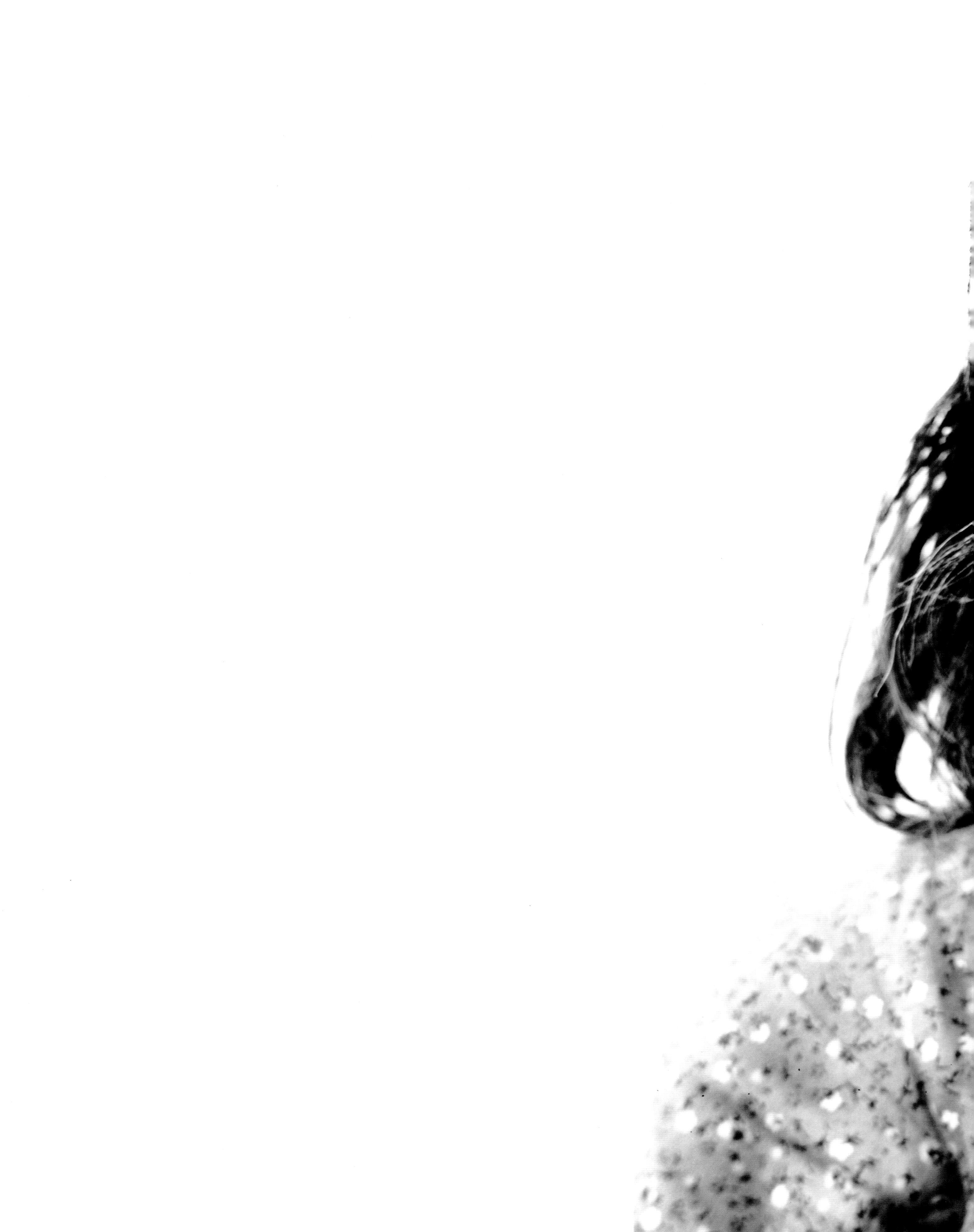

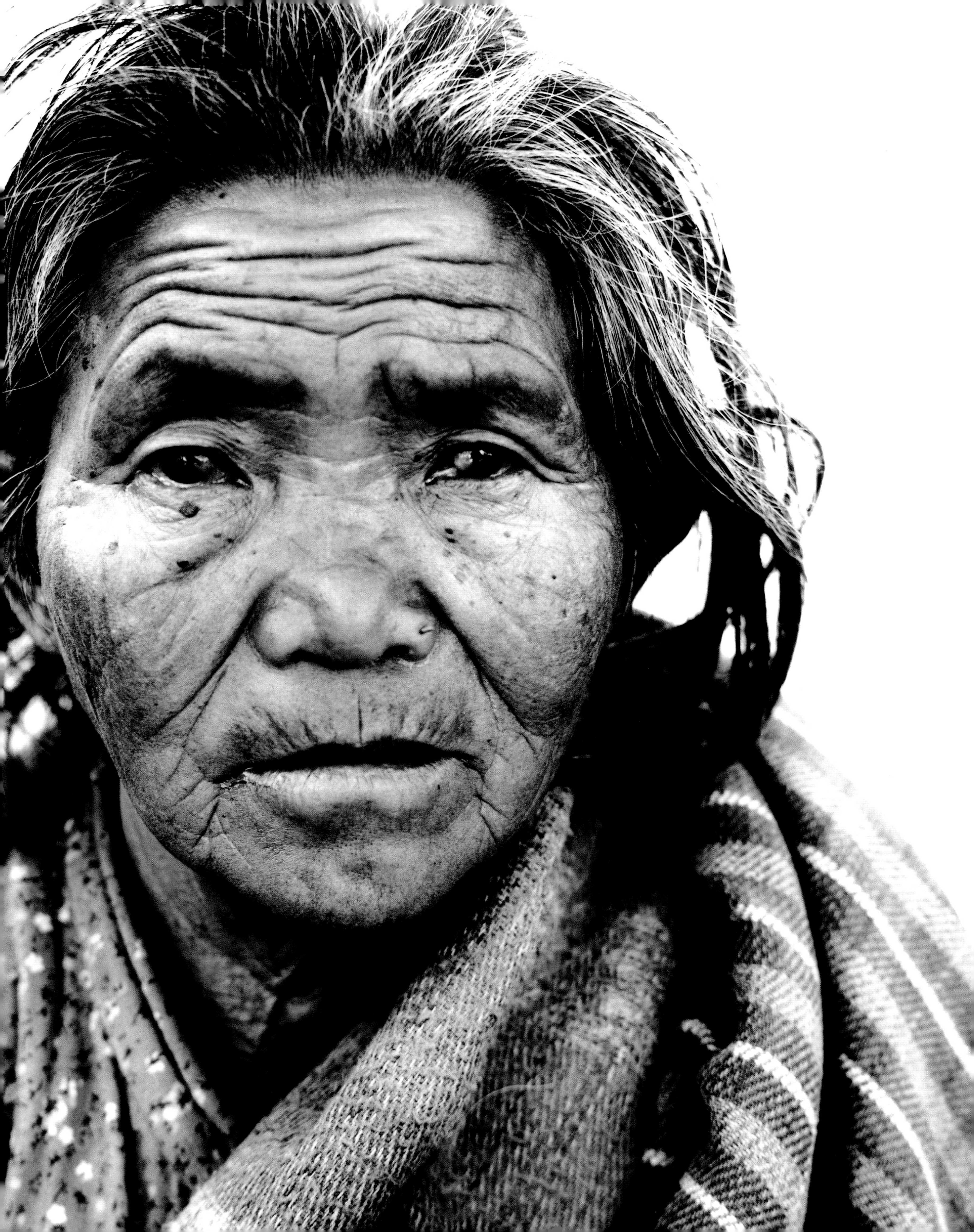

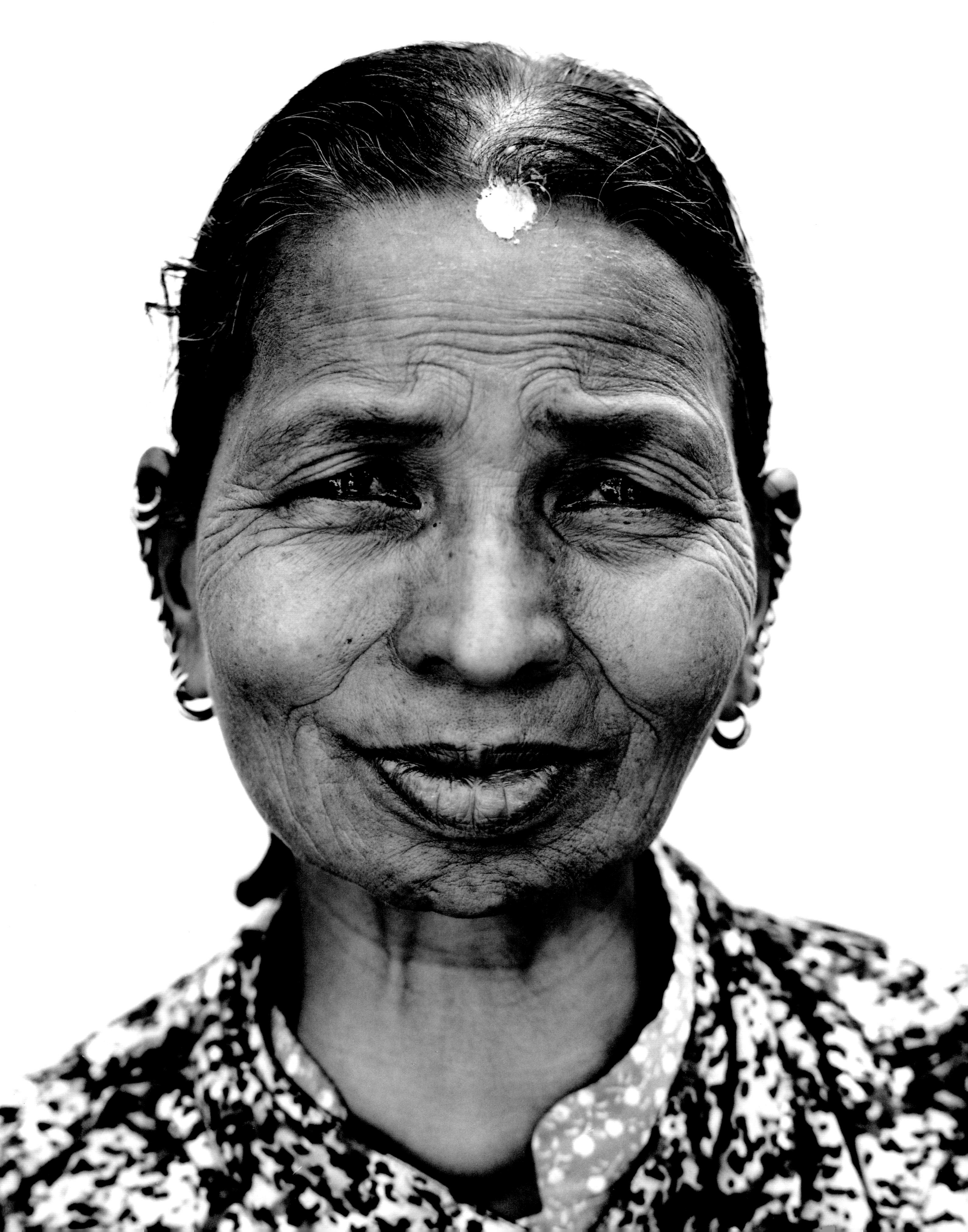

Nepal Newar Tribe

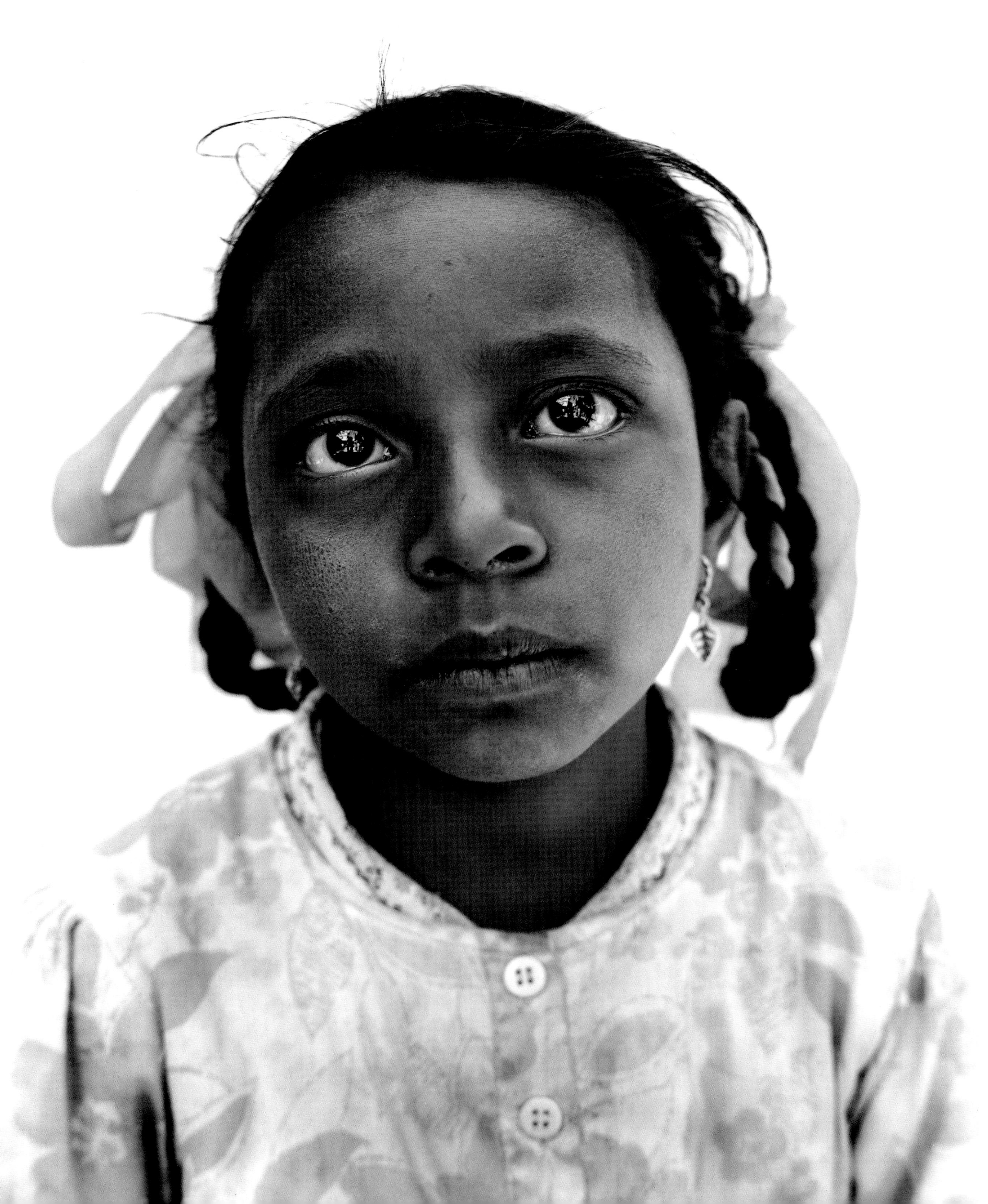

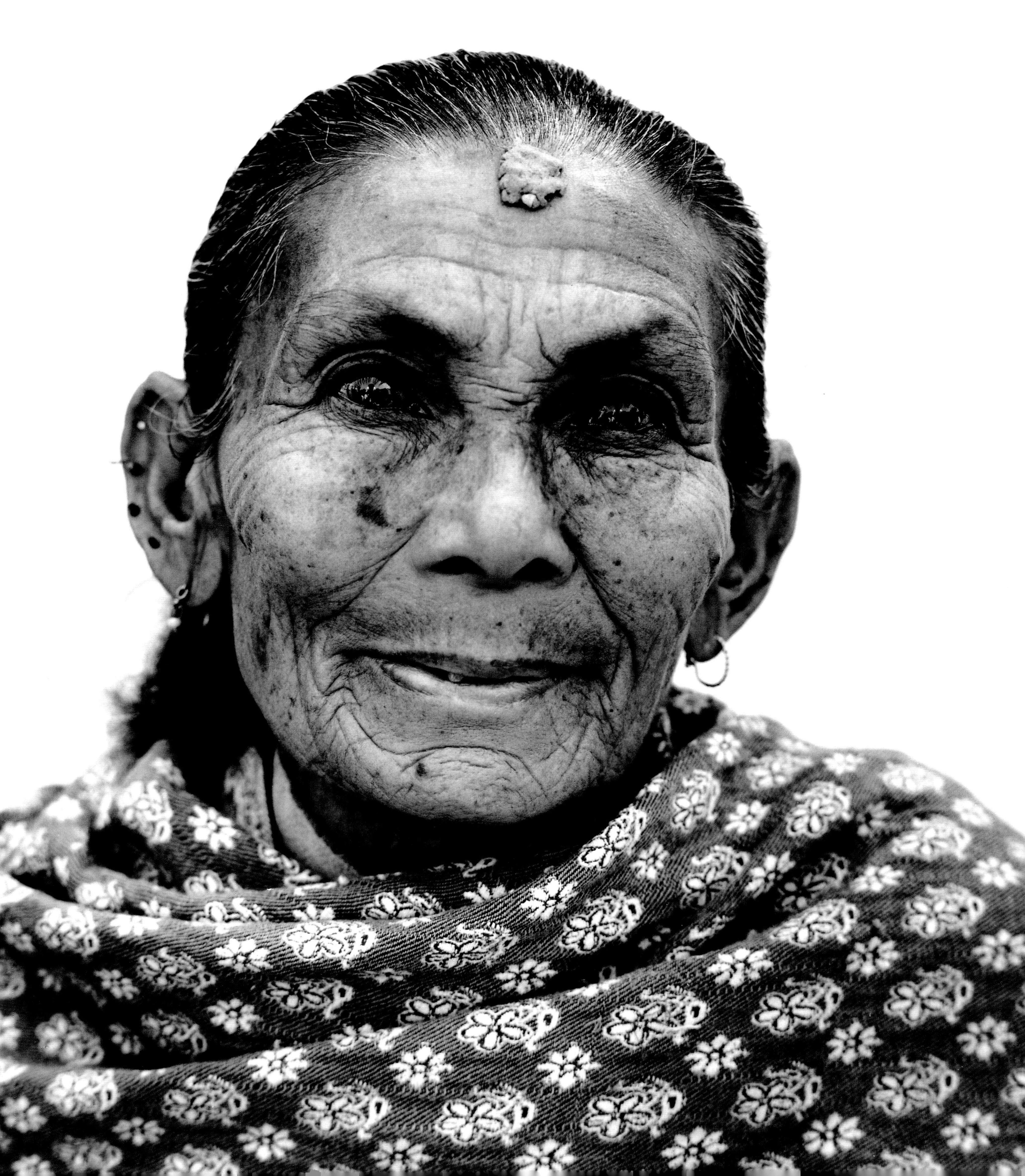

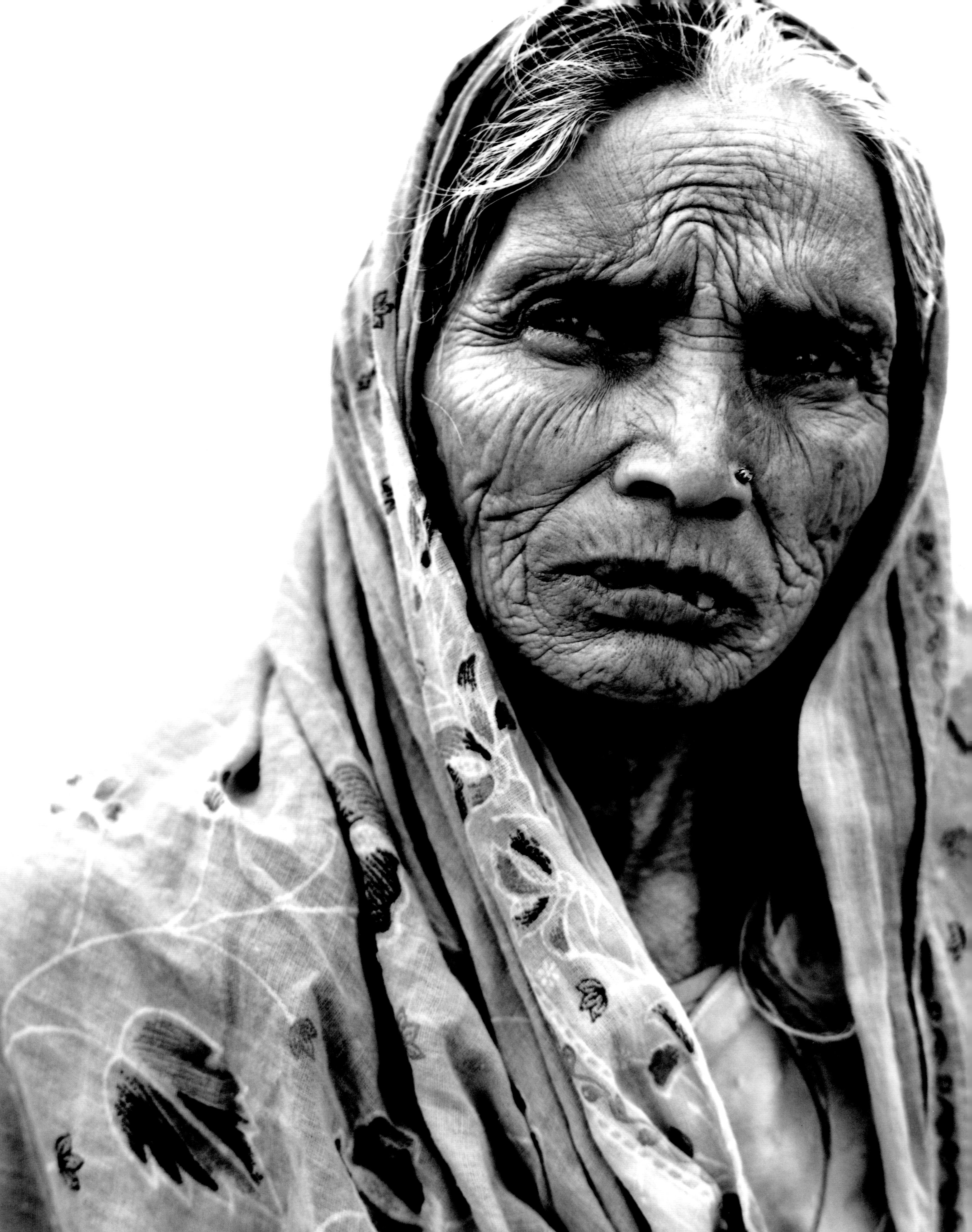

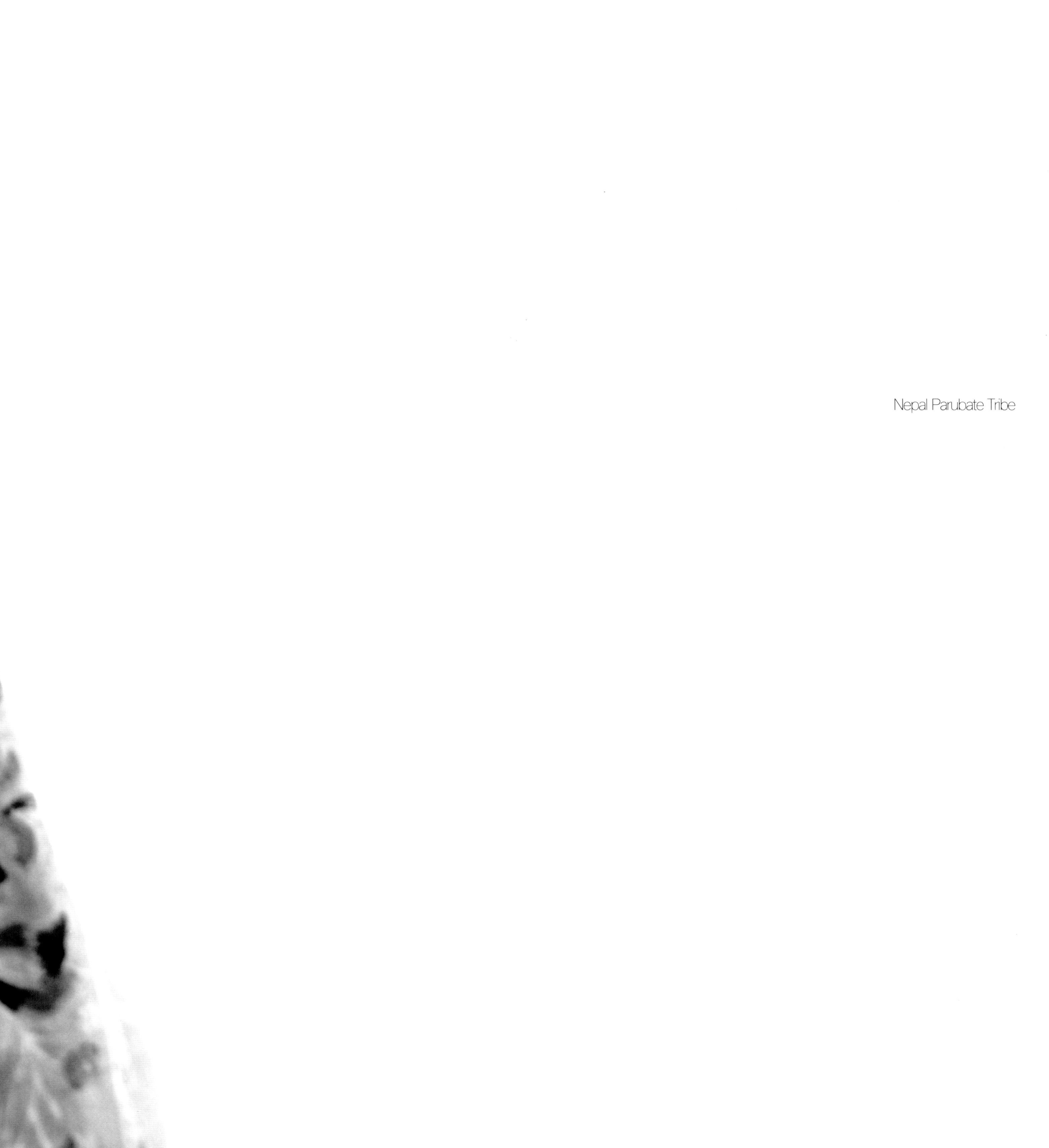

Nepal Parubate Tribe

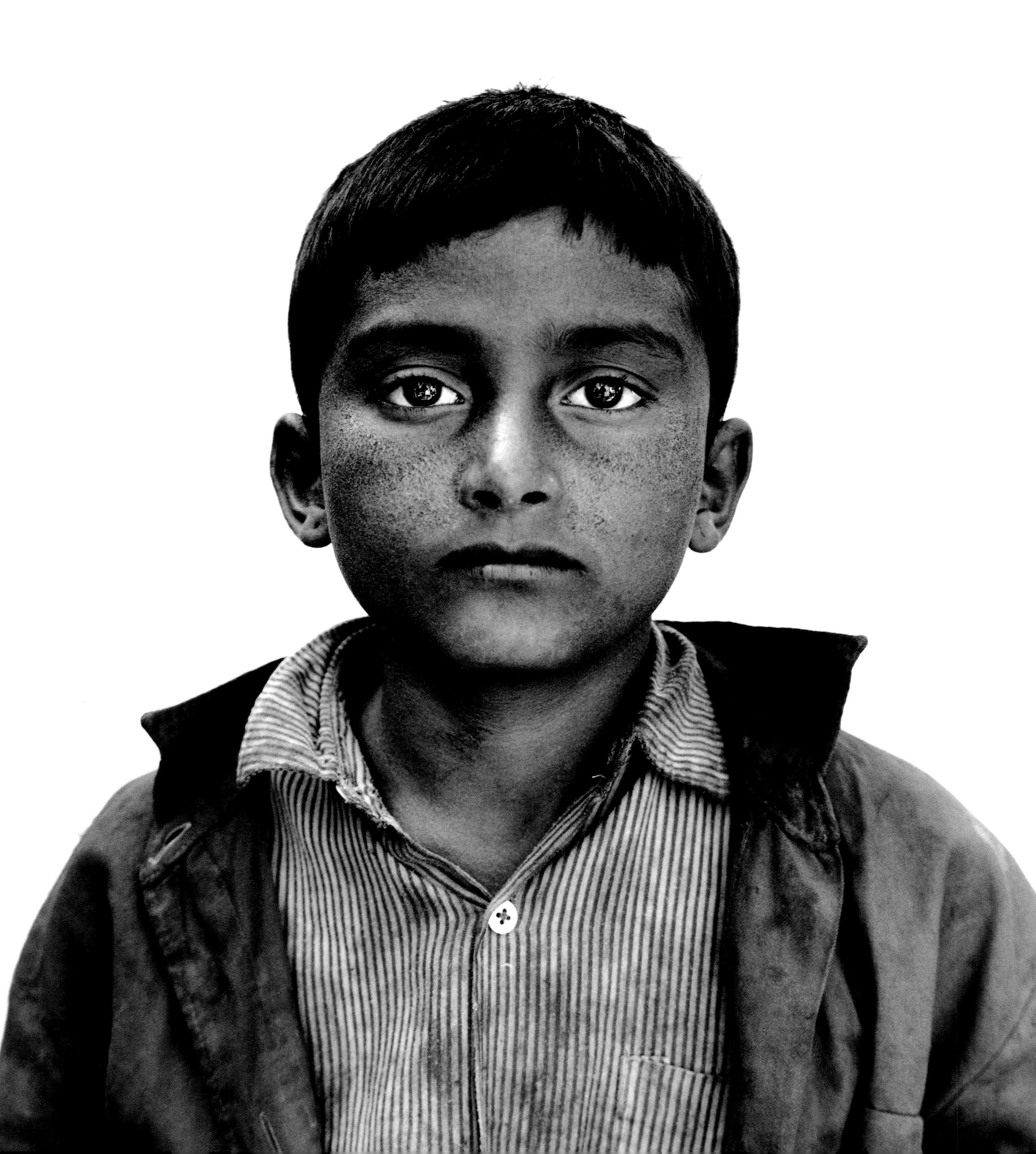

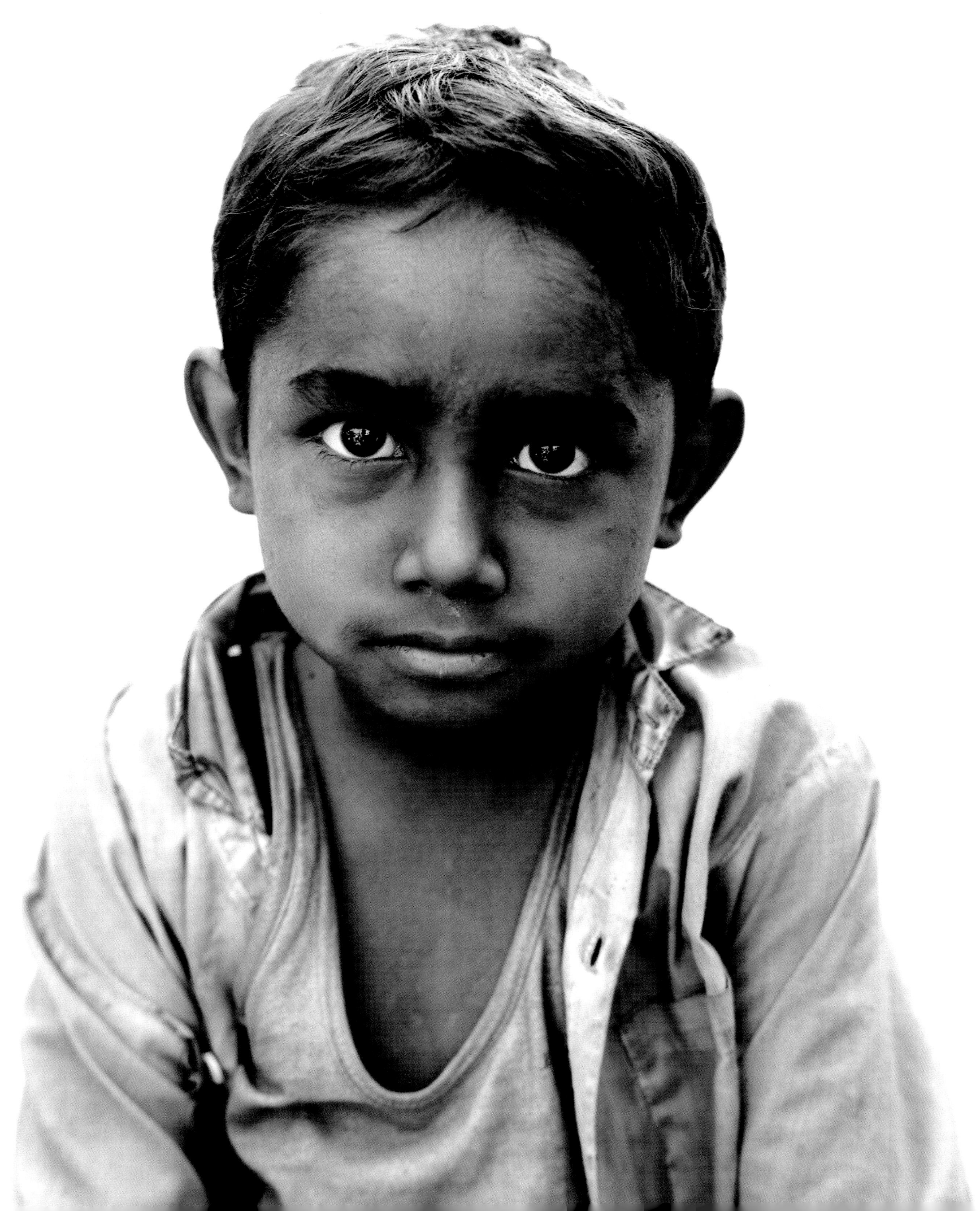

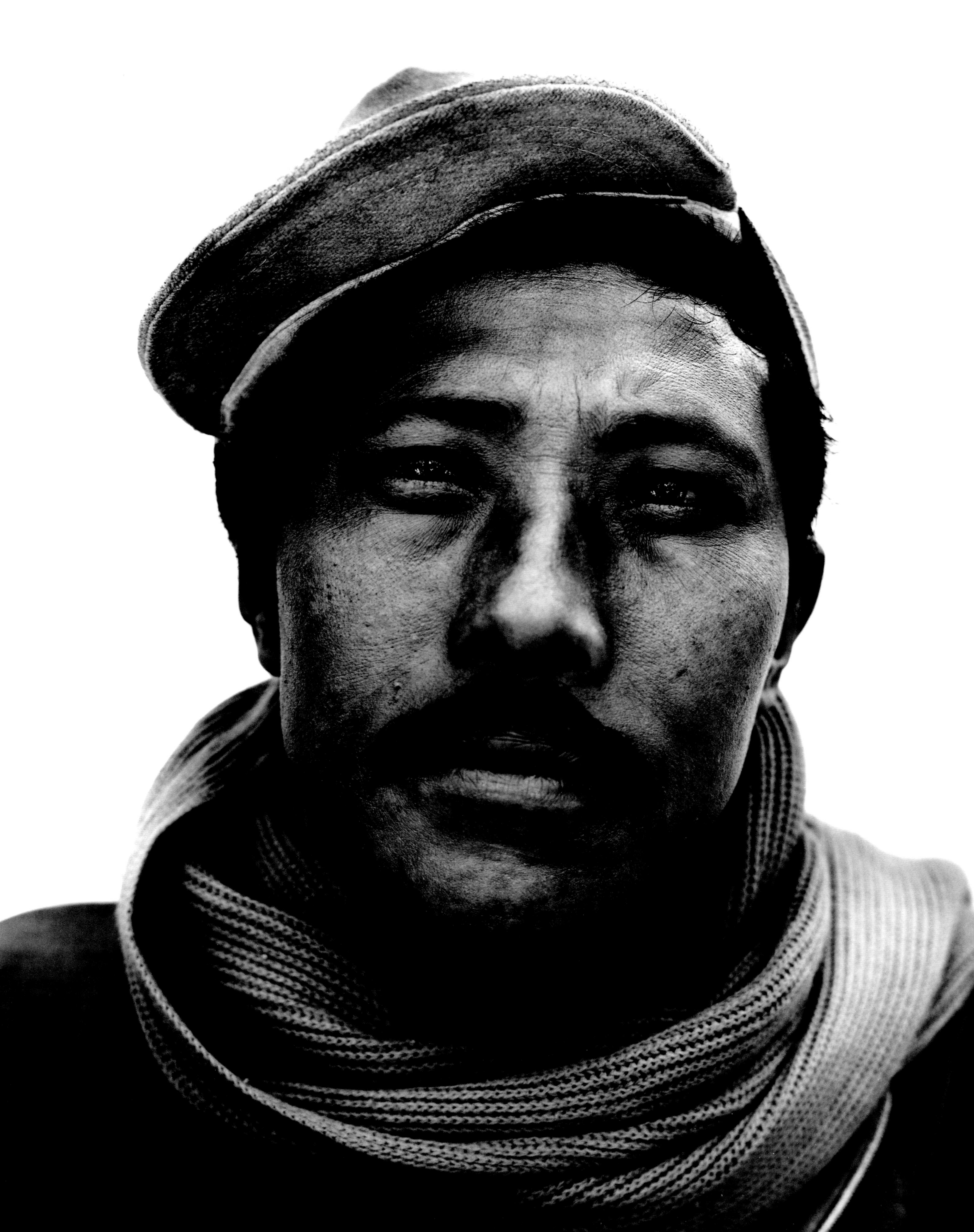

Nepal Tamang Tribe

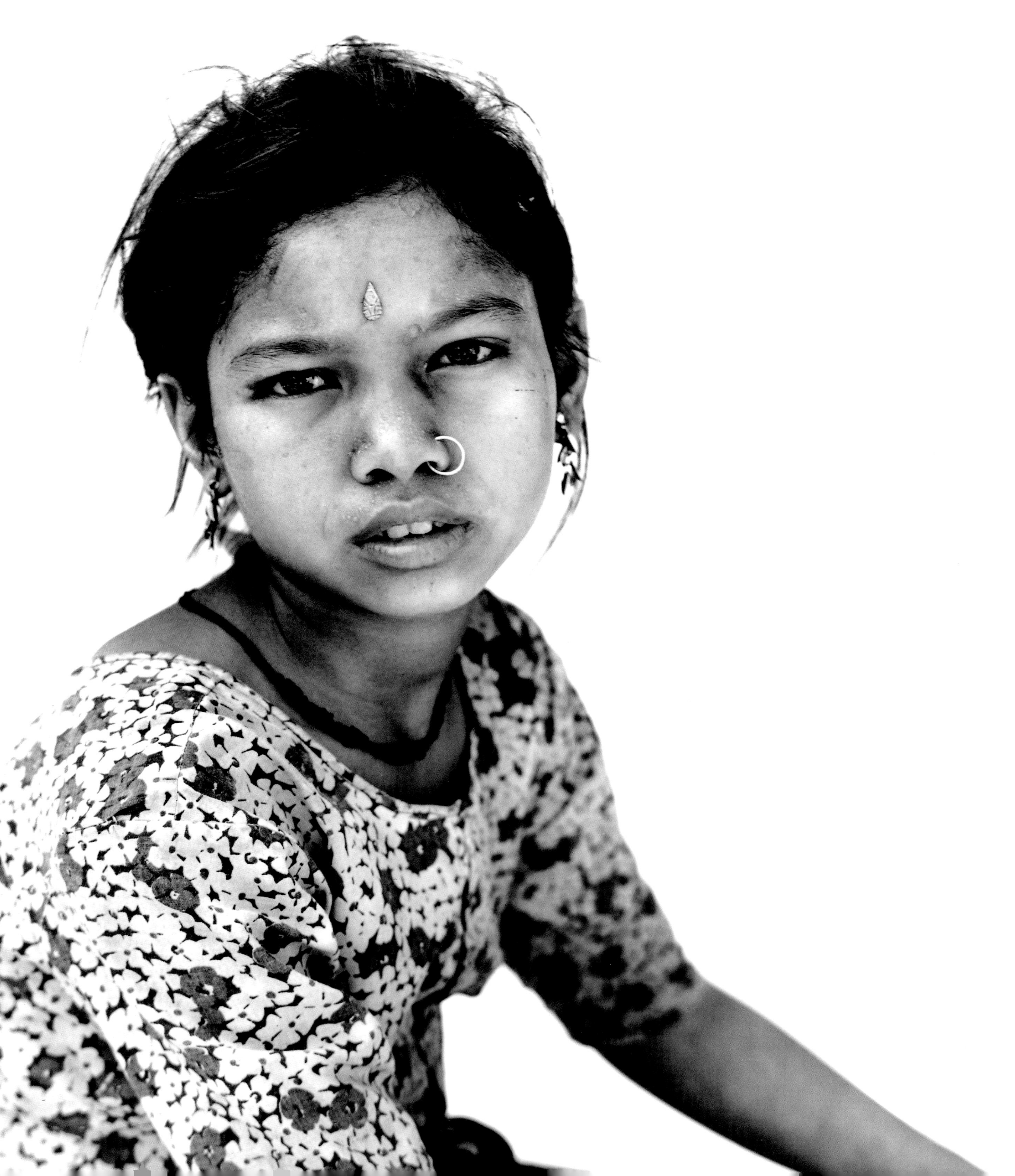

Nepal Tharu Tribe

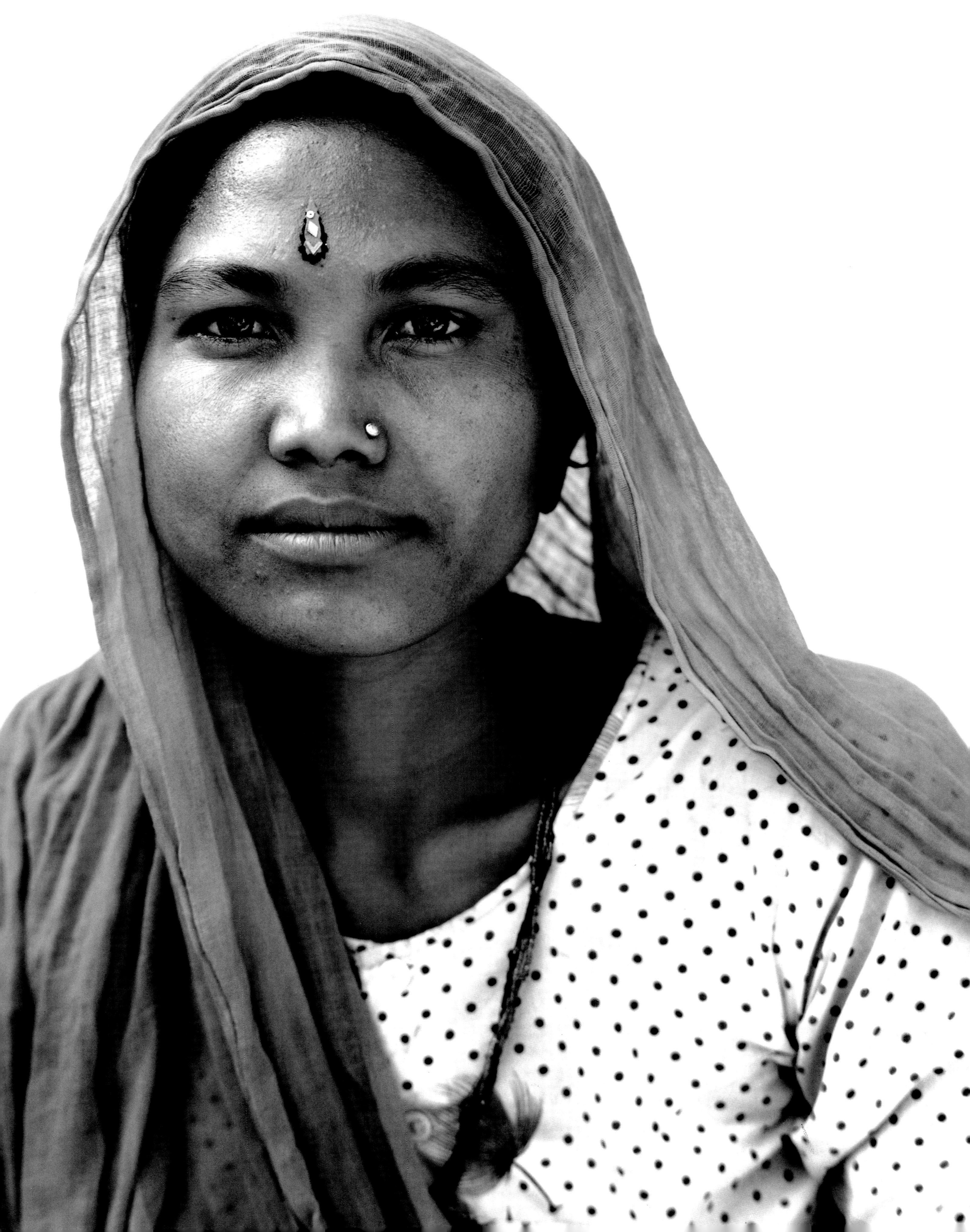

Thailand Lahu Tribe

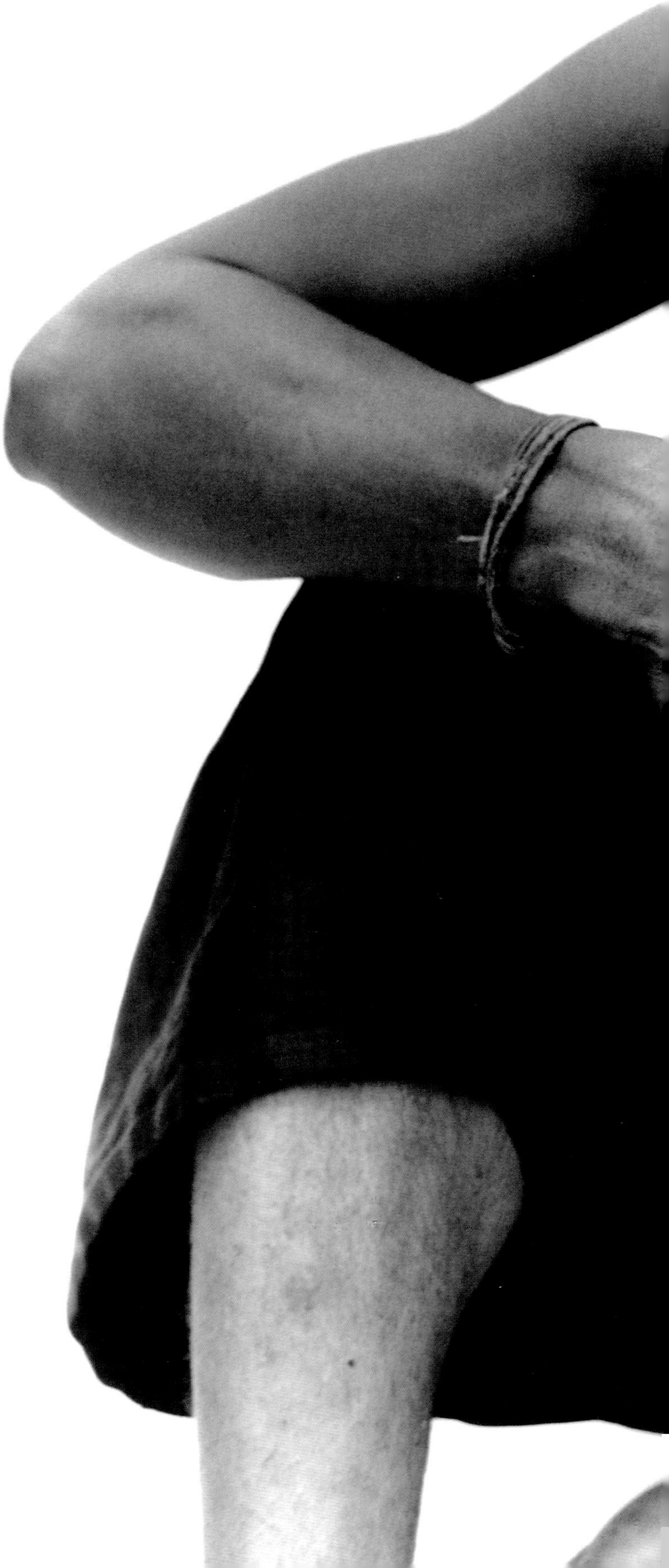

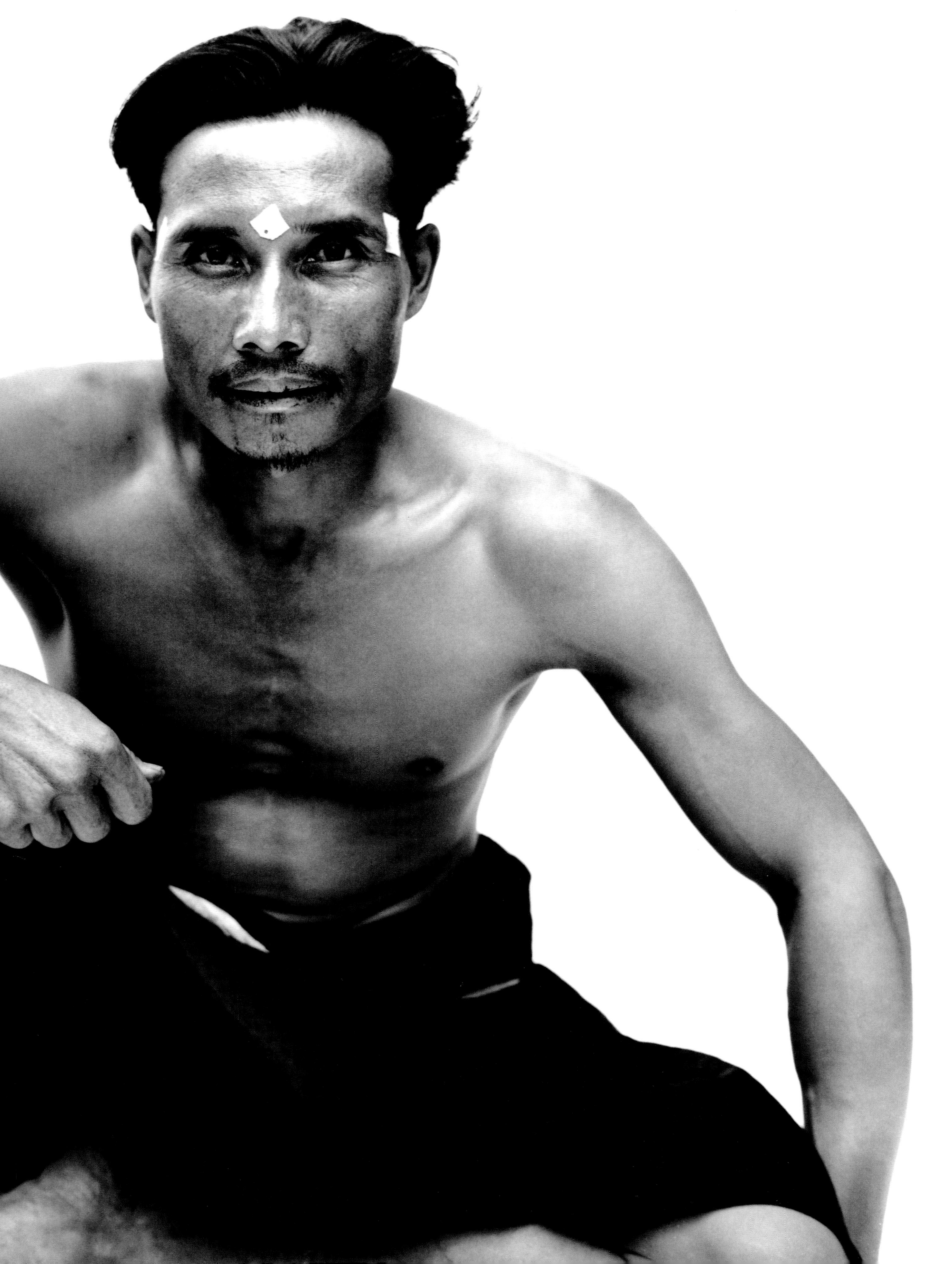

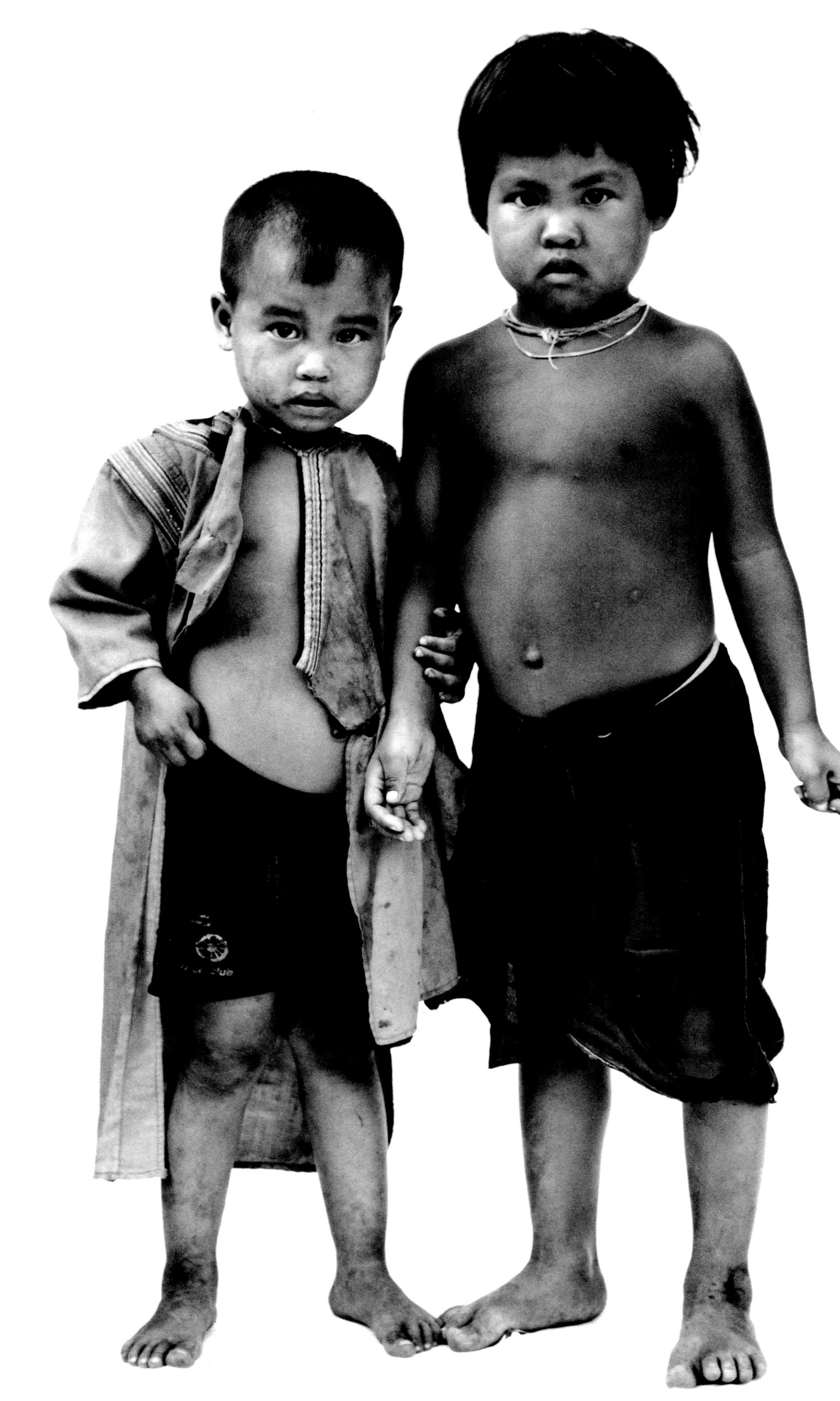

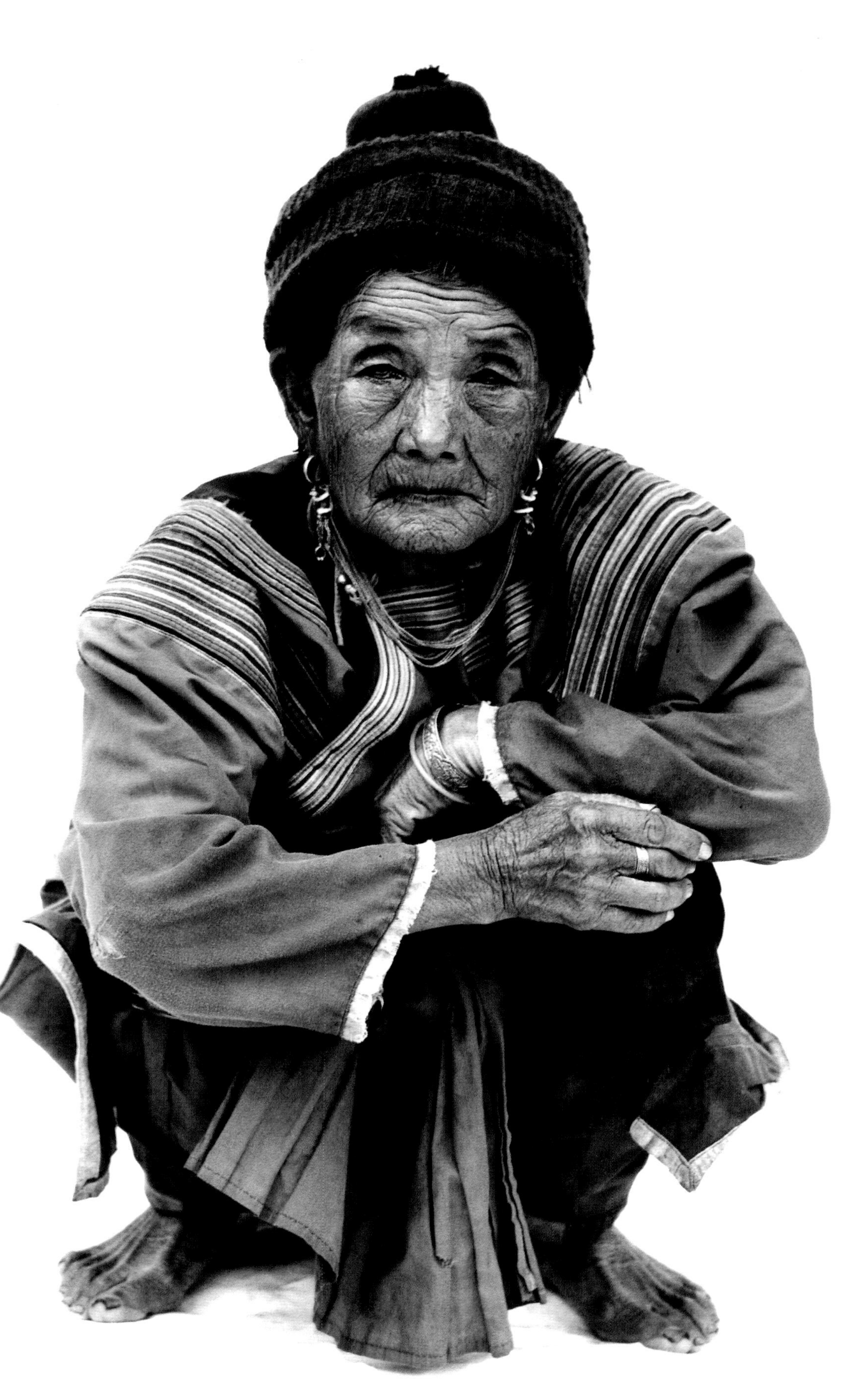

Thailand Lisu Tribe

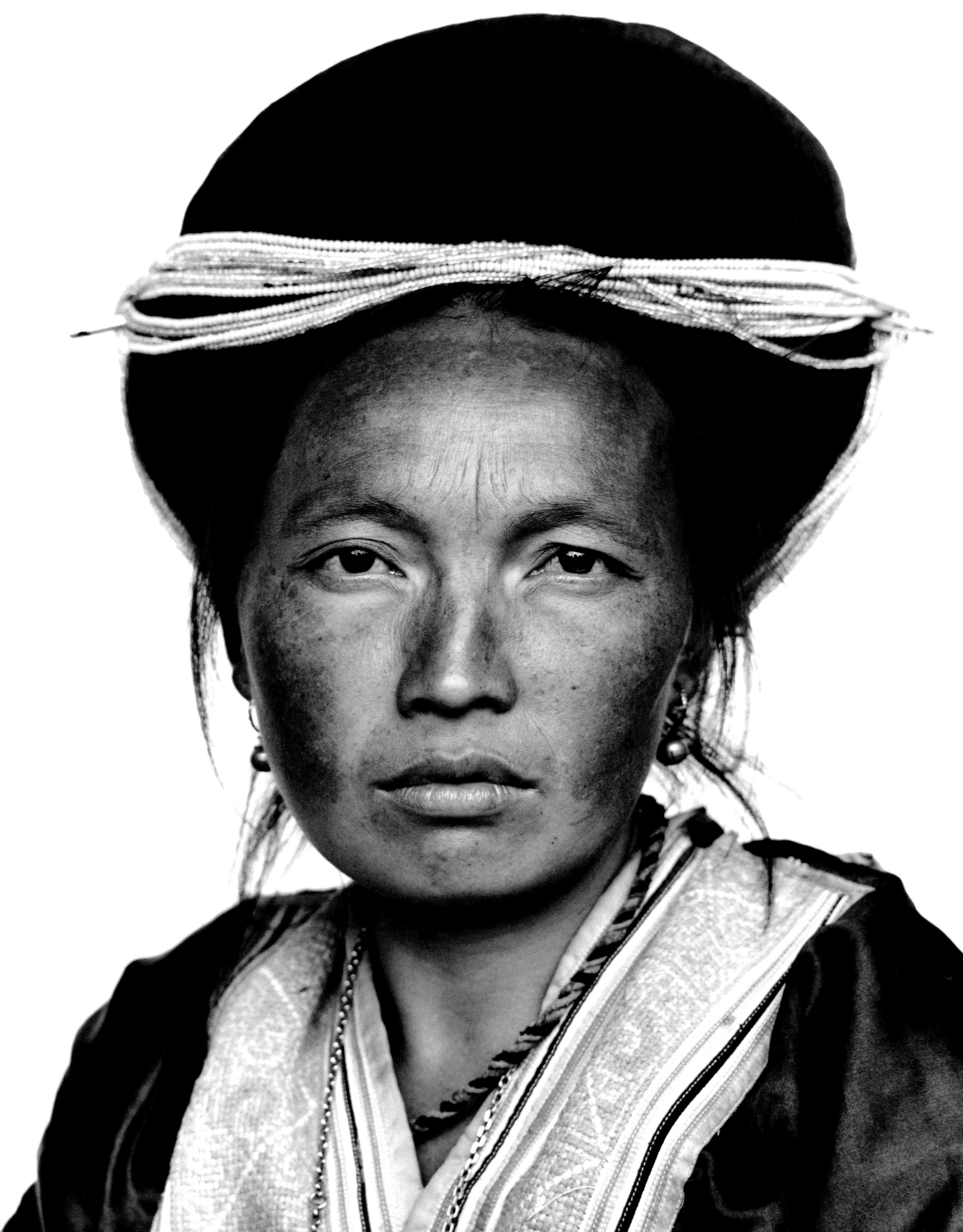

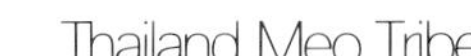

Thailand Meo Tribe

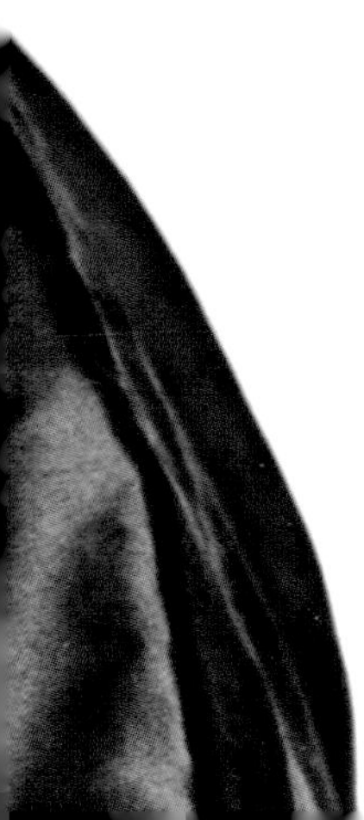

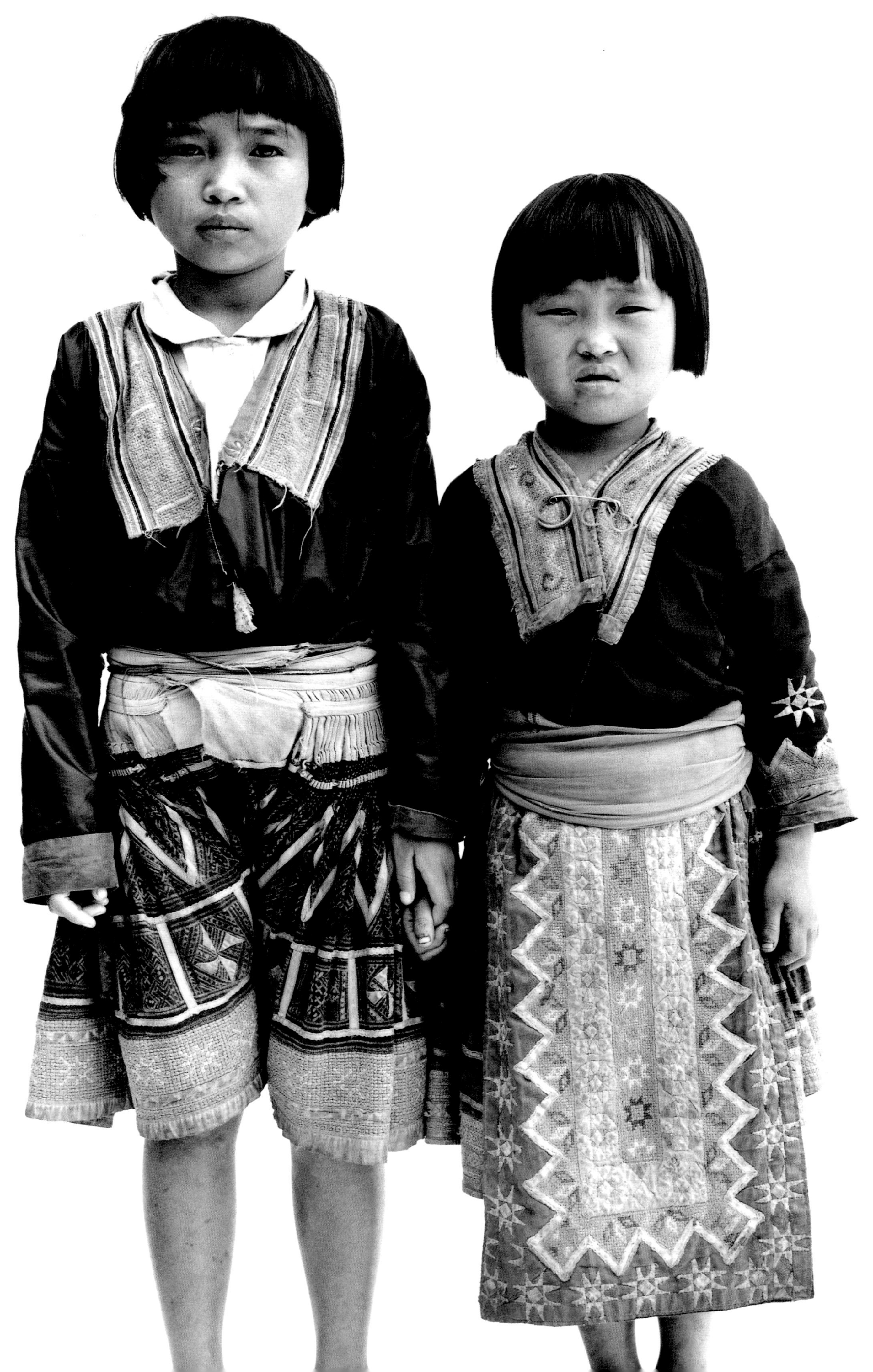

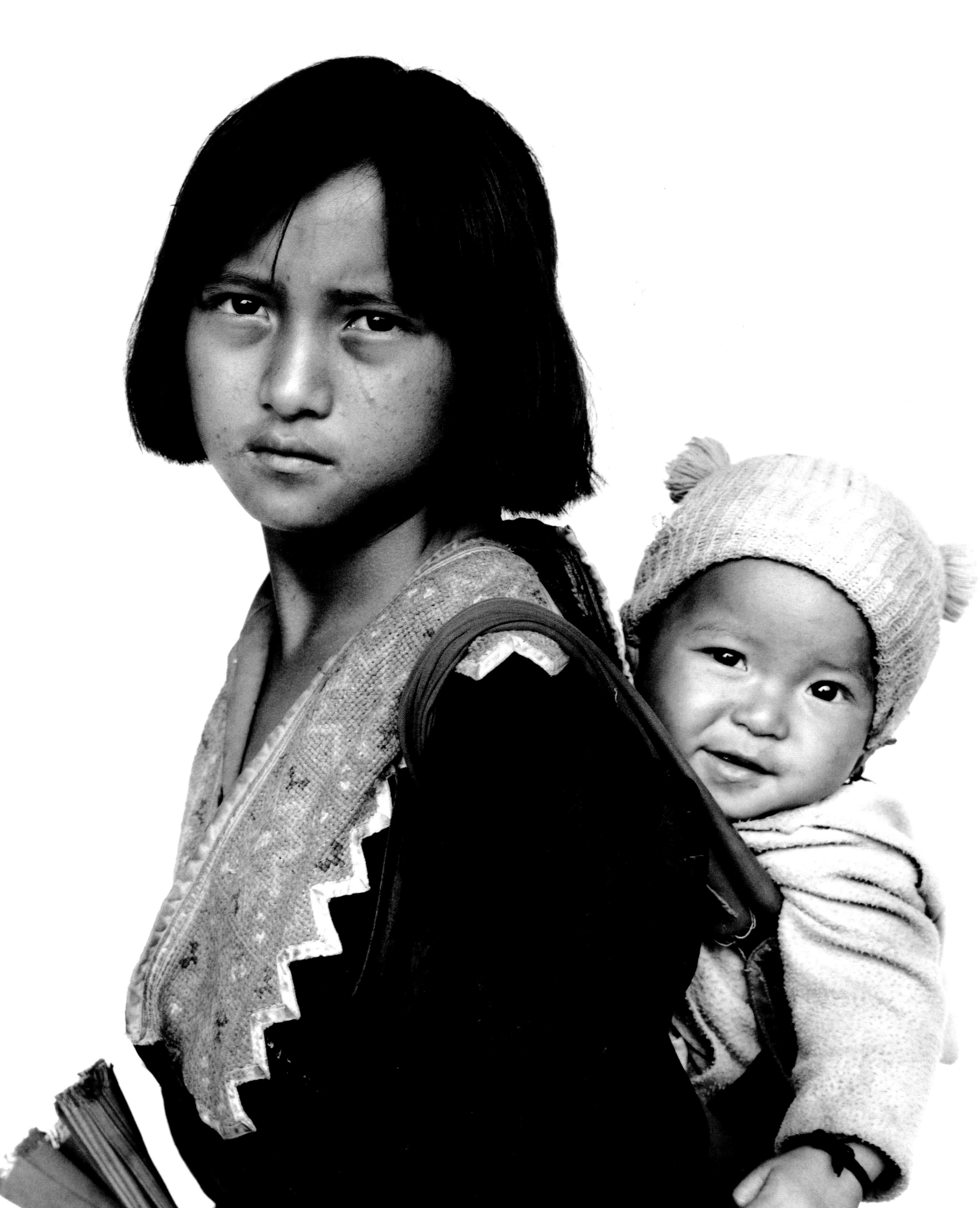

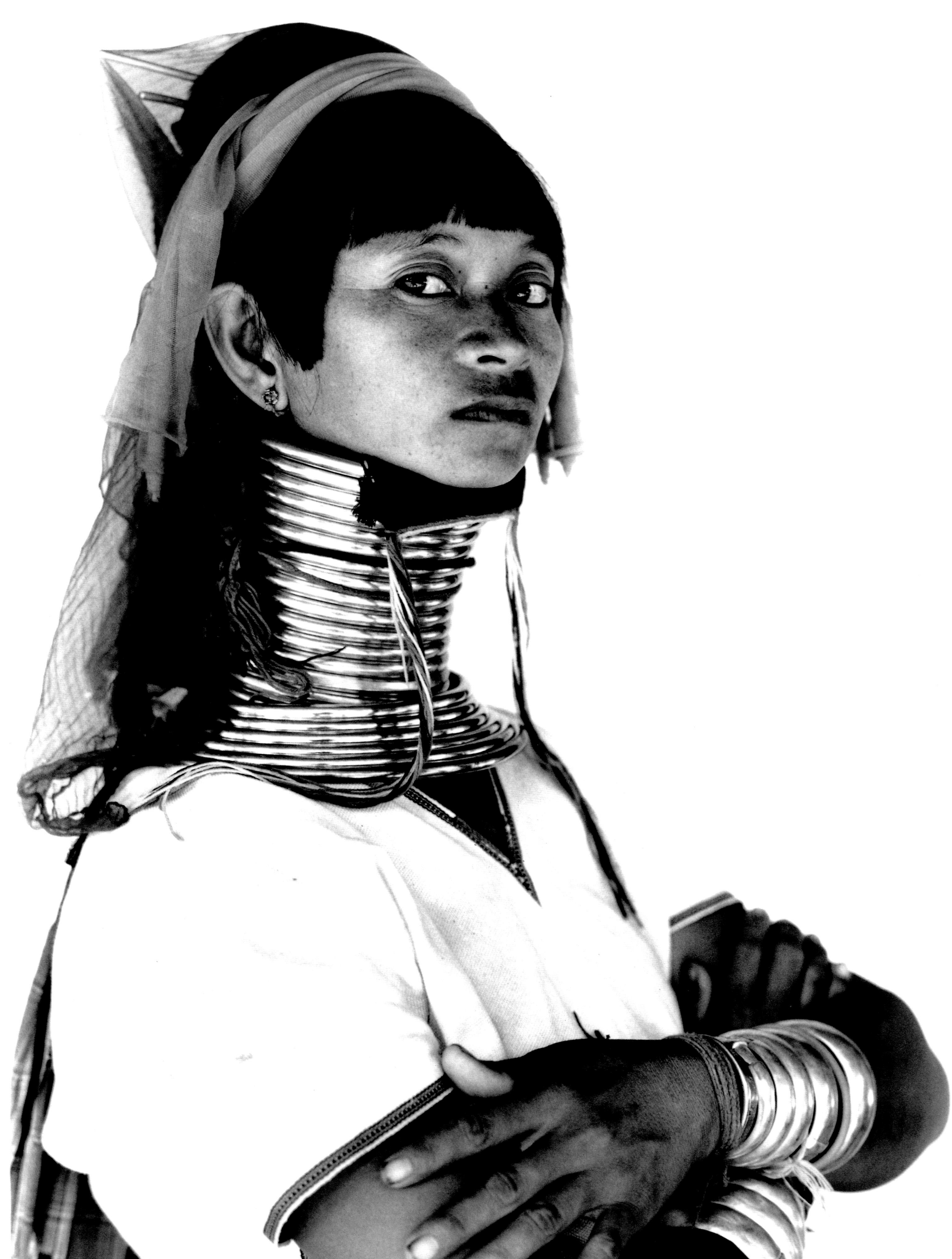

Thailand Padaung Tribe

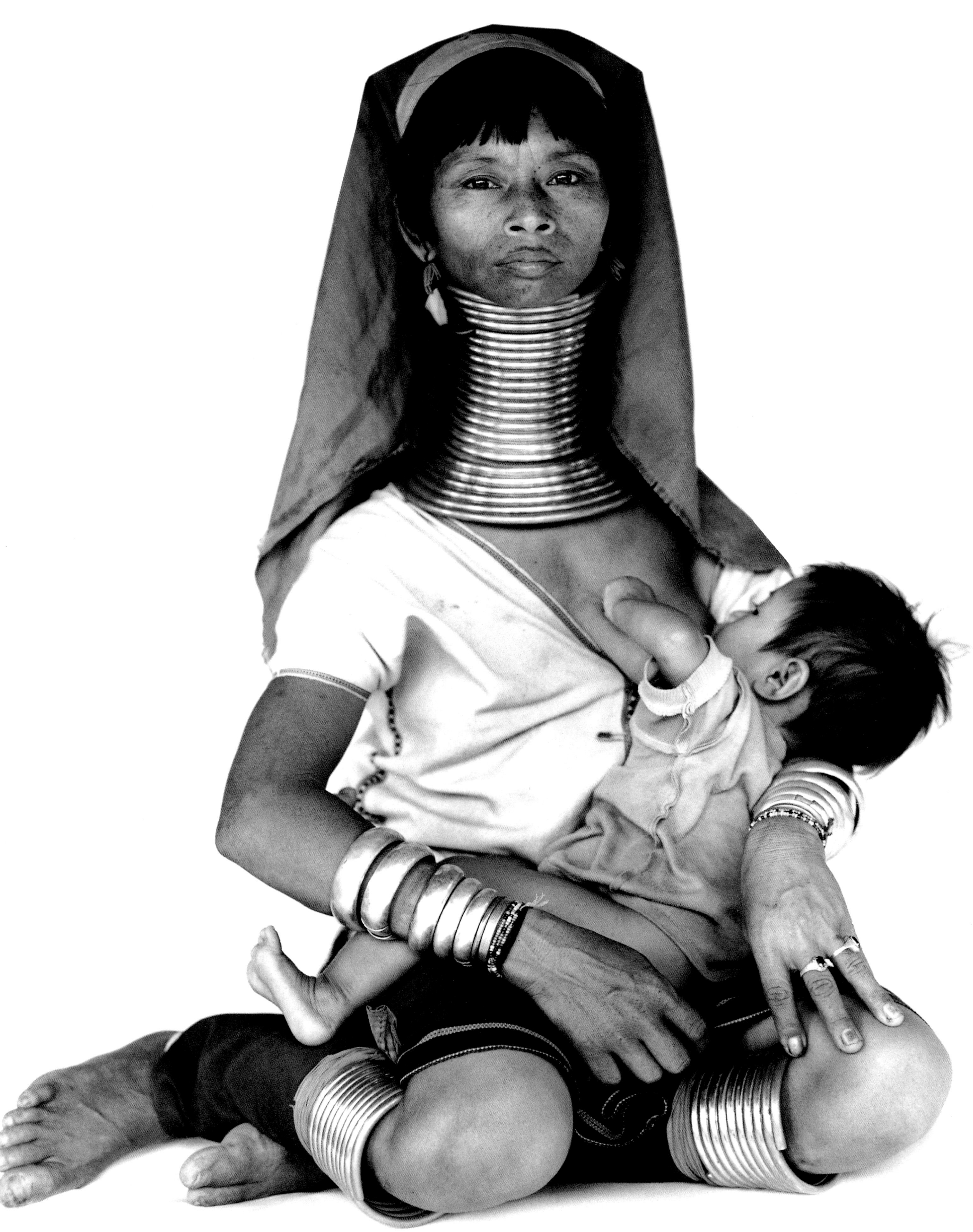

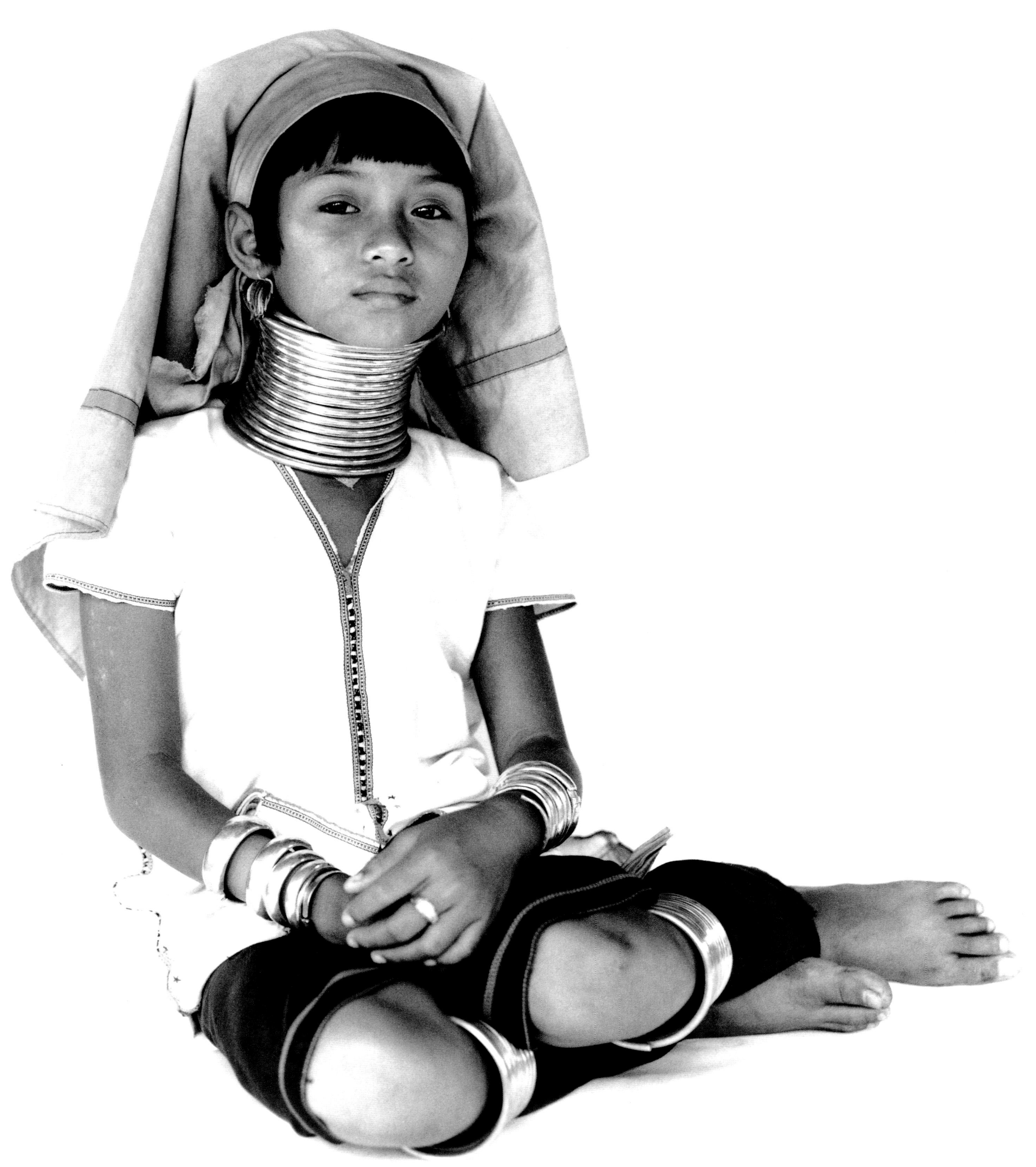

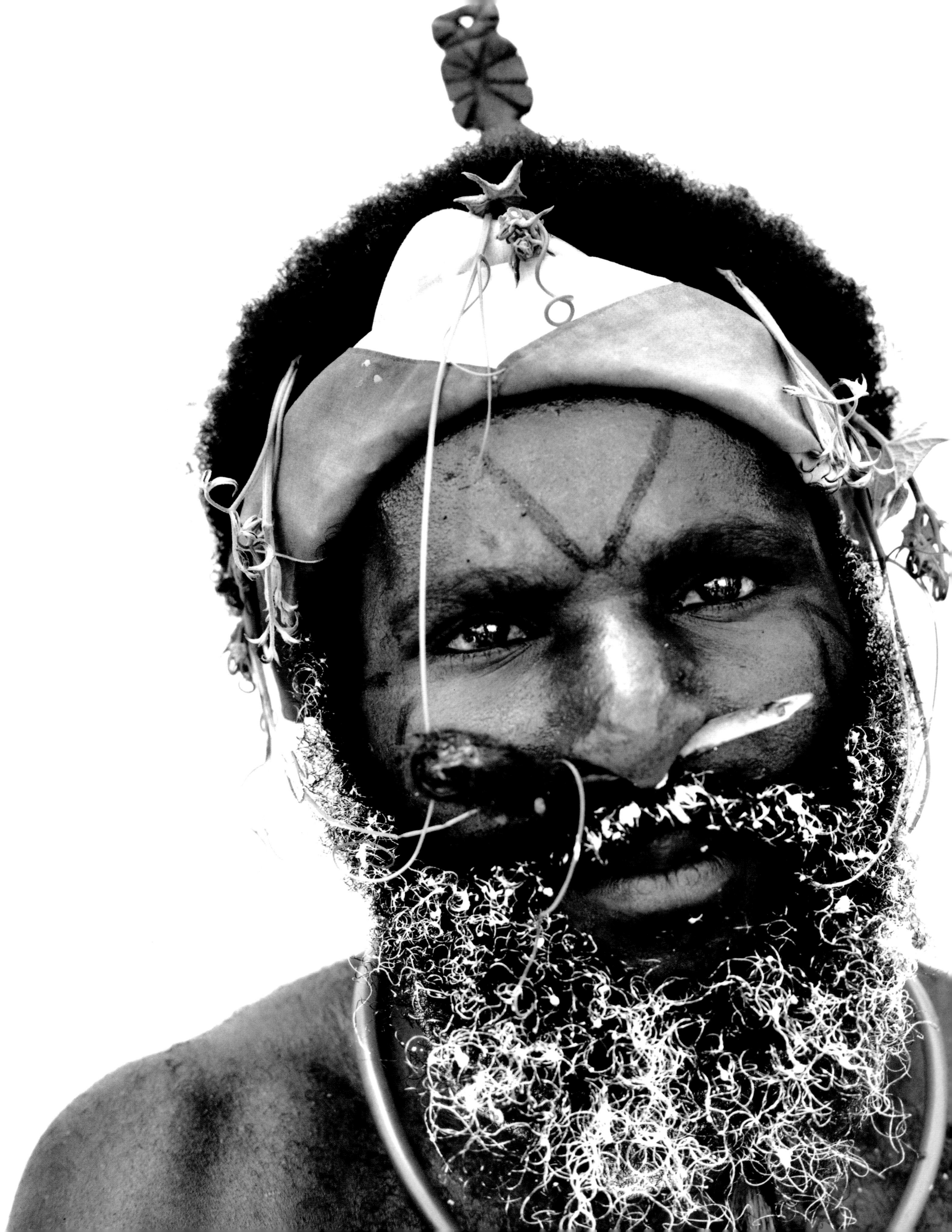

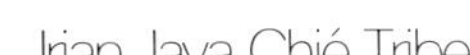

Irian Jaya Chié Tribe

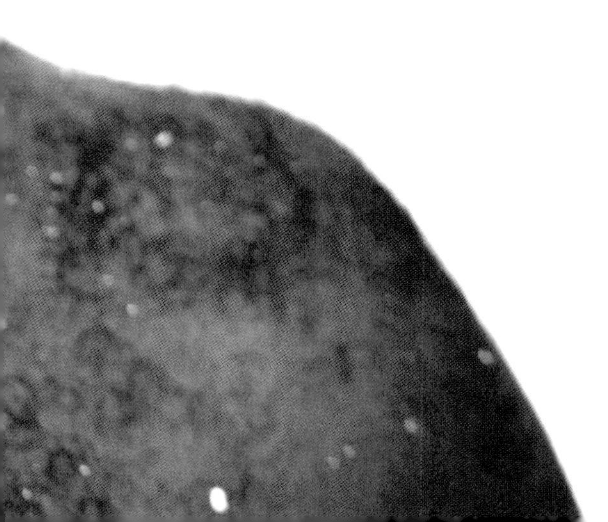

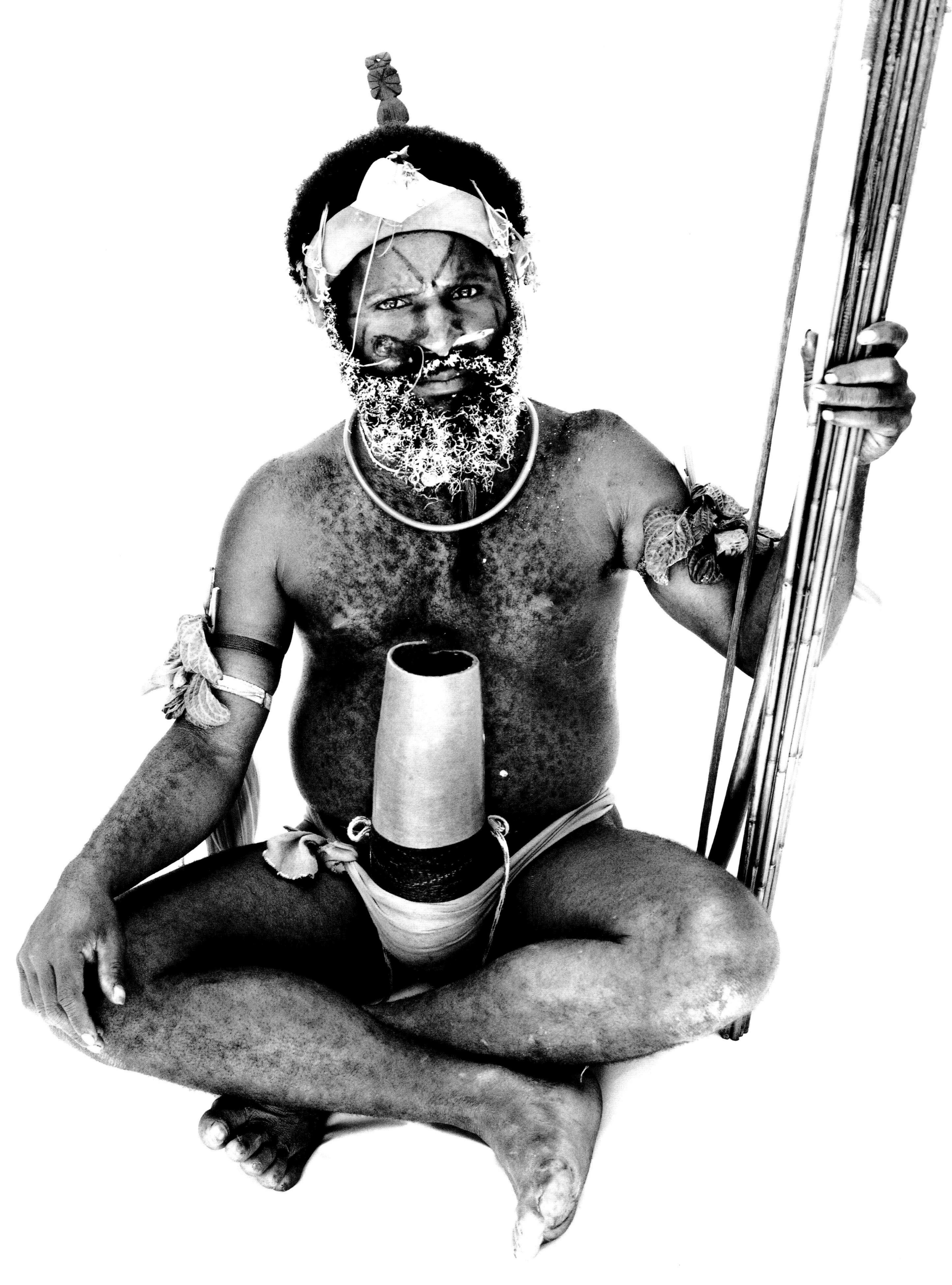

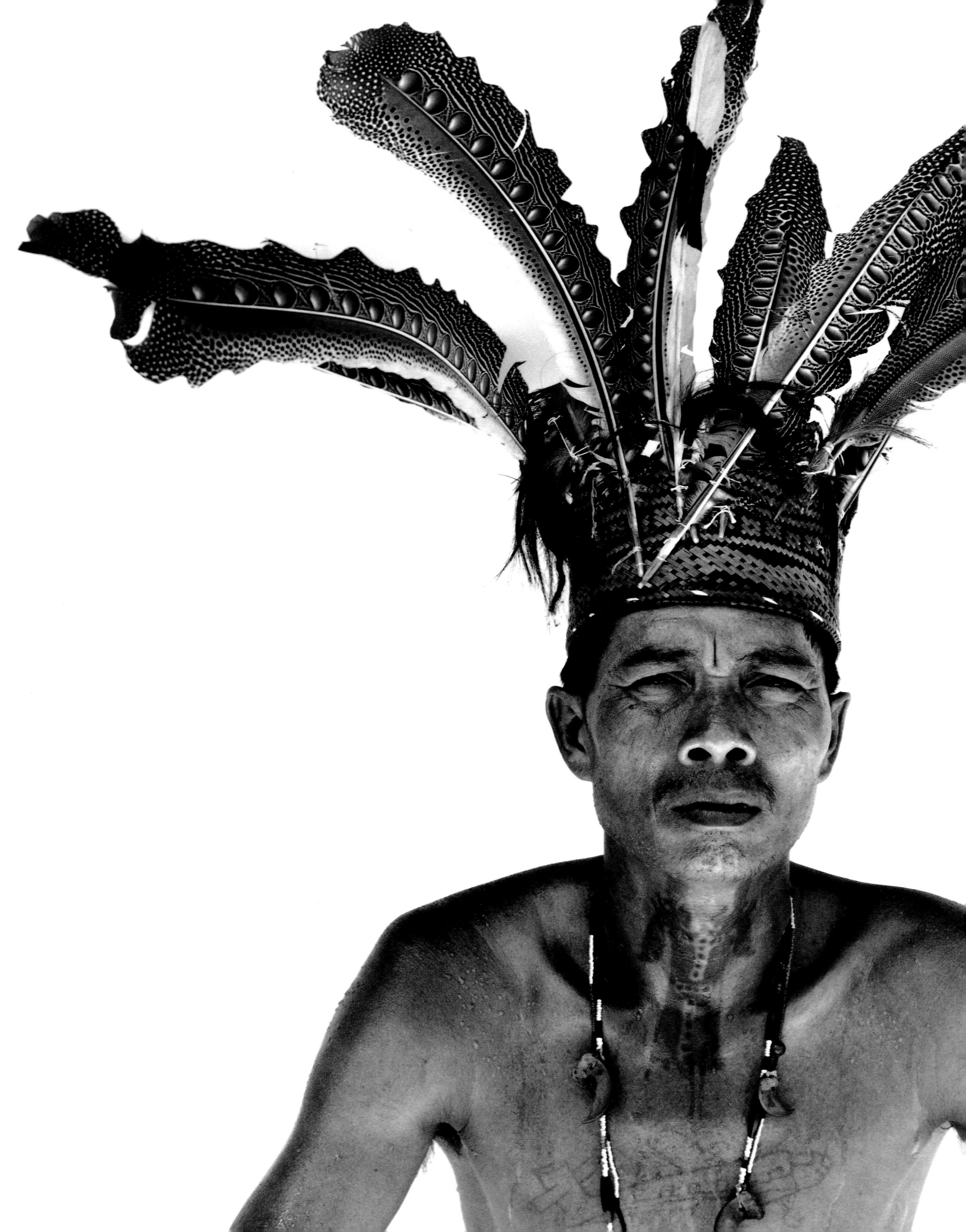

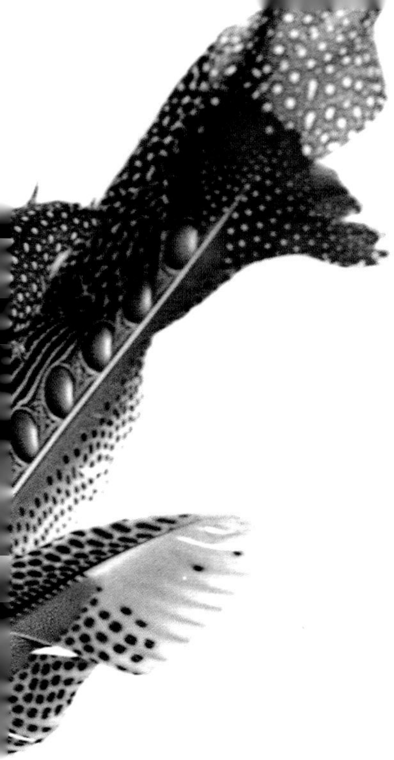

Borneo Iban Tribe

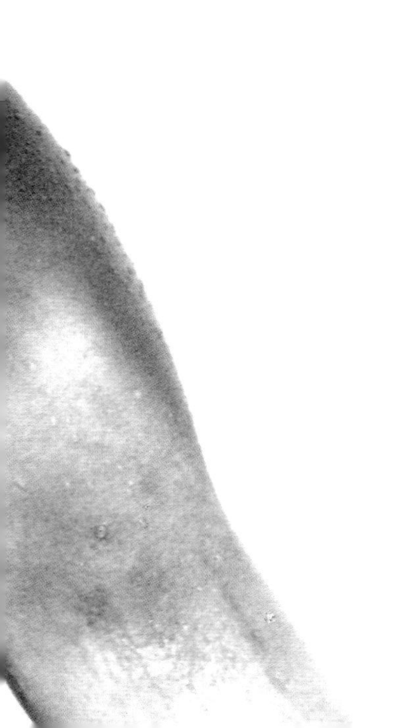

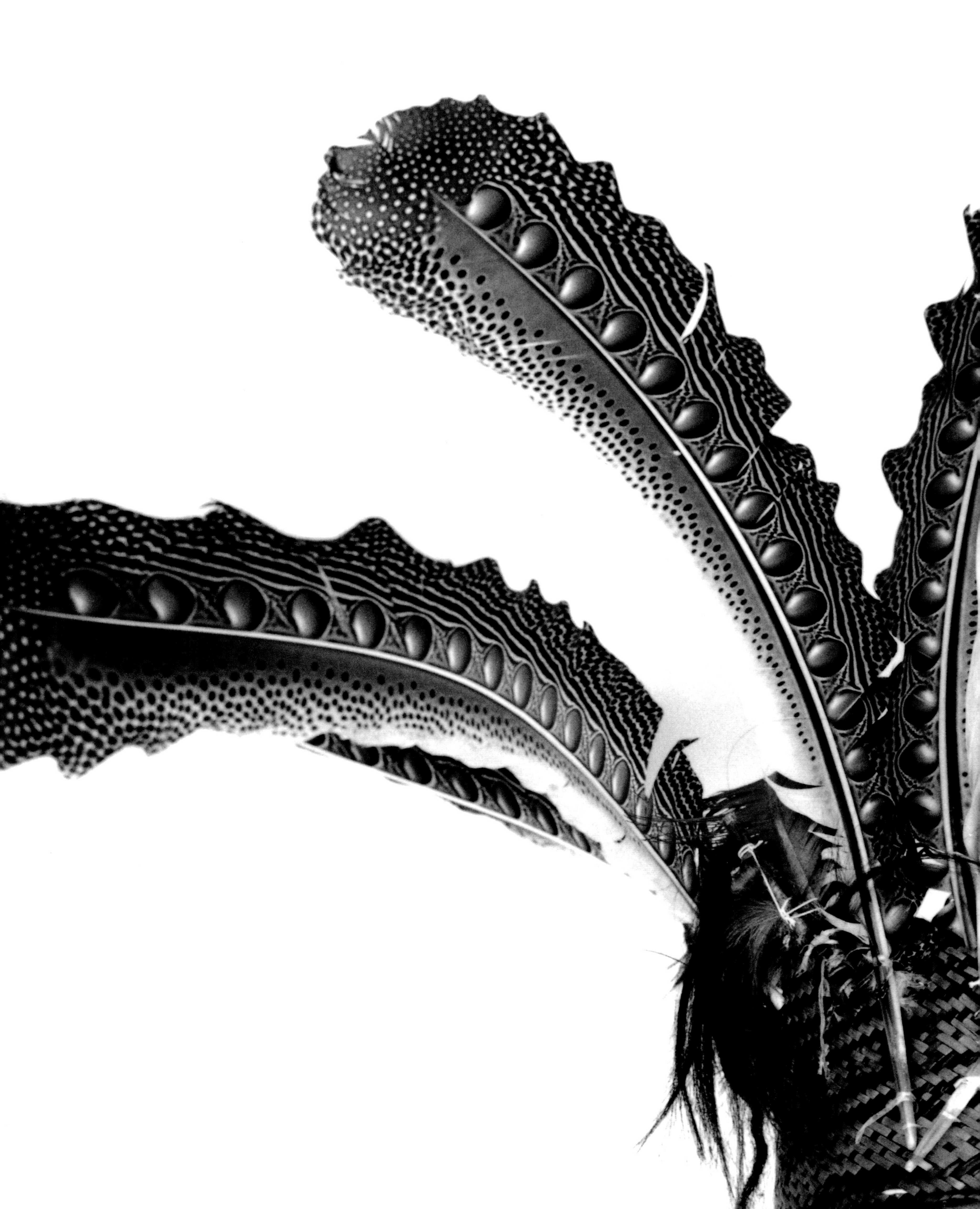

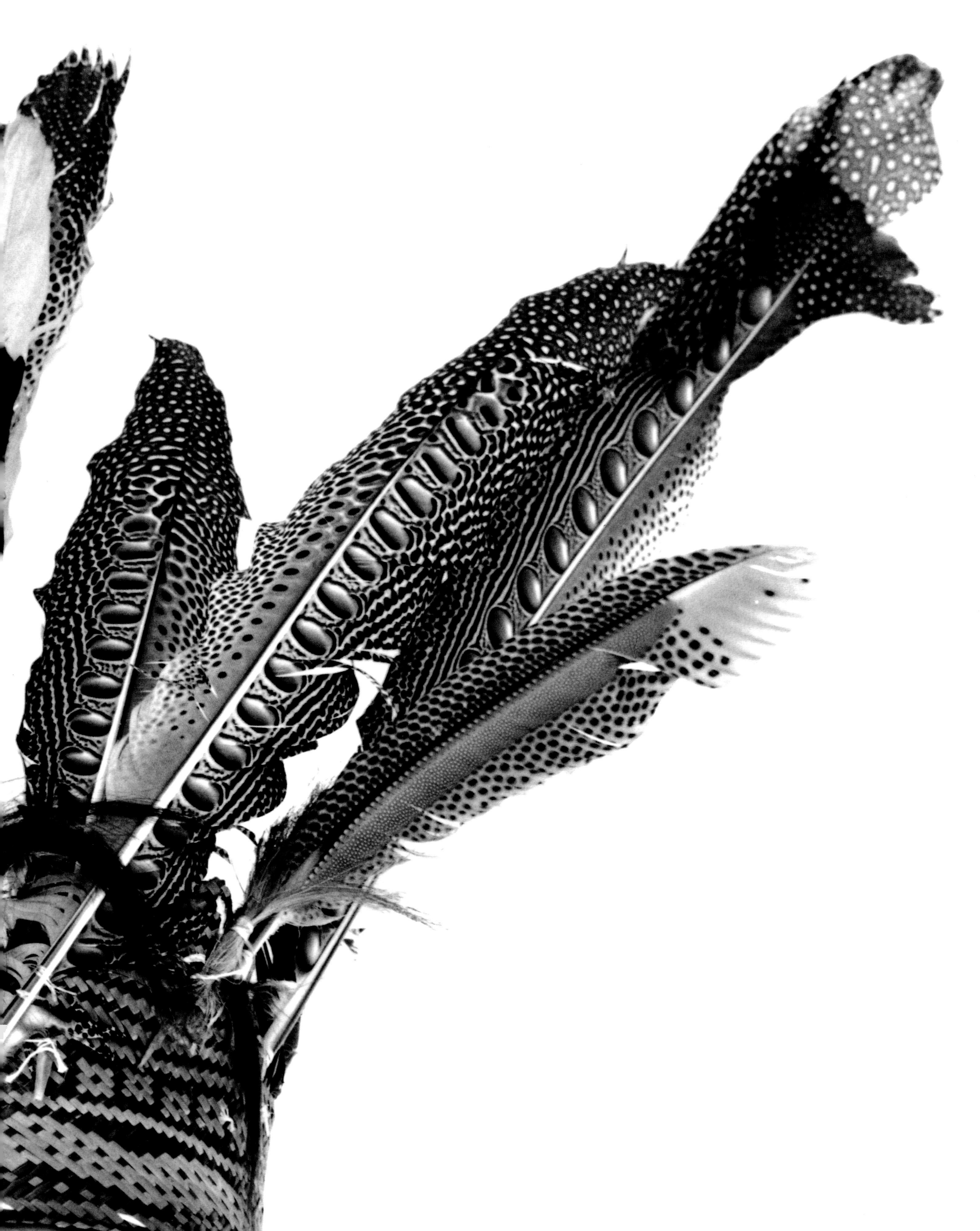

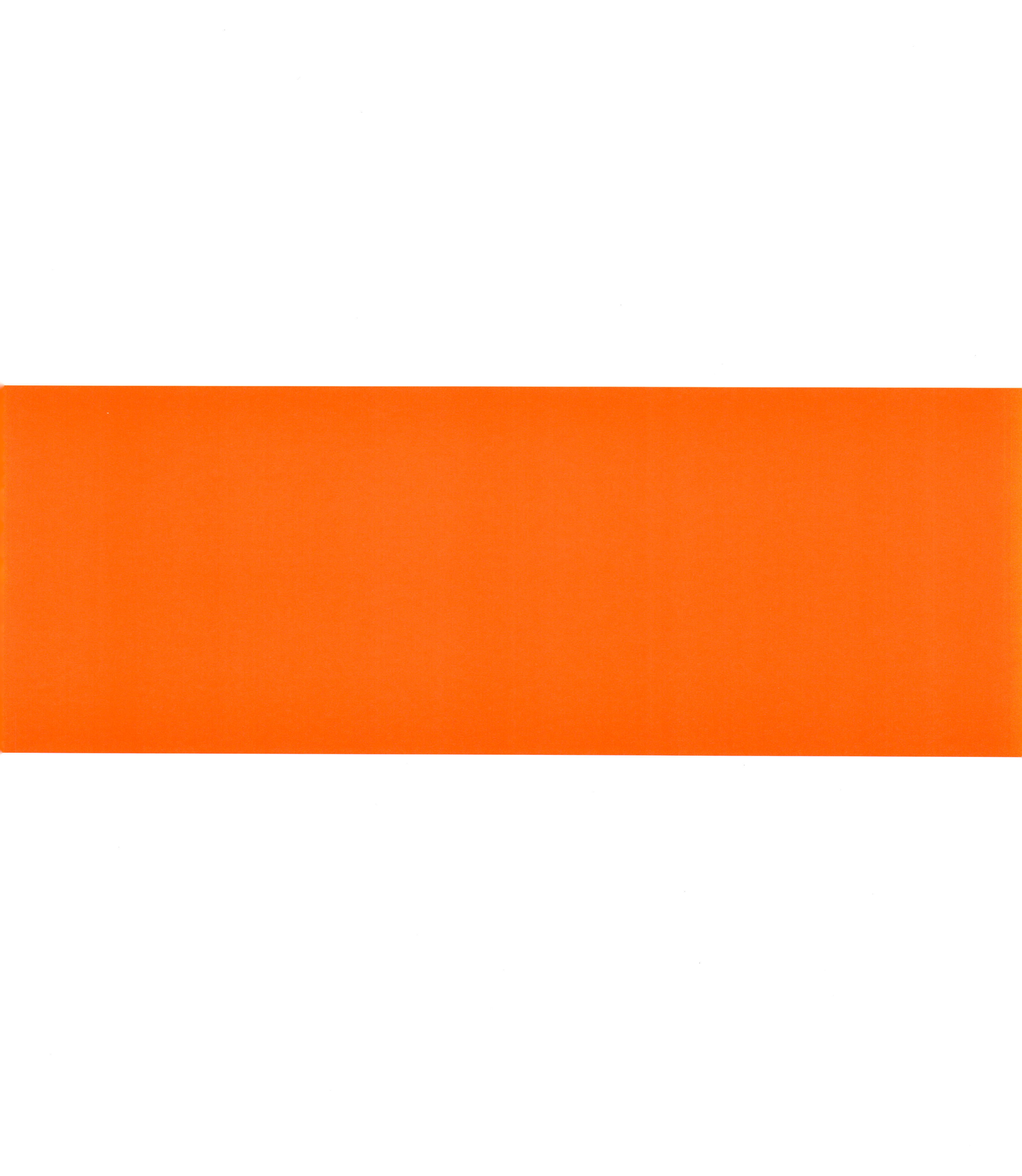

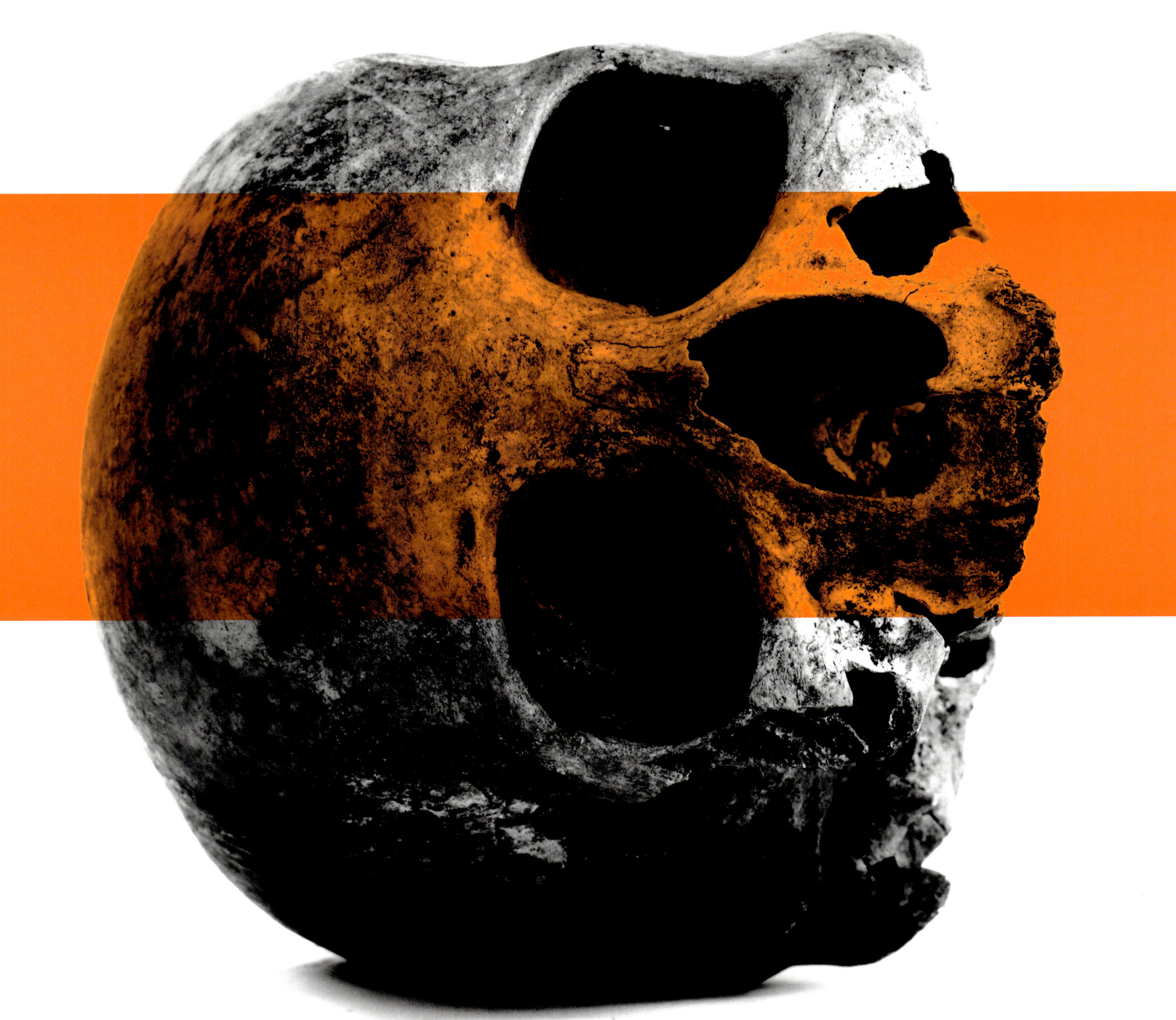

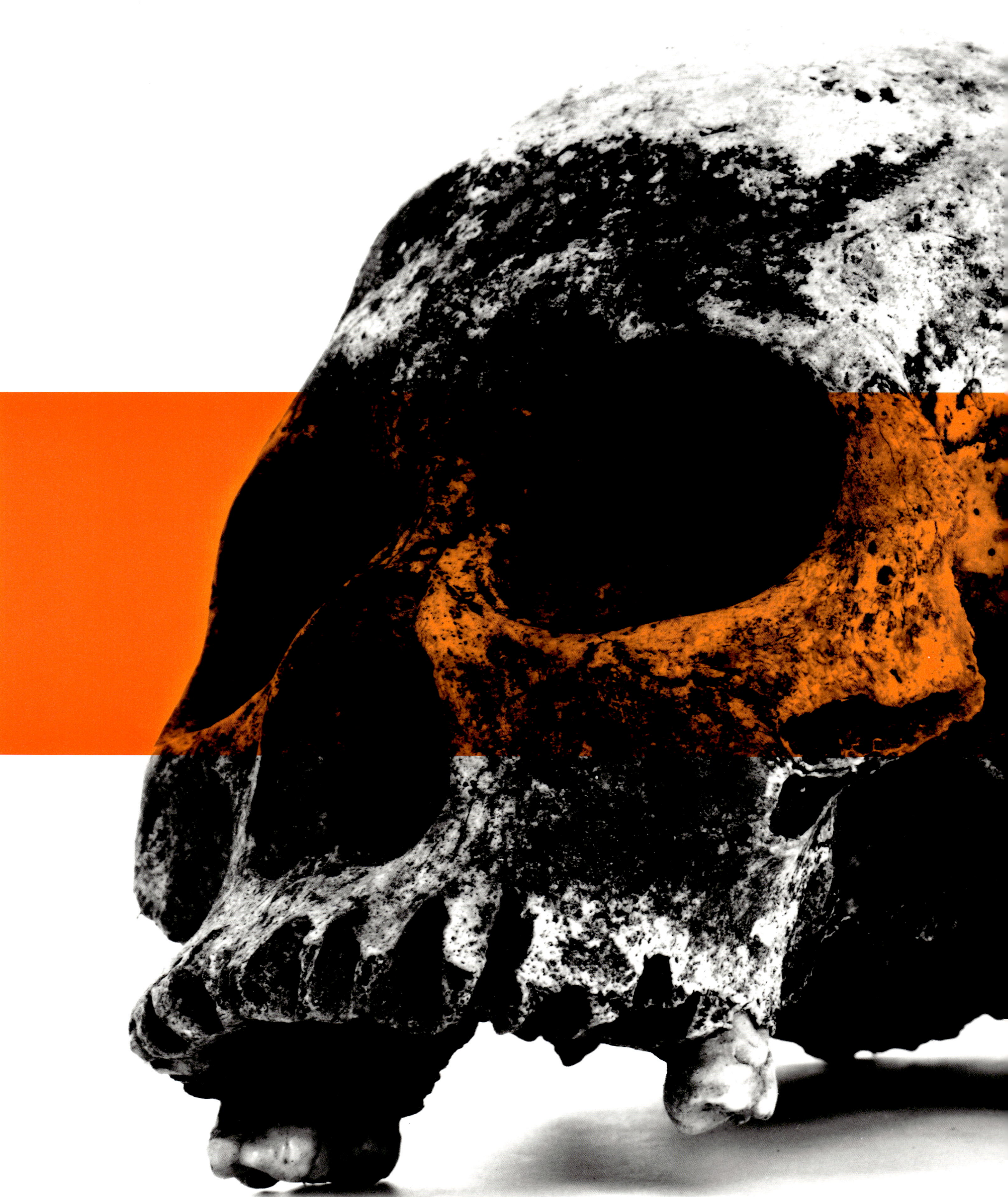

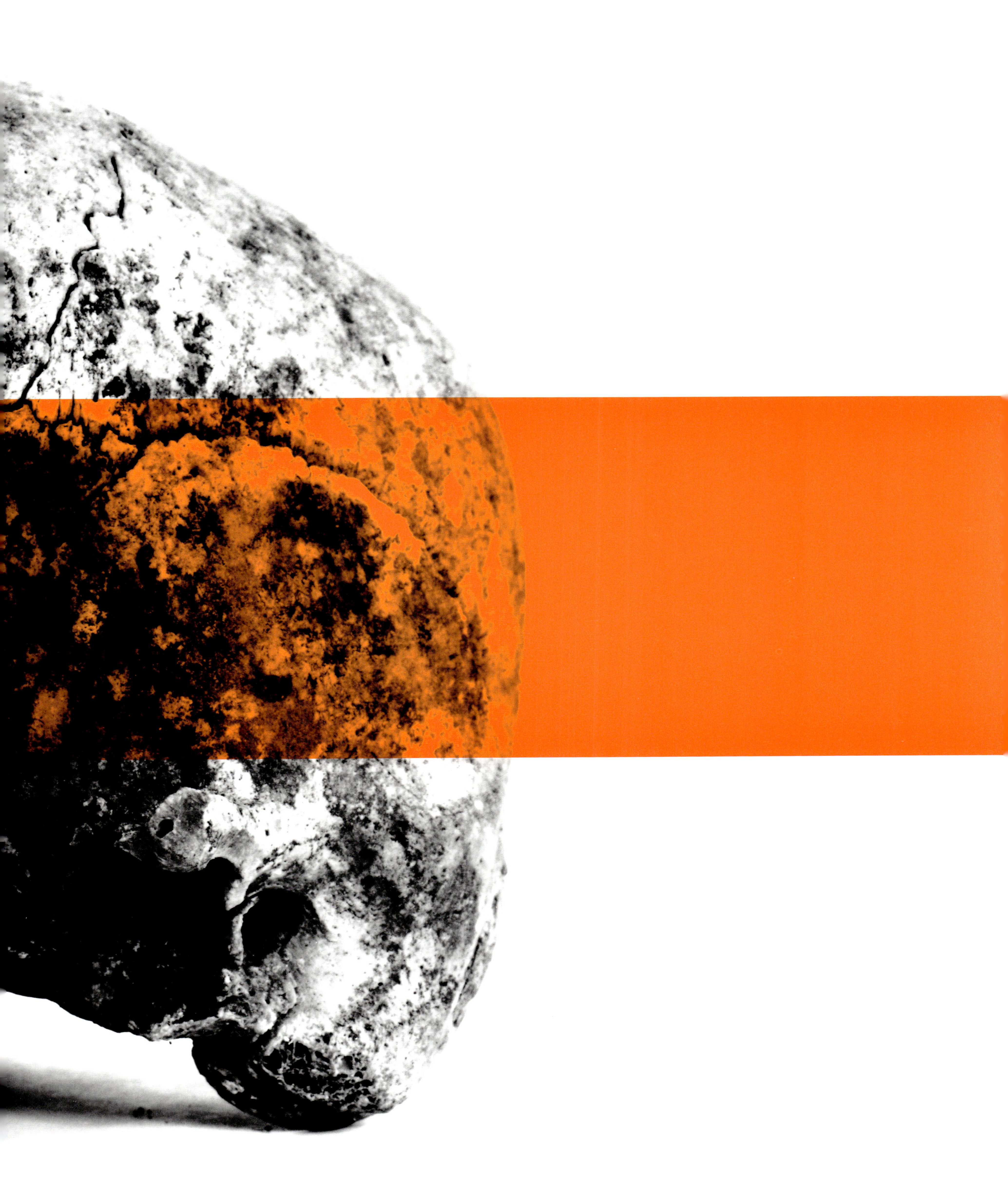

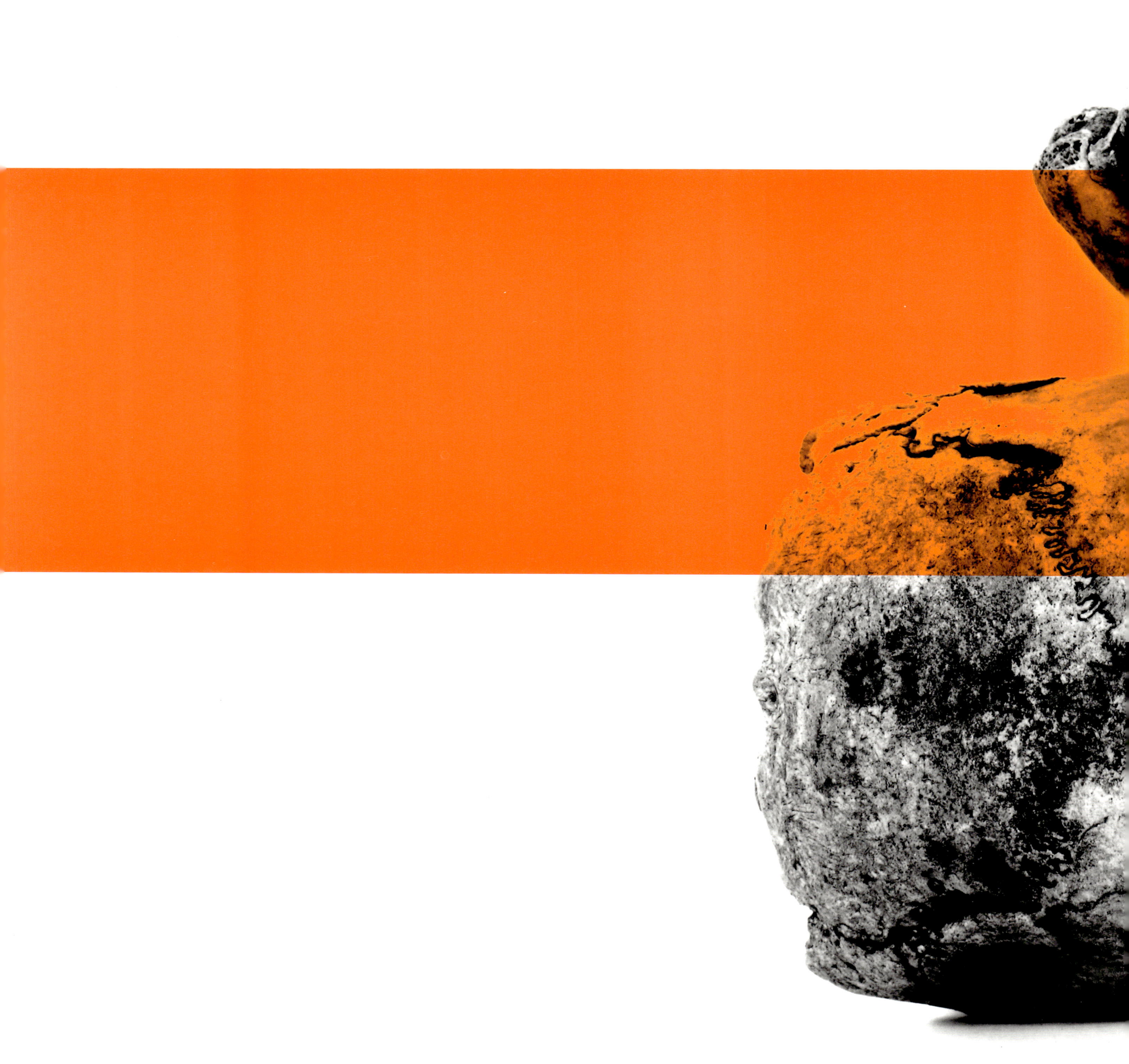

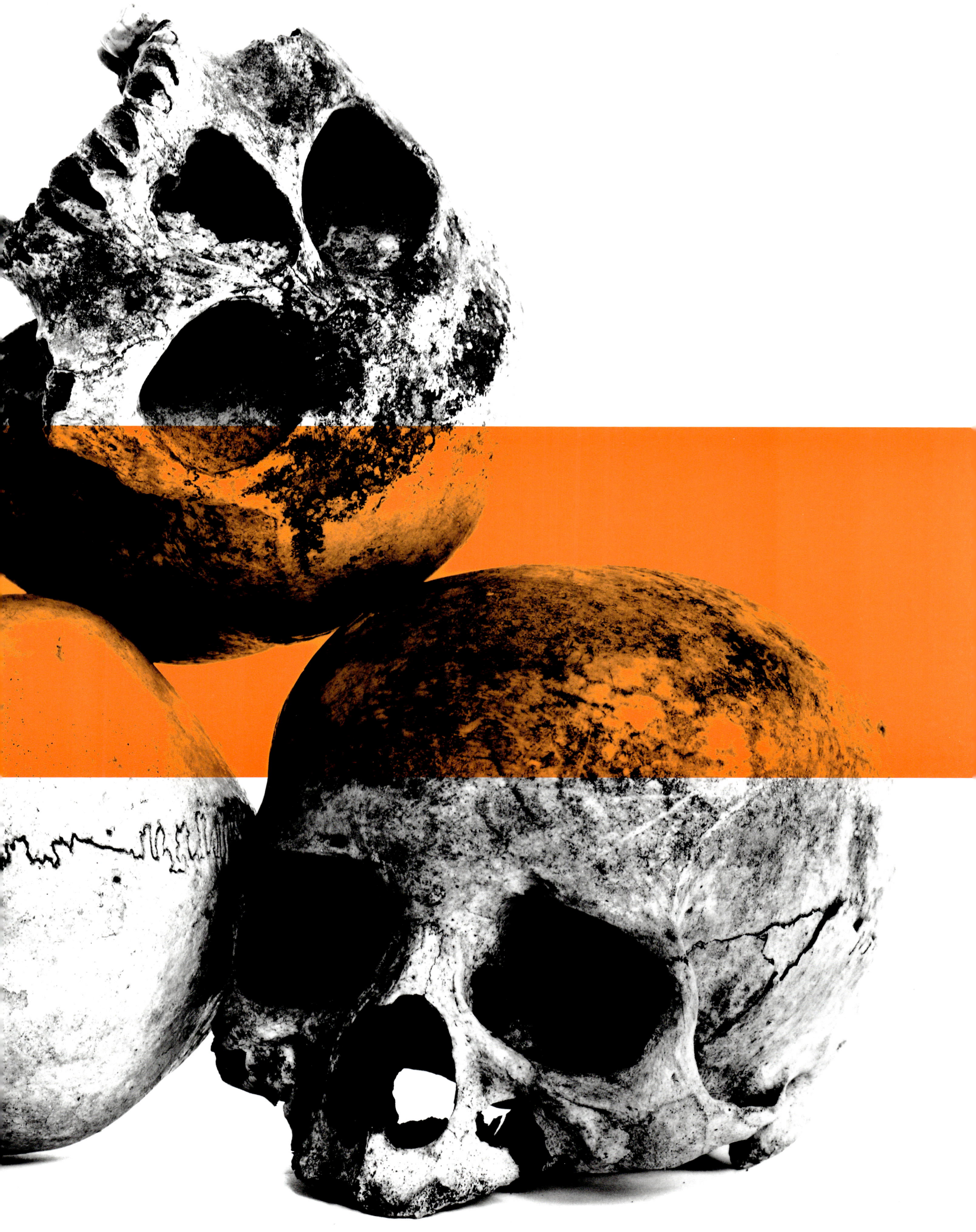

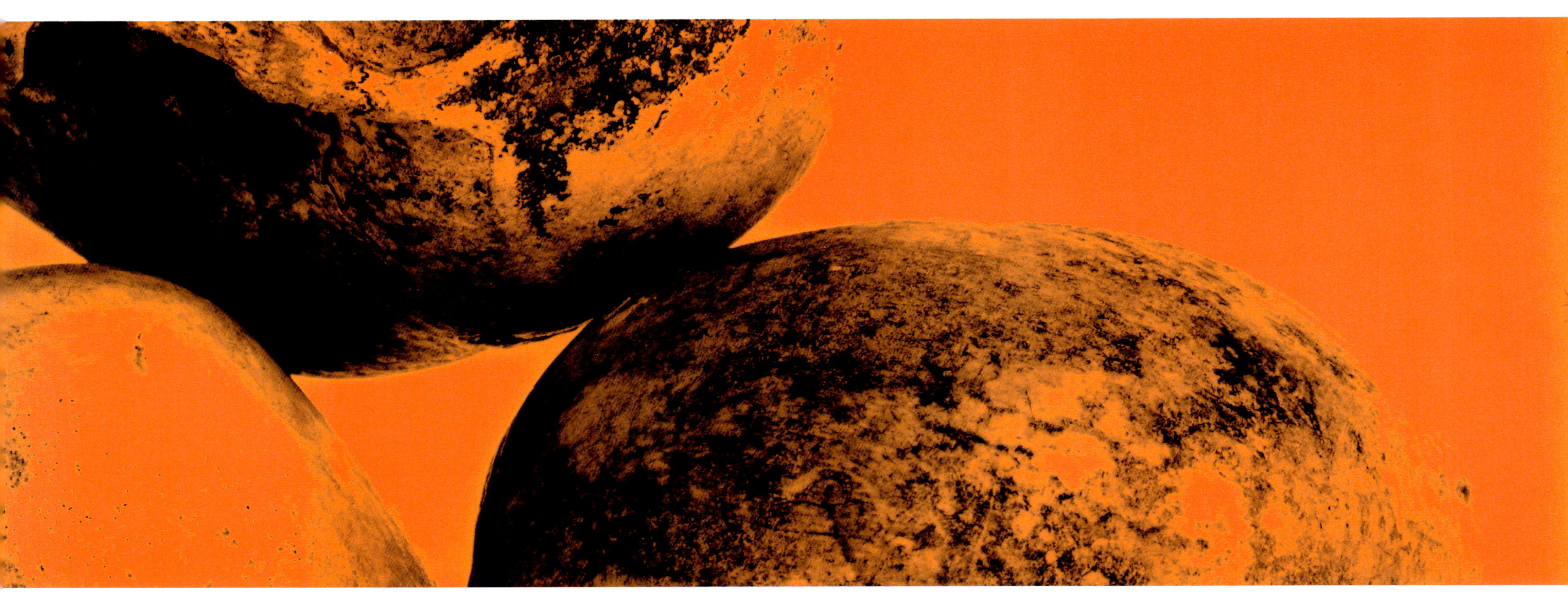